STRATEGIC INITIATIVES IN EVANGELICAL THEOLOGY

RETHINKING THE TRINITY & RELIGIOUS PLURALISM

AN AUGUSTINIAN ASSESSMENT

KEITH E. JOHNSON

Foreword by GEOFFREY WAINWRIGHT

IVP Academic
An imprint of InterVarsity Press
Downers Grove, Illinois

InterVarsity Press
P.O. Box 1400, Downers Grove, IL 60515-1426
World Wide Web: www.ivpress.com
E-mail: email@ivpress.com

InterVarsity Press® is the book-publishing division of InterVarsity Christian Fellowship/USA®, a movement of students and faculty active on campus at hundreds of universities, colleges and schools of nursing in the United States of America, and a member movement of the International Fellowship of Evangelical Students. For information about local and regional activities, write Public Relations Dept., InterVarsity Christian Fellowship/USA, 6400 Schroeder Rd., P.O. Box 7895, Madison, WI 53707-7895, or visit the IVCF website at <www.intervarsity.org>.

All scripture quotations, unless otherwise indicated, are from The Holy Bible, English Standard Version, *copyright © 2001 by Crossway Bibles, a division of Good News Publishers. Used by permission. All rights reserved.*

Design: Cindy Kiple

Images: The Three Angels of the Old Testament by Simon Ushakov at Russian State Museum, St. Petersburg, Russia. Scala/Art Resource, NY

ISBN 978-0-8308-3902-5

Printed in the United States of America ∞

 InterVarsity Press is committed to protecting the environment and to the responsible use of natural resources. As a member of Green Press Initiative we use recycled paper whenever possible. To learn more about the Green Press Initiative, visit <www.greenpressinitiative.org>.

Library of Congress Cataloging-in-Publication Data

Johnson, Keith E.
    Rethinking the Trinity and religious pluralism: an Augustinian assessment/Keith E. Johnson; foreword by Geoffrey Wainwright.
        p. cm.
    Includes bibliographical references and index.
    ISBN 978-0-8308-3902-5 (pbk.: alk. paper)
    1. Trinity—History of doctrines. 2. Augustine, Saint, Bishop of Hippo. 3. Religious pluralism. I. Title.
    BT111.3.J64 2011
    231'.04409015—dc22

2011013674

P	20	19	18	17	16	15	14	13	12	11	10	9	8	7	6	5	4	3	2	1
Y	27	26	25	24	23	22	21	20	19	18	17	16	15	14	13	12	11				

CONTENTS

◆

FOREWORD

Over the course of the twentieth century, theologians from across wide swaths of Christianity came to a renewed appreciation of the doctrine of the Trinity for a right understanding of the faith, worship, life and witness of the church. Presaged among Protestants already in the 1930s by Karl Barth's opening declaration in his *Church Dogmatics* that in and through the Word of God incarnate, narrated and preached, it is God himself who stands self-revealed as Father, Son and Holy Spirit, biblical scholars rediscovered the three-personed God in the composition, content and interpretation of the Scriptures. On the Catholic side Karl Rahner, in a famous essay around the time of the Second Vatican Council, argued that only a proper correspondence between the triune God at work in the world and God *in se* could save Christianity from being mistaken for an undifferentiated monotheism. Scattered westward after the Russian revolution, over the second half of the twentieth century Eastern Orthodox theologians gradually gained a hearing for their insistence that a strong pneumatology was necessary to a rounded trinitarianism and helped toward the revival of patristic theology in general.

The rediscovery of the Trinity was not limited to academic theologians or even dogmaticians. It both prompted and benefited from other movements in the wider life of the church and the churches. Thus, on the ecumenical front, an early member of the YMCA from Geneva, Maximilien Perret, reported to the Evangelical Alliance: "It is Jesus Christ whom we want to serve, Jesus Christ true God and true man, Jesus Christ great God and Saviour, to whom we give the same honour, praise, glory and worship for ever and ever, as to the Father and to the

Son and to the Holy Spirit"; and when the International Missionary Council became integrated with the World Council of Churches in 1961, the latter's basis of membership was formulated thus: "The World Council of Churches is a fellowship of churches which confess the Lord Jesus Christ as God and Saviour according to the Scriptures and therefore seek to fulfill together their common calling to the glory of the one God, Father, Son, and Holy Spirit." In their search to restore the unity of the church, the churches came to see—with, for instance, Lesslie Newbigin in *The Household of God* (1953)—that a fully ecumenical church would need to be "people of God," "body of Christ," "community of the Spirit," all three at once.

Again, the liturgical movement which spread throughout the Roman Catholic Church and in many Protestant churches profited from renewed interest in the patristic period. The trinitarian structures of baptism and the Eucharist, as affirmed in the "Lima text" of Faith and Order (*Baptism, Eucharist and Ministry*, 1982), were brought to clearer expression in revised rites and service books. It would be hard to overestimate the importance of St. Basil the Great's treatise *On the Holy Spirit* in regard to the patterns of the church's worship: since the gifts of God reach us through the Son in the Spirit, it is appropriate that our thanks and petitions offered in the Spirit mount through the Son to the Father; when it is a matter of the praise and glory of God *in se*, it is right that our address should consider the three persons of the Godhead conjunctively, as in the "Glory be to the Father and to the Son and to the Holy Spirit, as it was in the beginning, is now, and ever shall be."

We have thereby already glimpsed the importance of the doctrine of the Trinity for the right understanding of God, for ecumenical ecclesiology and for liturgical renewal. The same is the case with regard to the reading of the human condition and the purpose that God has in store for our kind and our world. Anthropology, soteriology and eschatology all come into play when the teaching and witness of the church is considered. Trinitarian doctrine properly stands in service to the story of God's engagement with the world as experienced, told and interpreted by the apostolic and patristic writers, on guard against inadequacies, exaggerations and distortions. Here the Christian message itself is at stake, both as to its content and as to the modes and methods of its propagation.

As his own guide in trinitarian doctrine, Keith Johnson takes St. Augustine, whose teaching has lately received much varied attention. Our author rightly refuses to overplay the differences in nuance between the Eastern fathers and the North African master of the West, both Catholic and Protestant. Augustine's scriptural exegesis and hermeneutics remain firmly at the basis of that great father's more systematic and even speculative trinitarian reflections, and Johnson has drawn appropriate lessons from that procedure.

The rediscovery of the Trinity was not without its dangers. In the present book Johnson brings a truly rediscovered doctrine of the Trinity to bear upon a topic that was of course a question for the early church, has recurred at points in subsequent history and has now—in an epoch of global awareness—attracted renewed attention over the past couple of generations, namely, the relation between the Christian faith and "other religions." He does not limit himself to an easy critique of those who have taken an alleged trinitarianism as the welcome door into "religious pluralism." Rather he engages critically with a number of serious Christian theologians who have sought to apply versions of trinitarian doctrine in quite sophisticated ways to the salvific process of God with the world. Mark Heim's notion of differing "religious ends" is seen to threaten the integrity of the Trinity not only in the range of operative eschatology but even in the inner life of God. Amos Yong's one-sided emphasis on the work of the Spirit to the neglect of the work of the Son risks segregating the two "Hands" of the Father and dividing their saving operation into two separate economies. Jacques Dupuis, by putting at risk the unity of the Son's person in and beyond the incarnation, may have threatened the unique sufficiency precisely of Jesus Christ as the mediator of salvation, such as the Roman Congregation for the Doctrine of the Faith in its *"Dominus Iesus"* declaration

(2000) found it necessary to insist upon. Raimundo Panikkar's three-fold "theandric spirituality" among the religions of the world would benefit from a more stringent application of St. Augustine's grammar of the *vestigia Trinitatis,* or "traces of the Trinity," than Ewert Cousins has thought to provide.

Constructively, it is clearly to the connection between the Trinity and missiology that the research and reflections of Keith Johnson in the present book will make a particularly important contribution. The propagation of the gospel requires respect for humankind's creation in the image of God, acknowledgement of our universal fall and thus the revelatory and redemptive history of the triune God with the world along his chosen paths as normatively set out in the Jewish and Christian Scriptures. This is the God encountered in the related missions of the Son and of the Spirit. This is the God confessed by the church in the Nicene, Constantinopolitan and Chalcedonian councils, and it is the God so understood whose cosmic triumph is finally awaited. This is the God to be preached to all.

In the latter part of his book, Keith Johnson draws together several areas besides immediate missionary preaching and evangelism where a sound doctrine of the Trinity can and should be invoked for the inter-related ends of God's glory and our salvation. As writings on the Trinity continue to multiply in contemporary theology, a second contribution of Johnson's is to raise important concerns about the discipline that is required in the doctrine's application to a variety of topics. In particular, he warns against any facile appeals directly to the immanent Trinity that appear to bypass the economic, or at least fail to respect its epistemic priority. While, ontologically speaking, the cooperation of the three divine persons in works toward the world is grounded in a patterned perichoresis in their inner life, our graced participation in the life of God must—for its knowledge and exercise—follow the route of redemption and restoration enacted by the triune God in his economy of salvation. The very understanding of ourselves—our existence, our vocation, our destiny—depends on the God revealed and active in that

economy of salvation. Our corresponding practice envisions and anticipates the ultimate glorification of the God whom we may have at least
begun to worship in spirit and in truth.

The doctrine of the Trinity has long represented a central interest in
Keith Johnson's studies, research and teaching. He has taught on the
topic both at Duke University and at the Reformed Theological Seminary (Orlando). He presently serves as the national director of theological education for the U.S. Campus Ministry of Campus Crusade for
Christ. As a Methodist, I am confident that Keith Johnson's book will
stand as a faithful guide for present and future believers on the road
toward what John Wesley describes at the conclusion of his sermon
"The New Creation": "And to crown all, there will be a deep, an intimate, an uninterrupted union with God, a constant communion with
the Father and his Son Jesus Christ, through the Spirit; a continual
enjoyment of the Three-One God, and of all the creatures in him!"

Geoffrey Wainwright

PREFACE

As a result of globalization and mass migration, Western Christians live in an increasing pluralistic environment. Increased awareness of religious diversity raises some challenging questions for the church. In such a context, can one continue to affirm that Jesus Christ is the universal Savior for all peoples? How are adherents of non-Christian religions to be viewed? Are they lost souls who need to be snatched from error, or should they be viewed as anonymous members of the church? What role, if any, do non-Christian religions play in the divine economy of salvation? These questions were made palpable to me over years through numerous conversations about the claims of Christ with non-Christian university students. Formally, these questions are discussed under the rubric of the "Christian theology of religions."

I was first introduced to trinitarian approaches to the theology of religions in a graduate course on the doctrine of the Trinity with Geoffrey Wainwright. I decided to explore the relationship between trinitarian doctrine and the Christian theology of religions in my master's thesis, which was titled "Toward a Theology of Religions via the Doctrine of the Trinity" (2002). In my thesis I examined the function of trinitarian doctrine in the proposals of Jacques Dupuis and Mark Heim. That investigation left me with a series of unanswered questions.

When I began doctoral study, I decided to pursue these questions further. Initially I envisioned that I would clarify certain pitfalls on the way to a more adequate trinitarian grammar for a Christian theology of religions. I immersed myself in the classical trinitarian tradition (especially the formative patristic period). My engagement with these classical theologians—particularly Augustine—had an unanticipated result. Not only did I become deeply suspicious of the way trinitarian doctrine is being employed in the theology of religions, but I also began to notice that the trinitarian problems I encountered were not limited to reflection on religious diversity. Similar methodological problems encumber attempts to relate the doctrine of the Trinity to a host of other issues (e.g., personhood, gender, politics, church, society, etc.). This narrative of my developing interests finds systematic embodiment in the thematic questions and overall structure of the present writing. *Rethinking the Trinity and Religious Pluralism* represents a revised and expanded version of my dissertation completed at Duke University in 2007.

This investigation is not merely about the theology of religions. It is also about the doctrine of the Trinity. Through an Augustinian engagement with the trinitarian doctrine in several recent proposals in the Christian theology of religions, this study will raise crucial questions regarding the function of trinitarian doctrine.[1] It is ironic that the theologian whose teaching was allegedly responsible for the "marginalization" of the Trinity might have something important to teach us about what it means for this doctrine to be relevant.

Apart from the support and encouragement of a number of people, this project would not have been possible. I want to express deep appreciation to my doctoral adviser, Geoffrey Wainwright, who graciously contributed the foreword to this book. Not only did his courses give me a vision for the doxological nature of theology, but he has also helped me see how the discipline of theology can and should serve the church. His seminar on the Trinity kindled my interest in trinitarian doctrine and provided impetus for this present investigation. Thank you Reinhard Huetter for suggesting that Augustine's trinitarian theology might provide the thematic center for my project, and Warren Smith for spending an entire semester helping me work through the trinitarian texts of Justin Martyr, Clement of Alexandria, Irenaeus, Tertullian, Origen, Athanasius, Basil of Caesarea, Gregory of Nyssa, Gregory of Nazianzus, Hilary of Poitiers and Augustine. My thanks also to

---

[1]The nature of my Augustinian evaluation will be explained in the introduction.

J. Kameron Carter for introducing me to the intricacies of medieval vestige tradition. Over a two-month period we carefully worked through Bonaventure's *Itinerarium Mentis in Deum* in a graduate seminar. I want to thank Lewis Ayres for sharing his research on Augustine's trinitarian doctrine with me, and Harold Netland for introducing me to the Christian theology of religions a number of years ago through a course on the theology of John Hick at Trinity Evangelical Divinity School. My ongoing conversations with Scott Swain about trinitarian theology have sharpened this work. I am grateful to Gary Deddo at InterVarsity Press for his thoughtful input on this manuscript. He has been a joy to work with. Finally, I am filled with profound gratitude to my wife, Rhonda, for her unfailing love, encouragement and support throughout this project.

INTRODUCTION

Immanuel Kant declared that the doctrine of the Trinity "has no practical relevance."[1] Kant would be hard-pressed to make this criticism stick today. Contemporary theologians are driven by a quest to relate trinitarian doctrine to a wide variety of concerns. Books and articles abound on Trinity and personhood, Trinity and societal relations, Trinity and gender, Trinity and marriage, Trinity and church, Trinity and politics, Trinity and ecology, and so forth. Theologians of every stripe are attempting to relate trinitarian doctrine to a broad variety of issues. That the doctrine of the Trinity has garnered widespread interest in recent years is a welcome development; however, it is important remember the maxim: "All that glitters is not gold." Is it possible that this quest for relevancy might be leading us down the wrong path?

Recently a number of Christian theologians have suggested that the doctrine of the Trinity holds the key to new understanding of religious diversity. Although at one time this doctrine may have been viewed as a stumbling block to interreligious dialogue, the situation has dramatically changed. A number of Christian theologians have attempted to pave the way for a positive understanding of non-Christian religions within redemptive history by appealing to the Trinity. According to one theologian,

> God has something to do with the fact that a diversity of independent ways of salvation appears in the history of the world. This diversity reflects the diversity or plurality within the divine life itself, of which the Christian doctrine of the Trinity provides an account. The mystery of the Trinity is for Christians the ultimate foundation for pluralism.[2]

---

[1]Immanuel Kant, *The Conflict of the Faculties*, trans. Mary J. Gregor (New York: Abaris, 1979), pp. 65-67.

[2]Peter C. Hodgson, "The Spirit and Religious Pluralism," in *The Myth of Religious Superiority:*

Similarly, "The diversity and communion of persons in the Godhead offer the proper key—to be explored hereafter—for understanding the multiplicity of interrelated divine self-manifestations in the world and in history."[3] Finally,

> It is impossible to believe in the Trinity *instead* of the distinctive religious claims of all other religions. If Trinity is real, then many of these *specific* religious claims and ends must be real also. . . . The Trinity is a map that finds room for, indeed requires, concrete truth in other religions.[4]

Although substantial differences exist among these proposals, they share an important feature in common—namely, a conviction that the doctrine of the Trinity provides the basis for a positive appraisal of non-Christian religions. It is my contention that this assumption merits careful scrutiny. The purpose of this book is to offer a critical assessment of the use of the doctrine of the Trinity in the Christian theology of religions. I will argue (1) that there is good reason to question the assertion that the Trinity provides the foundation for affirming the validity of non-Christian religions; (2) that recent attempts to employ trinitarian doctrine to this end are undermining classical Christian teaching regarding the Trinity; and (3) that misuse of trinitarian doctrine in the theology of religions reflects broader methodological problems in contemporary theology.

What difference does it make if a handful of theologians misconstrue this doctrine in addressing pressing questions of religious diversity? Perhaps the simplest response is to say that the gospel is ultimately at stake. It is instructive to remember that early trinitarian controversies were driven by soteriological concerns: Who must Christ *be* in order to *do* what Christ did? Because the Trinity represents a presupposition of

---

Multifaith Explorations of Religious Pluralism, ed. Paul F. Knitter (Maryknoll, N.Y.: Orbis, 2005), p. 136.

[3]Jacques Dupuis, *Toward a Christian Theology of Religious Pluralism* (Maryknoll, N.Y.: Orbis, 1997), p. 208.

[4]Mark Heim, "The Depth of the Riches: Trinity and Religious Ends," *Modern Theology* 17 (2001): 22.

the gospel,[5] distortions of this doctrine inevitably lead to a distorted gospel.[6]

Also at stake in this investigation is how we construe the "relevance" of trinitarian doctrine. In a review article titled "The Trinity: A New Wave?" Karen Kilby points out that as interest in the Trinity has grown, theologians have not paid adequate attention to the question of how this doctrine should function.[7] Should it regulate the way Christians talk about God, the way they read Scripture and the way they worship, or should it serve as a "launching pad for useful ideas" such as "relatedness" (or, in the case of this inquiry, "religious diversity")?[8] Kilby's question is crucial. This investigation will raise important questions regarding the proper function of trinitarian doctrine.

Drawing upon the trinitarian teaching of St. Augustine, I will critically examine four recent proposals in the Christian theology of religions: S. Mark Heim's trinitarian theology of religious ends, Amos Yong's pneumatological theology of religions, Jacques Dupuis's Christian theology of religious pluralism, and Raimundo Panikkar's trinitarian account of religious experience. Several factors shaped my selection of these theologians. First, I limited my investigation to proposals that explicitly appeal to the doctrine of the Trinity. Second, I focused on proposals that attempt to operate within the bounds of historic trinitarian orthodoxy. Third, I selected theologians who represent diverse ecclesial affiliations.[9] Finally, I wanted to select a set of proposals that would provide a representative cross-section of contemporary use of trinitarian doctrine in the Christian theology of religions. The proposals outlined earlier represent just such a cross-section. Mark Heim's

---

[5]See Fred Sanders, *The Deep Things of God: How the Trinity Changes Everything* (Wheaton, Ill.: Crossway, 2010), esp. chaps. 3-4.

[6]See Kevin J. Vanhoozer, *The Drama of Doctrine: A Canonical-Linguistic Approach to Christian Theology* (Louisville: Westminster John Knox, 2005), pp. 42-44.

[7]Karen Kilby, "The Trinity: A New Wave?" *Reviews in Religion and Theology* 7 (2000): 378-81.

[8]Ibid., p. 381.

[9]Mark Heim is Baptist. Amos Yong is Pentecostal. Jacques Dupuis and Raimundo Panikkar are Catholic.

trinitarian account of religious ends represents one of the most sophisticated attempts to date to employ a doctrine of the Trinity as constitutive ground for a Christian theology of religions. Amos Yong has developed one of the most advanced pneumatological approaches. Whereas trinitarian *pneumatology* represents the key to Yong's proposal, trinitarian *Christology* provides the key to Jacques Dupuis's proposal. On this basis, Dupuis makes a vigorous case for the salvific role of non-Christian religions in the economy of salvation. Raimundo Panikkar's trinitarian account of religious experience represents the strongest exemplar of a proposal that appeals to the logic of the "vestige" tradition.

Why bring the teaching of a late-fourth-century bishop into conversation with contemporary reflection on religious diversity? There are at least five reasons Augustine's theology provides a helpful basis for evaluating the trinitarian doctrine in the Christian theology of religions. First, Augustine stands at an important point in the development of trinitarian doctrine. The fourth century played a crucial role in solidifying the key elements of what we retrospectively call trinitarian orthodoxy.[10] Writing in the wake of conciliar developments at Nicaea (325) and Constantinople (381), Augustine's teaching on the Trinity represents a mature expression of the pro-Nicene theology that emerged in the latter decades of the fourth century among Latin and Greek speaking Christians.[11] Second, Augustine has been recognized as a "Doctor of the Church," that is, a reliable authority whose doctrine reflects the teaching of Scripture and creedal expressions of Christian orthodoxy. Not only do medieval theologians like Thomas Aquinas engage Augustine as an authority on matters of trinitarian doctrine but the Reformers do as well.[12] Third, Augustine's teaching on the Trinity is one

---

[10]For an overview of these developments, see Lewis Ayres, *Nicaea and Its Legacy: An Approach to Fourth-Century Trinitarian Theology* (New York: Oxford University Press, 2004).

[11]For a discussion of pro-Nicene theology, see chap. 2.

[12]It is important to remember the Reformers were not opposed to tradition as a guide to reading Scripture. What they opposed was tradition as a second source of revealed truth standing over and against Scripture. Heiko Oberman distinguishes two understandings of the relationship of Scripture and tradition that provide a backdrop for Reformation debates. According to "Tradition I," Scripture and tradition coincide in such a way that tradition simply represents

of the most influential in the Western church.[13] In turning to Augustine, we draw upon what is arguably the most representative version of trinitarian doctrine in the history of the church among Catholics and Protestants. Moreover, there is an ecumenical advantage in appealing to Augustine's theology. Despite popular claims to the contrary (see the appendix), Augustine shares much in common with the Greek-speaking theologians of the East (e.g., the Cappadocians).[14] Indeed, much of the critique I will offer of contemporary use of trinitarian doctrine in the Christian theology of religions could have been made in conversation with the Cappadocians. Finally, the essential trinitarian issues raised in the theology of religions are addressed in one form or another in Augustine's writings (see the following paragraph). Indeed, the continuing value of Augustine's trinitarian theology will become evident in chapters three to five as we observe the kind of heavy lifting it is capable of doing.

Even if we grant these five points, isn't it anachronistic to ask what Augustine thought about the views of contemporary theologians addressing the theology of religions? My purpose is *not* to marshal an Augustinian critique of contemporary interpretations of religious diversity (i.e., exclusivism, inclusivism and pluralism). I am not asking, What would Augustine think of Jacques Dupuis's inclusive pluralism? but rather, From an Augustinian perspective, how adequate is the trinitarian theology that supports Dupuis's proposal? To this end, my inves-

Scripture properly interpreted. According to "Tradition II," Scripture and tradition represent distinct sources of revelation. (The "II" in Tradition II stands for two sources whereas "Tradition I" is a single source view.) The Council of Trent embraces "Tradition II" while the Reformers hold to "Tradition I." As Oberman explains, during the Reformation and Counter-Reformation, "We are here not confronted with the alternatives of Scripture and tradition but with the clash of two radically different concepts of tradition: Tradition I and Tradition II" (Heiko A. Oberman, *The Dawn of the Reformation: Essays in Late Medieval and Early Reformation* [Edinburgh: T & T Clark, 1986], p. 283; see also Heiko A. Oberman, *Forerunners of the Reformation: The Shape of Late Medieval Thought* [Cambridge: James Clark, 2002], pp. 51-66).

[13]Of course, not everyone views Augustine's influence as positive. A detailed discussion of contemporary criticisms of Augustine's trinitarian theology can be found in the appendix.

[14]It is important not to read later theological differences that develop between the East and West back into the fourth and fifth centuries.

tigation is structured around an Augustinian assessment of three fundamental trinitarian issues in the Christian theology of religions: (1) the relationship of the economic Trinity and the immanent Trinity; (2) the relations among the divine persons (internally, apart from creation; and externally, in creation, providence, and redemption); and (3) the search for reflections of the Trinity (*vestigia trinitatis*) in human experience.[15] That these indeed are crucial issues in the theology of religions will be argued in the chapters that follow.

Because of his role as Doctor of the Church (*Doctor Ecclesiae*), medieval theologians treated Augustine as a reliable authority whose teaching on the Trinity may be employed as a foundational element in theological argumentation because is it seen as a faithful expression of Scripture and conciliar teaching.[16] This medieval practice offers an apt analogy for my engagement with Augustine in the chapters that follow. Augustine's teaching on the Trinity will function as "first principles" in the assessment to be developed in chapters three to five. In the spirit of *ressourcement,* I want to appropriate one of the treasures of the church for the sake of its theological renewal.[17]

Two twentieth-century developments provide a key context for my investigation: the trinitarian revival and the rise of the Christian theology of religions. These developments will be explored in chapter one. In chapter two I will offer a brief introduction to Augustine's teaching on the Trinity. I will identify four factors that provide important context for understanding his trinitarian doctrine and briefly survey one of

---

[15]My investigation is Augustinian in the narrow sense that I will draw exclusively on Augustine's trinitarian theology and *not* later interpreters of Augustine like Thomas Aquinas. Unless otherwise indicated, I will be referring to the teaching of the bishop of Hippo when I use the term *Augustinian.*

[16]This is not to suggest that they viewed Augustine's doctrinal statements as possessing the same kind of authority as Scripture. Rather they possessed a "probable" authority—something less than the ultimate authority of Holy Scripture but certainly much more than untested theological opinions.

[17]*Ressourcement* (French) denotes a return to the roots, a rediscovery of earlier sources. The term *La Ressourcement* was used to describe a movement that emerged among Catholics in Western Europe in the early part of the twentieth century that emphasized returning to early sources (Scripture, tradition and creeds) for the sake of theological renewal.

the key sources for his teaching on the Trinity—*De trinitate*.[18] The formal content of Augustine's trinitarian theology will be presented in chapters three to five. I have structured the order of these chapters to follow the way Augustine treats these topics in *De trinitate*.

Arguably, the relationship between the economic Trinity and the immanent Trinity represents a key point of debate in contemporary theology. This debate is directly relevant to the theology of religions. In chapter three I will explore the relationship between the economic Trinity and the immanent Trinity in the work of Mark Heim. In conversation with Augustine, I will argue that Heim's "theology of religious ends" ultimately severs the immanent Trinity from the economic Trinity.

Assumptions about the relations of the divine persons also play an important role in several recent proposals. In chapter four I will explore the relations among Father, Son and Holy Spirit in Jacques Dupuis's Christian theology of religious pluralism and Amos Yong's pneumatological theology of religions. In conversation with Augustine, I will argue that Yong and Dupuis offer inadequate accounts of relations of the divine persons.

A number of Christian theologians have suggested that trinitarian structures can be discerned in non-Christian religions and that this reality bears witness to the validity of non-Christian religions. In chapter five I will examine this assumption in the work of Raimundo Panikkar and his interpreter Ewert Cousins. In conversation with Augustine I will argue that Panikkar's trinitarian account of religious experience undermines the basic grammar of the vestige tradition.

In chapter six I will explore the implications of my investigation for the Christian theology of religions and contemporary theology. One might be tempted to assume that the trinitarian problems I document in the pages to follow are limited to a select group of theologians reflecting on religious diversity; however, such an assumption would be

---

[18]Augustine, *The Trinity*, trans. Edmund Hill (Brooklyn: New City Press, 1991).

mistaken. After summing up my evaluation of Heim, Yong, Dupuis and Panikkar, I will demonstrate that similar problems can also be seen in attempts to relate the doctrine of the Trinity to a variety of other concerns. I will close by considering how Augustine might lead us to rethink the purpose(s) of trinitarian doctrine.

At the end of *Rethinking the Trinity and Religious Pluralism*, I have added an appendix addressing contemporary criticisms of Augustine. According to his critics, Augustine's trinitarian theology begins with a unity of divine substance (which he allegedly prioritizes over the divine persons), his trinitarian doctrine is shackled to Neo-Platonic philosophy, his "psychological analogy" veers toward modalism and he severs the life of the triune God from the economy of salvation. These criticisms can be found in works of Colin Gunton, Cornelius Plantinga, Catherine LaCugna and Karl Rahner. I will engage a key spokesperson for these criticisms, Colin Gunton, in order to draw attention to some of the ways Augustine is characteristically misread in contemporary theology.

1

THE TURN TO THE TRINITY
IN THE THEOLOGY
OF RELIGIONS

◆

Two contemporary developments provide an important context for my Augustinian assessment of trinitarian doctrine in the Christian theology of religions: the twentieth-century trinitarian revival, and the rise of the Christian theology of religions. The purpose of this chapter is to survey these developments.

THE CONTEMPORARY TRINITARIAN REVIVAL

A number of excellent studies have been written chronicling the renaissance of trinitarian theology in the twentieth century. There is no need to repeat at length what others have said.[1] For our purposes it will suffice briefly to examine the work of Karl Barth and Karl Rahner, with specific attention to several themes that have shaped the character of the contemporary trinitarian revival.[2]

---

[1]See Claude Welch, *In This Name: The Doctrine of the Trinity in Contemporary Theology* (New York: Charles Scribner's, 1952); John Thompson, *Modern Trinitarian Perspectives* (New York: Oxford University Press, 1994); Geoffrey Wainwright, "The Ecumenical Rediscovery of the Trinity," *One in Christ* 34 (1998): 95-124; and Stanley J. Grenz, *Rediscovering the Triune God: The Trinity in Contemporary Theology* (Minneapolis: Fortress, 2004).

[2]A discussion of the extent to which trinitarian doctrine was actually marginalized in various

Karl Barth. The twentieth-century trinitarian revival was energized on the Protestant side by the work of Karl Barth.[3] In his massive *Church Dogmatics*, Barth introduces the doctrine of the Trinity as a foundational element of his prolegomena. This move is driven by the assumption that it is impossible to reflect on the nature of Christian doctrine apart from the material content of Christian doctrine.[4] More specifically, Barth insists that we cannot think about the nature of revelation apart from the One who is revealed *in* revelation.[5] Three questions naturally arise as we consider the nature of revelation. Who is revealed? How does revelation happen? What is the result of revelation? The answer to the first question is that "*God* reveals himself."[6] The answer to the second is that "He reveals himself *through himself.*"[7] The answer to the third is that "He reveals *himself.*"[8] For Barth, God is the *subject* of revelation, the *act* of revelation and the *object* of revelation. "It is from this fact," explains Barth, "that we learn we must begin the doctrine of

---

ecclesial contexts in the early part of the twentieth century lies outside the scope of this investigation (see Bruce D. Marshall, "Trinity," in *The Blackwell Companion to Modern Theology*, Blackwell Companion to Religion, ed. Gareth Jones [Malden, Mass.: Wiley-Blackwell, 2004], pp. 183-203). What is clear is that a trinitarian revival emerged in the twentieth century and that the work of Barth and Rahner exerted significant influence on the character of this revival. One compelling exception to the marginalization thesis can found in the writings of the Dutch theologian Hermann Bavinck. Written almost forty years before Barth, Bavinck's *Reformed Dogmatics* is deeply trinitarian (see Herman Bavinck, *Reformed Dogmatics*, vols. 1-4, ed. John Bolt, trans. John Vriend [Grand Rapids: Baker Academic, 2003-2008]; for a discussion of Bavinck's doctrine of the Trinity, see Bavinck, *Reformed Dogmatics*, vol. 2, *God and Creation*, pp. 256-334).

[3]For a brief overview of Barth's life and theology, see Robert W. Jenson, "Karl Barth," in *The Modern Theologians: An Introduction to Christian Theology in the Twentieth Century*, ed. David F. Ford, 2nd ed. (Cambridge, Mass.: Blackwell, 1997), pp. 21-36.

[4]Commenting on his approach, Barth explains, "The most striking anticipation of this kind will consist in the fact that we shall treat the whole doctrine of the Trinity and the essentials of Christology in this connection, namely as constituent parts of our answer to the question of the Word of God. We cannot pose the questions of formal dogma without immediately entering at these central points upon material dogma" (Karl Barth, *Church Dogmatics* 1/1, *The Doctrine of the Word of God*, trans. G. W. Bromiley, 2nd ed. [Edinburgh: T & T Clark, 1975], p. 44).

[5]Ibid., p. 295.

[6]Ibid., p. 296.

[7]Ibid.

[8]Ibid.

revelation with the doctrine of the triune God."[9] When we recognize that "to the same God who in unimpaired unity is the Revealer, the revelation and the revealedness, there is also ascribed in unimpaired differentiation within Himself this threefold mode of being," we are brought directly to the problem of the Trinity.[10]

Barth's decision to locate the doctrine of the Trinity in his prolegomena stood in contrast to a well-established practice of discussing God's existence, nature and attributes prior to any discussion of God's triunity. Because the doctrine of the Trinity "is what basically distinguishes Christian doctrine of God as Christian," it must be given a place of priority.[11] Barth's concern is not merely chronological. He insists that the doctrine of the Trinity should shape all theological reflection: "In giving this doctrine a place of prominence our concern cannot be merely that it have this place externally but rather that its content *be decisive and controlling for the whole of dogmatics*."[12] In the latter context Barth presents the doctrine of the Trinity as both an interpretation of and prerequisite for revelation.

Barth's methodological claim that the doctrine of the Trinity should be "decisive and controlling" for all theological reflection may well represent one of his most significant contributions to the twentieth-century trinitarian revival. Robert Jenson explains that what is noteworthy about Barth's doctrine of the Trinity is not its content, which "turns out to be a fairly standard Augustinian doctrine,"[13] but rather his theologi-

---

[9]Ibid.

[10]Ibid., p. 299.

[11]Ibid., p. 301.

[12]Ibid., p. 303 (italics added).

[13]Jenson, "Karl Barth," p. 32. Barth offers the following summary of his trinitarian doctrine: "Generally and provisionally we mean by the doctrine of the Trinity the proposition that He whom the Christian church calls God and proclaims as God, the God who has revealed Himself according to the witness of Scripture, is the same in unimpaired unity and yet also the same thrice in different ways in unimpaired distinction. Or, in the phraseology of the church's dogma of the Trinity, the Father, the Son and the Holy Spirit in the biblical witness to revelation are the one God in the unity of their essence, and the one God in the biblical witness to revelation is the Father, the Son and the Holy Spirit in the distinction of His persons" (Barth, *Church Dogmatics* 1/1, pp. 307-8). We can see the Augustinian influence on Barth's thought mostly clearly in the final sentence.

cal method.[14] Contemporary theologians have learned from Barth "that this doctrine has and must have explanatory and regulatory use in the whole of theology, that it is not a separate puzzle to be solved but the framework within which all theology's puzzles are to be solved."[15]

Karl Rahner. The trinitarian revival was invigorated on the Catholic side through the work of Karl Rahner.[16] In 1967 Rahner wrote what proved to be an influential essay on the Trinity that was first published in German in a multivolume work titled *Mysterium Salutis* and later translated into English and published as a stand-alone book.[17] In this essay Rahner laments the marginalization of the Trinity in the church:

> All of these considerations should not lead us to overlook the fact that, despite their orthodox confession of the Trinity, Christians are, in their practical life, almost mere "monotheists." We must be willing to admit that, should the doctrine of the Trinity have to be dropped as false, the major part of religious literature could well remain virtually unchanged.[18]

According to Rahner, at least three factors contributed to marginalization of trinitarian doctrine: (1) a trend, beginning in medieval theology texts, of separating discussion of trinitarian doctrine from discussion of the economy of salvation (e.g., the incarnation), (2) increased preoccupation with the immanent Trinity, and (3) a tendency to treat the doctrine of God under two headings, first from the standpoint of

---

[14]Jenson, "Karl Barth," p. 33.

[15]Ibid., p. 31.

[16]Inasmuch as the doctrine of the Trinity constitutes formal dogma for the Catholic Church, it would be inappropriate to speak, in any formal sense, about the doctrine being recovered among Catholics. Certainly the doctrine was not lost. Rahner, as we will see, speaks in terms of the marginalization of the doctrine. Alongside the work of Rahner, Vatican II played an important role in stimulating the trinitarian revival among Catholics. A trinitarian framework shapes many of the conciliar documents.

[17]Karl Rahner, "Der dreifaltige Gott als transzendenter Urgrund der Heilsgeschichte," in *Mysterium Salutis: Grundriß heilsgeschichtlicher Dogmatik*, vol. 2, *Die Heilsgeschichte vor Christus*, ed. Johannes Feiner and Magnus Löhrer (Einsiedeln: Benziger Verlag, 1967), pp. 317-401; Karl Rahner, *The Trinity*, trans. Joseph Donceel (New York: Crossroad, 1999).

[18]Rahner, *Trinity*, pp. 10-11.

the divine essence (*De Deo Uno*) and then only secondarily from the standpoint of the divine persons (*De Deo Trino*).[19]

According to Rahner, the first step in recovering the significance of the Trinity for the Christian life is recognizing that this doctrine is a mystery of salvation: "The isolation of the treatise of the Trinity *has* to be wrong. There *must* be a connection between Trinity and man. The Trinity is a mystery of *salvation,* otherwise it would never have been revealed."[20] Reconnecting the Trinity and salvation requires that we recognize the unity of the *economic* Trinity and the *immanent* Trinity.[21]

> The *basic thesis* which establishes this connection between the treatises and presents the Trinity *as* a mystery of salvation (its reality and not merely as a doctrine) might be formulated as follows: *The "economic" Trinity is the "immanent" Trinity and the "immanent" Trinity is the "economic" Trinity.*[22]

According to Rahner, the unity of the economic and the immanent Trinity can be seen most clearly in case of the incarnation. Who Jesus is and what he does, as a human, reveals the eternal Logos. As a result, "we can assert, in the full meaning of the words: here the Logos with God and the Logos with us, the immanent and the economic Logos, are strictly the same."[23] Rahner suggests that the incarnation represents a single instance of a broader phenomenon: the self-communication of the triune God. In God's self-communication, each of the divine persons communicates himself to human beings in a way that reflects the particularity of that divine person.[24]

Rahner insists that all trinitarian reflection (and, for that matter, dogmatic presentation) must begin with the self-revelation of the triune

---

[19]Ibid., pp. 15-24.

[20]Ibid., p. 21.

[21]The economic Trinity refers to God's self-revelation through creation, providence and redemption, while the immanent Trinity denotes the intratrinitarian life of the three divine persons apart from creation and redemption.

[22]Rahner, *Trinity*, pp. 21-22.

[23]Ibid., p. 33.

[24]"These three self-communications are the self-communication of the one God in three relative ways in which God subsists" (Rahner, *Trinity*, p. 35).

God in the economy of salvation, and only thereafter move to a doctrine of the immanent Trinity. Thus, the divine "missions" should constitute the starting point of theological reflection. Following this methodology Rahner develops his constructive doctrine of the Trinity beginning with God's economic "self-communication." On the one hand, God's self-communication is one; it possesses an inner unity. At the same time, God's self-communication involves two fundamental modalities—truth and love. Rahner claims that these self-differentiations (truth and love) must belong to God *in himself.* Otherwise God's communication would not be a genuine self-communication: "For those modalities and their differentiation either are in God himself (although we first experience them from our point of view), or they exist only in us, they belong only to the realm of creatures as effects of the divine creative activity."[25] If the latter were the case, no genuine *self*-communication would exist. God would be present only as represented by a creature. If there is to be an authentic self-communication, God must not merely be the "giver," he must also be the "gift." Genuine self-communication means that God reveals himself *as God* through his self-communication. It is because of God's immanent self-communication that God can freely communicate himself in the economy.

Implications. Barth and Rahner share several important assumptions that have shaped (and continue to shape) the contemporary trinitarian revival.[26] First, both share a vision for recovering the centrality of trinitarian doctrine for the life of the church. Arguably, this vision fuels the contemporary quest for establishing the relevance of trinitarian doctrine. Second, both believe that the doctrine of the Trinity should play a governing role in Christian theology. Barth expresses this conviction

---

[25]Ibid., p. 100.

[26]This is not to suggest that all their shared assumptions have proved influential. For example, both Barth and Rahner were quite hesitant to speak of the Father, Son and Holy Spirit as "persons" in the post-Enlightenment sense of the word. Barth preferred to speak of the divine hypostases as "modes of being" while Rahner preferred the term "distinct manners of subsisting." In contrast to Barth and Rahner, many contemporary theologians—especially "social" trinitarians—speak quite freely about Father, Son and Spirit as "persons" in the strongest possible sense.

when he says that trinitarian doctrine should be "decisive and controlling for the whole of dogmatics."[27] We can see the outworking of Barth's
assumption in contemporary attempts to identify the implications of
the doctrine of the Trinity for human personhood, worship, ecclesiology, missions, marriage, ethics, societal relations, political theory, non-
Christian religions and the like. Third, both posit a close relationship
between the economic and the immanent Trinity. Barth articulates a
"rule" that is quite similar to Rahner's: "But we have consistently followed the rule, which we regard as basic, that statements about the divine modes of being antecedently in themselves cannot be different in
content from those that are to be made about their reality in revelation."[28]
Rahner's rule about the relationship between the economic Trinity and
the immanent Trinity has sparked extensive debate among contemporary theologians (see chap. 3). Finally, Barth and Rahner both emphasize the *epistemic* priority of the economic Trinity (God's self-revelation
in the economy of salvation) and present their trinitarian doctrine in a
way that underscores this basic assumption. Rahner's presentation
moves from God's "self-communication" in the economy of salvation to
the intratrinitarian "self-communication" that grounds it. Similarly, in
his *Church Dogmatics* Barth discusses each divine "mode of being" under
two headings—first, from the standpoint of the economic Trinity (e.g.,
"God as Reconciler") and then from the standpoint of the immanent
Trinity (e.g., "The Eternal Son"). The critical link for Barth between
the economic and the immanent Trinity can be found in the phrase
antecedently in himself. For example, the Son can be our Reconciler only
because "antecedently in himself" apart from his salvific action on our
behalf, he is the eternal Son.[29] For Barth the relationship of the economic to the immanent Trinity is irreversible: the immanent consti-

---

[27]Barth, *Church Dogmatics* 1/1, p. 303.
[28]Barth continues, "All our statements concerning what is called the immanent Trinity have
    been reached simply as confirmations or underlinings or, materially, as the indispensable
    premises of the economic Trinity" (Barth, *Church Dogmatics* 1/1, p. 479).
[29]Ibid., pp. 414-16.

tutes the ontological ground for the economic.[30] With this background in mind, we will now turn our attention to another key development in twentieth-century theology.

THE CHRISTIAN THEOLOGY OF RELIGIONS

The Christian theology of religions, which should be distinguished from the "history of religions" and the "philosophy of religion," emerged as a distinct theological discipline following Vatican II.[31] Questions discussed under the rubric of the theology of religions include the following: Under what circumstances may individuals experience salvation apart from the witness of the church? To what extent, and on what basis, can we recognize elements of truth and goodness in non-Christian religions? To what extent, if any, is the triune God active in non-Christian religions? What role, if any, do non-Christian religions play in salvation history? To what end, and on what basis, should Christians enter into dialogue with adherents of other religions? Finally, to what extent can we incorporate non-Christian religious practices into the development of indigenous churches in missionary contexts? These questions cannot be avoided in the increasingly globalized world we live in.[32]

---

[30]It should be noted that important epistemological differences exist between Rahner and Barth, on the one hand, and the classical (pre-Enlightenment) theology on the other. Rahner and Barth operate within a post-Kantian epistemological context in which Kant's distinction between the *noumenal* and *phenomenal* realms provides the context for understanding the relationship between divine reality and dogmatic concepts, such as immanent Trinity and the economic Trinity.

[31]Several thinkers have rightly noted that Vatican II represented a "watershed" event in the history of the church (see Miikka Ruokanen, *The Catholic Doctrine of Non-Christian Religions According to the Second Vatican Council* [New York: E. J. Brill, 1992], p. 8). This is not to suggest that theological reflection on the relationship of Christianity to other religions did not exist prior to Vatican II. What is unique following Vatican II is the emergence of the "theology of religions" as a new theological discipline. For a discussion of the development of this new discipline, see Veli-Matti Kärkkäinen, *An Introduction to the Theology of Religions: Biblical, Historical and Contemporary Perspectives* (Downers Grove, Ill.: InterVarsity Press, 2003).

[32]This is not to suggest that an awareness of religious diversity is somehow novel in the history of the church. The early church proclaimed its *kerygma* in a syncretistic environment that recognized "many gods and many lords" (see Bruce W. Winter, "In Public and in Private: Early Christians and Religious Pluralism," in *One God, One Lord: Christianity in a World of Religious*

Exclusivism, inclusivism and pluralism. Debate regarding the relationship of Christianity to other religions has taken place under the rubric of the exclusivist-inclusivist-pluralist typology. *Exclusivism* is associated with the view that salvation can be found only through the person and work of Jesus Christ, and that saving grace is not mediated through the teachings and practices of non-Christian religions.[33] *Inclusivism* generally refers to the view that Christian salvation extends beyond the visible boundaries of the church and that non-Christian religions may play some positive role in God's purposes for humanity.[34] Although they agree that salvation extends beyond the witness of the church, inclusivists are divided on the question of whether non-Christian religions *qua* religions constitute channels through which saving grace is mediated. In a variety of forms, inclusivism has gained momentum among Protestants and Catholics since Vatican II. As an interpretation of religion *pluralism* denotes the viewpoint that all religions represent equally valid means to salvation (which is construed in a variety of ways).[35]

Although the exclusivist-inclusivist-pluralist typology has framed debate regarding the relationship of Christianity to other religions for

---

Pluralism, ed. Andrew D. Clarke and Bruce W. Winter [Grand Rapids: Baker, 1992], pp. 125-48).

[33]Exclusivism is sometimes confused with restrictivism (i.e., the view that only those who express *explicit* faith in Christ can be saved); however, as the term is used in the broader discussion of the relationship between Christianity and other religions, exclusivism does not necessarily entail a particular view regarding the fate of the unevangelized. For example, Alister McGrath, who holds an exclusivist (or, as he prefers, *particularist*) view, adopts an agnostic stance regarding the fate of the unevangelized (see Alister McGrath, "A Particularist View: A Post-Enlightenment Approach," in *More Than One Way? Four Views of Salvation in a Pluralistic Word*, ed. Dennis L. Okholm and Timothy R. Phillips [Grand Rapids: Zondervan, 1995], pp. 151-209).

[34]See Harold A. Netland, *Encountering Religious Pluralism: The Challenge to Christian Faith and Mission* (Downers Grove, Ill.: InterVarsity Press, 2001), p. 52. While the precise boundary between exclusivism and inclusivism is difficult to discern for reasons I will outline later, one element that clearly distinguishes exclusivists from inclusivists is their perspective regarding the salvific role of non-Christian religions.

[35]The pluralist position is perhaps best exemplified in the writings of John Hick (see John Hick, *An Interpretation of Religion: Human Responses to the Transcendent* [New Haven, Conn.: Yale University Press, 1989]).

almost two decades, at least three limitations beset it.[36] First, several proposals cannot be easily located under any of these positions. For example, Karl Barth is typically identified as an exclusivist; however, to the extent Barth may legitimately be characterized as a universalist, his position defies easy categorization. Second, even among theologians who explicitly align themselves with one of the three positions outlined here, considerable diversity exists in the substance of their proposals. For example, Mark Heim claims that while Christians will experience salvation (in a Christian sense), adherents of other religions will experience other positive ends that are distinct from salvation.[37] Jacques Dupuis claims that non-Christian religions constitute channels through which their adherents will experience Christian salvation.[38] Although he acknowledges the universal presence of the Spirit in non-Christian religions, Gavin D'Costa insists that saving grace is not mediated through non-Christian religions.[39] All three of these thinkers broadly identify themselves as "inclusivists," yet their constructive proposals differ significantly.[40] Heim affirms multiple religious ends while Dupuis claims that only one positive end exists (i.e., communion with the triune God). Dupuis affirms that non-Christian religions mediate salvific grace, while D'Costa rejects this claim. Differences such as these suggest that explanatory power of the exclusivist-inclusivist-pluralist typology has become limited. Although some theologians believe that the exclusivist-inclusivist-pluralist typology is still useful, others have

---

[36]Alan Race is frequently credited for bringing this typology into prominence (see Alan Race, *Christians and Religious Pluralism: Patterns in the Christian Theology of Religion* [Maryknoll, N.Y.: Orbis, 1982]).

[37]S. Mark Heim, "Salvations: A More Pluralistic Hypothesis," *Modern Theology* 10 (1994): 343-60.

[38]Jacques Dupuis, *Toward a Christian Theology of Religious Pluralism* (Maryknoll, N.Y.: Orbis, 1997), pp. 203-390.

[39]Gavin D'Costa, *The Meeting of Religions and the Trinity* (Maryknoll, N.Y.: Orbis, 2000), pp. 101-16.

[40]In fairness to Gavin D'Costa, it should be noted that while he previously identified himself as an inclusivist, he has more recently distanced himself from this label—both because he rejects the typology on which it is based and also because he believes that inclusivism has become increasingly associated with a position he rejects, namely, that salvation is mediated through non-Christian religions (see ibid., pp. 99, 116).

attempted to develop alternative paradigms.[41] Finally, use of the label "exclusivism" within the threefold typology obscures the fact that each of these positions is exclusivist in a fundamental sense. Gavin D'Costa advances this thesis as the basis for a penetrating critique of a pluralist interpretation of religious diversity. Drawing on the work of John Milbank and Alasdair MacIntyre, D'Costa argues that there is no such thing as a "non-tradition-specific" account of religion, and that pluralism "represents a tradition-specific approach that bears all the same features as exclusivism—except that it is western liberal modernity's exclusivism."[42] Inclusivism fares no better, according to D'Costa, because it too is exclusivist in that it offers a tradition-specific account of religious diversity. Inclusivism "collapses" into exclusivism in three important ways.[43] First, inclusivists hold that their position is ontologically and epistemologically correct. Second, the claims of inclusivists are inseparably linked to Christ and the church in ways that are similar to exclusivism. Finally, both exclusivists and inclusivists offer tradition-specific interpretations of religion and defend these interpretations against conflicting interpretations.

The turn to the Trinity in the theology of religions. Raimundo Panikkar is frequently identified as one the first contemporary theologians explicitly to employ a doctrine of the Trinity as constitutive ground for a Christian theology of religions. In 1968 Panikkar wrote an essay titled "Toward an Ecumenical Theandric Spirituality," which was later

---

[41]For supporters of the former see Paul Griffiths, *Problems of Religious Diversity* (Malden, Mass.: Blackwell, 2001), pp. 22-65, 138-69; and Perry Schmidt-Leukel, "Exclusivism, Inclusivism, Pluralism: The Tripolar Typology—Clarified and Reaffirmed," in *The Myth of Religious Superiority: Multifaith Explorations of Religious Pluralism*, ed. Paul F. Knitter (Maryknoll, N.Y.: Orbis, 2005), pp. 13-27. One alternative typology that has gained prominence employs the categories of "ecclesiocentrism," "Christocentrism" and "theocentrism." Veli-Matti Kärk-käinen, following Jacques Dupuis, endorses this typology (see Kärkkäinen, *Introduction to the Theology of Religions*, pp. 23-27, 165-73). The ecclesiocentric-Christocentric-theocentric typology does not appear to offer any substantive improvement on the exclusivism-inclusivism-pluralism typology.

[42]D'Costa, *Meeting of Religions*, p. 22. It is important to distinguish the fact of plurality (empirical pluralism) from "religious pluralism" as a philosophical interpretation of religion. When I am speaking of the former I will generally employ the phrase "religious diversity."

[43]Ibid.

developed into a book under the title *The Trinity and the Religious Experience of Man*.[44] Panikkar suggests that the doctrine of the Trinity provides an integrating model for human spirituality in which the Father, Son and Holy Spirit are identified with three distinct forms of religious experience ("iconolatry," "personalism" and "mysticism"). In 1970, Ewert Cousins wrote an essay titled "The Trinity and World Religions"[45] in which he commends Panikkar's proposal and attempts to build on it by linking it to "three universalizing currents in the history of Trinitarian theology": the medieval vestige doctrine, the trinitarian doctrine of creation in the Greek theologians and the Western doctrine of appropriation.[46] Cousins argues that when Panikkar's proposal is situated within the context of these three "universalizing currents," his proposal can be seen to possess a legitimate basis in the history of Christian theology.[47]

The following year (1971), in his address to the World Council of Churches Central Committee, Georges Khodr suggested that trinitarian pneumatology may provide a way forward in dealing with the relationship of Christianity to other religions.[48] Central to Khodr's proposal is a trinitarian distinction between an economy of the Son and an economy of the Spirit: "The Spirit is present everywhere and fills everything by virtue of an economy distinct from that of the Son."[49] Because "the Spirit operates and applies His energies in accordance with His own economy," one could "regard the non-Christian religions as points where His inspiration is at work."[50] Although it did not prove to be immedi-

---

[44]Raymond Panikkar, "Toward an Ecumenical Theandric Spirituality," *Journal of Ecumenical Studies* 5 (1968): 507-34; and Panikkar, *The Trinity and the Religious Experience of Man: Person-Icon-Mystery* (New York: Orbis, 1973). Panikkar's proposal will be discussed in greater detail in chap. 5.

[45]Ewert Cousins, "The Trinity and World Religions," *Journal of Ecumenical Studies* 7 (1970): 476-98.

[46]Ibid., p. 484.

[47]Ibid., p. 492.

[48]Georges Khodr, "Christianity and the Pluralistic World—The Economy of the Holy Spirit," *Ecumenical Review* 23 (1971): 125-26.

[49]Ibid.

[50]Ibid., p. 126.

ately influential, Khodr's essay influenced the development of subsequent pneumatological approaches to the theology of religions.[51]

Over the next twenty years, little was written explicitly linking trinitarian doctrine to the theology of religions. A new wave of appeal to doctrine of the Trinity began in 1990 with the publication of *Christian Uniqueness Reconsidered: The Myth of a Pluralistic Theology of Religions.*[52] This book contains a collection of essays that were written in response to *The Myth of Christian Uniqueness: Toward a Pluralistic Theology of Religions.*[53] The first section of *Christian Uniqueness Reconsidered* contains three essays under the heading "The Trinity and Religious Pluralism." In the first essay, "Trinity and Pluralism," Rowan Williams appreciatively—though not uncritically—examines Panikkar's attempt to employ the Trinity as the foundation for religious pluralism.[54] Panikkar's book *The Trinity and the Religious Experience of Man* represents "one of the best and least read meditations on the Trinity in [the twentieth] century."[55] Although Panikkar's model "possess[es] a real consistency and plausibility," it requires "some specific clarifications precisely in the area of its fundamental Trinitarian orientation."[56] According to Williams, Panikkar helps Christians see that the doctrine of the Trinity need not be a stumbling block to interfaith dialogue but rather a resource.[57] In "Particularity, Universality, and the Religions," Christoph Schwöbel argues that neither exclusivism nor pluralism offer the proper foundation for interreligious dialogue because they both fail to provide an adequate account of "the complex relationship of particularity and

---

[51]Khodr's influence can be seen in Amos Yong's pneumatological theology of religions (see chap. 4).

[52]Gavin D'Costa, ed., *Christian Uniqueness Reconsidered: The Myth of a Pluralistic Theology of Religions* (Maryknoll, N.Y.: Orbis, 1990).

[53]John Hick and Paul F. Knitter, eds., *The Myth of Christian Uniqueness: Toward a Pluralistic Theology of Religions* (Maryknoll, N.Y.: Orbis, 1987).

[54]Rowan Williams, "Trinity and Pluralism," in *Christian Uniqueness Reconsidered: The Myth of a Pluralistic Theology of Religions*, ed. Gavin D'Costa (Maryknoll, N.Y.: Orbis, 1990), pp. 3-15.

[55]Ibid., p. 3.

[56]Ibid., p. 6.

[57]Ibid., p. 11.

universality in religions."[58] The exclusivist position affirms particularity while denying universality, while the pluralist position offers an account of universality that undermines particularity. A proper understanding of the relationship between the universal and particular is provided by the Christian doctrine of the Trinity.[59] Trinitarian faith requires Christians not only to recognize the distinctive particularity of their own faith but to affirm also the distinctive particularity of other faiths.[60] Alongside this particularity, the Christian faith also affirms a universal dimension grounded in the recognition that the God who is revealed in Jesus Christ through the Spirit is the "ground of all being, meaning and salvation."[61] Thus, the triune God is universally present and active "as creative, reconciling, and saving love."[62] The latter reality must be taken into account in order to arrive at a proper understanding of other religions.[63] All religions represent "human responses to the universal creative and redeeming agency of God."[64] Thus, although salvation may take place only though Christ, this does not mean one must be a member of a Christian church or accept Christian doctrine to experience it.[65] Perhaps the most important essay in this book attempting to relate trinitarian doctrine to the Christian theology of religions is "Christ, the Trinity and Religious Plurality" by Gavin D'Costa.[66] D'Costa argues that the concerns that animate the writers of *The Myth of Christian Uniqueness* are better addressed within a trinitarian framework. Within a trinitarian context "the multiplicity of religions takes

---

[58]Christoph Schwöbel, "Particularity, Universality, and the Religions: Toward a Christian Theology of Religions," in *Christian Uniqueness Reconsidered: The Myth of a Pluralistic Theology of Religions*, ed. Gavin D'Costa (Maryknoll, N.Y.: Orbis, 1990), p. 33.

[59]Ibid., p. 43.

[60]Ibid., p. 37.

[61]Ibid.

[62]Ibid., p. 38.

[63]Ibid., p. 39.

[64]Ibid., p. 43.

[65]Ibid., p. 41.

[66]Gavin D'Costa, "Christ, the Trinity and Religious Plurality," in *Christian Uniqueness Reconsidered: The Myth of a Pluralistic Theology of Religions*, ed. Gavin D'Costa (Maryknoll, N.Y.: Orbis, 1990), pp. 16-29.

on a special theological significance that cannot be ignored by Christians who worship a Trinitarian God."[67] According to D'Costa, the doctrine of the Trinity provides a key to understanding other religions because of the way it holds together particularity and universality.[68] On the one hand, this doctrine affirms that the triune God has been disclosed in the particularity of Jesus of Nazareth. On the other hand, it also affirms that God is continually revealing himself in human history through the presence and work of the Holy Spirit.[69] Because the work of the Spirit is not limited to institutional Christianity, trinitarian faith can engender open attitudes toward other religions:

> The significance of this Trinitarian ecclesiology is that if we have good reasons to believe that the Spirit and Word are present and active in the religions of the world (in ways that cannot, a priori, be specified), then it is intrinsic to the vocation of the church to be attentive to the world religions.[70]

The following year (1991), Ninian Smart and Stephen Konstantine published a book titled *Christian Systematic Theology in World Context*, in which they argue that the triune God, specifically the "social" Trinity, is the ultimate divine reality, which constitutes the ground of all religious experience.[71] Differing forms of spirituality arise from an experience of one of three "aspects of the divine life" of the triune God: (1) nonrelational, (2) relational, and (3) communal.[72] Diversity in the divine life grounds diversity in religious experience.[73] Buddhists, for example, apprehend the "non-relational" dimension of the divine life while Christians experience the "relational" dimension. Smart and Konstantine contend that these three "aspects" of the divine life are

---

[67]Ibid., p. 16.

[68]Ibid., p. 18.

[69]Ibid., p. 17.

[70]Ibid., p. 23.

[71]Social trinitarians view human community as a model for relations among the divine persons. Ninian Smart and Stephen Konstantine, *Christian Systematic Theology in World Context* (Minneapolis: Fortress, 1991).

[72]Ibid., p. 174.

[73]Ibid., pp. 173-74.

generated by the complex nature of God as Trinity.

During the same year, Paul Knitter wrote an essay titled "A New Pentecost? A Pneumatological Theology of Religions."[74] In this essay Knitter builds upon Georges Khodr's earlier proposal by suggesting that non-Christian religions represent the independent domain of the Spirit:

> If we can take the Spirit, and not the Word in Jesus Christ, as our start-ing point for a theology of religions, we can affirm the possibility that the religions are "an all-comprehensive phenomenon of grace"—that is, an economy of grace that is genuinely different from that made known to us through the Word incarnate in Jesus (in whom, of course, the Spirit was also active). And in that sense, the economy of religions is "independent"—that is, not to be submerged or engulfed or incorpo-rated into the economy of the Word represented in the Christian churches.[75]

Although Knitter did not further develop this trinitarian pneumatol-ogy, his proposal has been embraced by other theologians.[76]

In 1994 Pan-Chiu Lai published a revision of his doctoral disserta-tion under the title *Towards a Trinitarian Theology of Religions*.[77] The point of departure for Lai's investigation is the assumption that the two dominant positions in the theology of religions—"theocentrism" (pluralism) and "Christocentrism" (exclusivism)—are inadequate.[78] Whereas the theocentric position downplays the centrality of the in-carnation, the Christocentric position minimizes the role of the Holy Spirit.[79] Lai suggests that a trinitarian approach provides a way to in-tegrate and transcend theocentrism and Christocentrism, and that the resources for developing this kind of trinitarian approach can be found

---

[74]Paul F. Knitter, "A New Pentecost? A Pneumatological Theology of Religions," *Current Dia-logue* 19 (1991): 32-41.

[75]Ibid., p. 36.

[76]One example is the Pentecostal theologian Amos Yong.

[77]Pan-Chiu Lai, *Towards a Trinitarian Theology of Religions: A Study in Paul Tillich's Thought*, Studies in Philosophical Theology 8 (Kampen, Netherlands: Kok Pharos, 1994).

[78]Ibid., pp. 31-41.

[79]Ibid., p. 41.

in the theology of Paul Tillich.[80] According to Lai, an important shift in thought took place in Tillich's thinking between the second and third volumes of his *Systematic Theology*.[81] Tillich's early approach to non-Christian religions might aptly be characterized as Christocentric, inasmuch as it assumed the superiority of Christianity; however, in the third volume of his *Systematic Theology* Tillich adopted a pneumatological approach to other religions primarily because he recognized that Logos doctrine did not offer an adequate basis for affirming the validity of other religions. The universal economy of the Spirit played a key role in Tillich's new approach. According to Tillich, salvation occurs anywhere people encounter the "healing power" of Christ.[82] The Spirit represents the ultimate source of this healing power.[83] According to Lai, Tillich's theory of the Trinity has three implications for interreligious dialogue. First, his doctrine of the Trinity grounds the "possibility and autonomy of other ways of salvation" by avoiding "an exclusively Christocentric conception of the Trinity."[84] Second, by affirming that "the three *personae* of the divine Trinity represent three different characters of the divine revelation—the abysmal, logical and spiritual," Tillich is able to integrate a wide variety of religious experiences.[85] Finally, the "participatory ontology" that undergirds Tillich's understanding of the Trinity enables Christians to enter into dialogue based on the assumption that other traditions are "living religions" just like Christianity.[86]

In 1996, Jacques Dupuis published his "Christian theology of religious pluralism" which he grounds in trinitarian theology.[87] According

---

[80]Ibid., p. 43.

[81]Paul Tillich, *Systematic Theology*, 3 vols. (Chicago: University of Chicago Press, 1951-1963).

[82]Lai, *Towards a Trinitarian Theology of Religions*, p. 119. Although Christ represents the criterion for this healing, saving power is not limited to him. Only God is Savior. God saves through Christ.

[83]Ibid., p. 129.

[84]Ibid., pp. 160, 159, respectively

[85]Ibid. 160.

[86]Ibid., p. 164-65.

[87]Jacques Dupuis, *Toward a Christian Theology of Religious Pluralism* (Maryknoll, N.Y.: Orbis, 1996). Dupuis's proposal will be discussed at greater detail in chap. 4.

to Dupuis, the "Christian vision of the Triune God" opens the door for a "positive evaluation of other religious traditions."[88] It does so by providing an interpretive key: "From a Christian viewpoint the doctrine of the divine Trinity serves as the hermeneutical key for an interpretation of the experience of the Absolute Reality to which other religious traditions testify."[89] Dupuis appeals to the Trinity in at least five different ways. First, the Trinity constitutes the ontological basis for his proposal. According to Dupuis, "the mystery of the Triune God—Father, Son, Spirit—corresponds objectively to the inner reality of God, even though only analogically."[90] Second, Dupuis claims that all religious experience possesses a "trinitarian structure."[91] Third, the Trinity provides the "hermeneutical key" to relating the universality of God's saving will to the particularity of Christ, enabling one to move beyond an exclusivist approach to non-Christian religions without embracing a pluralist perspective. How does one affirm the universality of God's saving will while retaining the particularity of the Christ event? Simply by recognizing that the "two hands" of God—the Word and the Spirit—are universally present and active in other religions.[92] Fourth, Dupuis reinterprets the centrality of Christ through an appeal to the Trinity in such a way that he is able to affirm other saviors who somehow participate in the mediation of Christ.[93] Finally, religious plurality, as an empirical phenomenon, finds its ultimate basis in the plurality of divine life of the Trinity: "The diversity and communion of persons in the Godhead offer the proper key—to be explored hereafter—for understanding the multiplicity of interrelated divine self-manifestations in the world and in history."[94]

The following year a collection of ten essays from the Fifth Edin-

---

[88]Ibid., p. 313.
[89]Ibid., p. 264.
[90]Ibid., p. 259.
[91]Ibid., pp. 276-77.
[92]Ibid., p. 300.
[93]Ibid., pp. 205-6.
[94]Ibid., p. 208.

burgh Dogmatics Conference was published under the title *The Trinity in a Pluralistic Age*.[95] Kevin Vanhoozer explains that the purpose of the conference was to explore the implications of trinitarian thought for the present pluralistic context:

> Our working hypothesis is straightforward, but its implications are immense: the doctrine of the Trinity, with its dual emphasis on oneness and threeness as equally ultimate, contains unexpected and hitherto unexplored resources for dealing with the problems, and possibilities, of contemporary pluralism.[96]

A distinctive feature of this collection of essays is the way several contributors express concerns regarding contemporary appeal to the Trinity in the theology of religions. Three examples will suffice. Although he praises the trinitarian revival that has taken place, Lesslie Newbigin criticizes attempts on the part of key leaders in the ecumenical movement to commend a trinitarian approach to mission as an alternative to and replacement for a Christocentric model that emphasizes the universal lordship of Christ.[97] Such a move, he explains, would represent a "grave mistake."[98] In an essay titled "The Trinity and 'Other Religions,'" Stephen Williams raises important methodological questions regarding the appeal to the Trinity in the works of Raimundo Panikkar (*The Trinity and the Religious Experience of Man*) as well as Ninian Smart and Stephen Konstantine (*Christian Systematic Theology in World Context*): "One striking feature of both of these contributions is the absence of any discussion of the question of criteria. The criteriological question that must be answered is this: what enables something to count as a formulation of the doctrine of the Trinity?"[99] Although both Panikkar and Smart-Konstantine employ trinitarian terms and

---

[95]Kevin J. Vanhoozer, ed., *The Trinity in a Pluralistic Age* (Grand Rapids: Eerdmans, 1997).

[96]Ibid., p. x.

[97]Lesslie Newbigin, "The Trinity as Public Truth," in *The Trinity in a Pluralistic Age*, ed. Kevin J. Vanhoozer (Grand Rapids: Eerdmans, 1997), p. 7.

[98]Ibid., p. 8.

[99]Stephen Williams, "The Trinity and 'Other Religions,'" in *The Trinity in a Pluralistic Age*, ed. Kevin J. Vanhoozer (Grand Rapids: Eerdmans, 1997), p. 28.

identify triadic patterns, neither of them answers, or even attempts to answer, this question.[100] Finally, in an essay titled "Does the Trinity Belong in a Theology of Religions?" Kevin Vanhoozer explores several key trinitarian issues in the Christian theology of religions.[101] One issue concerns the relation of the Son and the Spirit in the economy of salvation. Vanhoozer expresses concern over the way many contemporary theologies treat the Spirit as "universalizer."[102] If the Spirit's activity truly is universal, one would not be able "to distinguish the divine from the demonic," nor would there be any good reason exist to limit the Spirit's work to the realm of religion.[103] Vanhoozer suggests that problematic accounts of the Spirit's universal work arise, at least in part, from a failure to consider how the Spirit relates to Christ: "Does not the narrative identification of the triune God present the Spirit as the Spirit of Christ—not simply the Logos, but the crucified and risen Christ?"[104] Contemporary theologians would benefit from reconsidering Reformed teaching regarding the "inseparability of Word and Spirit, and in particular its doctrine of the testimony of the Spirit, for a theology of religions."[105]

In 2000, two important books relating the trinitarian doctrine to the theology of religions were published: Gavin D'Costa's *The Meeting of Religions and the Trinity*, and Amos Yong's *Discerning the Spirit(s): A Pentecostal-Charismatic Contribution to a Christian Theology of Religions*.[106] In *The Meeting of Religions and the Trinity* D'Costa argues that pluralists like John Hick are really covert exclusivists and that the concerns which drive pluralist interpretations of religion (e.g., openness,

---

[100]Ibid., p. 29.

[101]Kevin J. Vanhoozer, "Does the Trinity Belong in a Theology of Religions? On Angling in the Rubicon and the 'Identity' of God," in *The Trinity in a Pluralistic Age*, ed. Kevin J. Vanhoozer (Grand Rapids: Eerdmans, 1997), pp. 41-71.

[102]Ibid., p. 62.

[103]Ibid., p. 63.

[104]Ibid., pp. 69-70.

[105]Ibid., p. 70.

[106]Gavin D'Costa, *The Meeting of Religions and the Trinity* (Maryknoll, N.Y.: Orbis, 2000); and Amos Yong, *Discerning the Spirit(s): A Pentecostal-Charismatic Contribution to a Christian Theology of Religions* (Sheffield, U.K.: Sheffield Academic Press, 2000).

tolerance and equality) are better addressed within the framework of a Roman Catholic trinitarian theology of religions. Central to D'Costa's trinitarian theology of religions is the universal presence of the Holy Spirit. Although he believes that the Spirit is universally present and active within non-Christian religions, D'Costa rejects the view that non-Christian religions, *qua* religions, constitute "vehicles of salvation" on the grounds that support for this view cannot be found in conciliar teaching.[107] D'Costa contends that that presence of the Spirit in non-Christian religions is "intrinsically trinitarian and ecclesiological."[108] As a result, the work of the Spirit outside the church must be analogous to the Spirit's work inside the church. Furthermore, he argues that the presence of the Spirit cannot be severed from the presence of Christ, the church and the kingdom.[109] Christian theologians, therefore, should avoid "abstract talk of the 'the Spirit in other religions.'"[110] In the process of constructing alternative theologies of religion, a number of Catholic thinkers—including Paul Knitter, Raimundo Panikkar and Jacques Dupuis—have severed "intrinsic relations" that obtain between the persons of the Trinity, the church and the presence of God in the world.[111] At least five implications flow from the universal presence of the Holy Spirit. First, it means that salvation is available (apart from the witness of the church) to adherents of non-Christian religions. Second, it means that the Spirit produces the presence of the kingdom and the church in an "inchoate" form among other religions.[112] Third, it suggests that through engagement with adherents of other religions, the church may be led more deeply into the life of the triune God: "The church, therefore, must be attentive to the possibility of God's gift of himself through the prayers and practices of other religions."[113] Fourth,

---

[107]D'Costa, *Meeting of Religions and the Trinity*, p. 105.
[108]Ibid., p. 110.
[109]Ibid., p. 111.
[110]Ibid., p. 128.
[111]Ibid., p. 110.
[112]Ibid., p. 116.
[113]Ibid., pp. 115-16.

as a result of the Spirit's universal presence, it is possible that Christians may observe "Christ-likeness" in adherents of other religions: "It must be clear from this that other religions, in keeping with their own self-understanding, may generate profoundly Christ-like behavior."[114] Finally, because the Spirit inspires every "authentic prayer," Christian participation in interreligious prayer may, in certain contexts, be appropriate.[115]

The universal presence of the Spirit also plays a central role in the work of Amos Yong. Although a number of Christian theologians have commended pneumatological approaches to non-Christian religions, *Discerning the Spirit(s)* represents the first book-length attempt to articulate a pneumatological theology of religions. In *Discerning the Spirit(s)* Yong argues that the Holy Spirit is present and active among adherents of non-Christian religions and that Christians must learn to discern the Spirit's presence.[116] The trinitarian pneumatology he outlines in *Discerning the Spirit(s)* builds on a distinction between an economy of the Word and the economy of the Spirit. Because the Spirit acts in an economy distinct from that of the Son, Christians should be able to identify aspects of the Spirit's work that are not constrained by the work of the Son. To this end, Yong outlines a process for discerning the "religious" activity of the Spirit among adherents of other religions that involves three elements (experiential, ethical and theological).

Perhaps the most sophisticated attempt to ground a Christian theology of religions in trinitarian doctrine came in 2001 with the publication of S. Mark Heim's *The Depth of the Riches: A Trinitarian Theology of Religious Ends*.[117] Heim claims that the quest for a Christian theology of religions generally proceeds from the unwarranted supposition that there can be only one religious end. In contrast, Heim argues for *mul-*

---

[114]Ibid., p. 129.

[115]Ibid., p. 152.

[116]Yong's proposal will be discussed at length in chap. 4.

[117]S. Mark Heim, *The Depth of the Riches: A Trinitarian Theology of Religious Ends*, Sacra Doctrina (Grand Rapids: Eerdmans, 2001). Heim's proposal will be discussed at length in chap. 3.

tiple religious ends. While Christians will experience salvation (i.e., communion with the triune God), adherents of other religions may experience other ends that must be distinguished from Christian salvation.[118] These alternate ends are rooted in the complex nature of the triune God. The divine life of the triune God is complex in that it is constituted by three dimensions. When a relation with God is pursued exclusively through one of the three dimensions, the result is a distinct religious end that cannot simply be subsumed under salvation (in the Christian sense).[119] Four kinds of human destiny may follow: Christian salvation, other religious ends, nonreligious destinies, and the negation of the created self.

In 2003 Michael Ipgrave wrote a book titled *Trinity and Inter Faith Dialogue* in which he presents the doctrine of the Trinity as a key "resource" for interfaith discussion.[120] This doctrine can be seen as a resource when we recognize that the Trinity represents "a universal pattern traceable in all religions."[121] Central to Ipgrave's proposal is a distinction between "Trinity" and "trinity." The former represents the divine persons of Christian revelation (Father, Son and Holy Spirit), while the latter "serves as a generic name for any triadic account of divinity sharing to some recognizable extent in the patterns of Christian understanding of the Trinity."[122] In short, Ipgrave proposes that we separate the structural or constitutive elements of the Trinity from confession that this trinitarian God has been revealed in Jesus Christ.[123] To this end, he identifies six foundational trinitarian elements as a basis for interfaith engagement, including "plurality" (divine reality involves

---

[118]Ibid., pp. 31-32.
[119]Ibid., pp. 167-68.
[120]Michael Ipgrave, *Trinity and Inter Faith Dialogue: Plenitude and Plurality*, Religions and Discourse 14 (New York: Peter Lang, 2003), p. 21.
[121]Ibid.
[122]Ibid., p. 12.
[123]"The coherence of this separation is shown by the possibility in principle of imagining a religious faith which taught that God was an eternal and co-equal 'trinity', differentiated as three persons and undivided in one substance, yet which made no reference to the event of Jesus Christ" (ibid., p. 25).

differentiation), "personality" (realities constituted by this differentiation are, in some sense, persons), "threeness" (there are exactly three differentiated persons), "equality" (patterns of equality mark these relationships), "necessity" (any differentiation must be necessary rather than contingent), and "immanence" (differentiation must obtain at every ontological level).[124] Through the six "trinitarian parameters," this doctrine provides the key to discussing the divine reality toward which human dialogue is directed. These trinitarian parameters can be identified and named in other religious traditions.[125] Ipgrave also suggests that the key elements of successful dialogue ("openness," "rationality" and affirming "religious experience") are grounded, respectively, in the Father, Son and Holy Spirit; thus, a trinitarian pattern shapes the dialogical process.[126]

One final work merits discussion. In 2004 Veli-Matti Kärkkäinen wrote *Trinity and Religious Pluralism: The Doctrine of the Trinity in Christian Theology of Religions*.[127] Kärkkäinen briefly explores nine recent attempts to relate trinitarian doctrine to a Christian theology of religions. Four are Roman Catholic (Karl Rahner, Jacques Dupuis, Gavin D'Costa, Raimundo Panikkar) while five are Protestant (Karl Barth, Wolfhart Pannenberg, Clark Pinnock, S. Mark Heim, John Hick).[128] Following his analysis of these nine theologians, Kärkkäinen examines recent dialogue between Roman Catholics and Muslims in France as a test case for a trinitarian theology of religions. He concludes by identifying a number of issues that need to be addressed "on the way

---

[124]Ibid., pp. 27-31.

[125]"Trinitarian doctrine makes a claim about the structure of the divine life: that the ultimate referent of religious language is in reality characterized by the patterns of Trinitarian diversity which mark the Christian understanding of God—patterns which I have identified in terms of six parameters. As this is so in reality, it is not unreasonable to expect some traces of this diversity to be found in the ways in which other religious traditions in turn speak of the divine plenitude" (ibid., pp. 336-37).

[126]Ibid., p. 325.

[127]Veli-Matti Kärkkäinen, *Trinity and Religious Pluralism: The Doctrine of the Trinity in Christian Theology of Religions* (Burlington, Vt.: Ashgate, 2004).

[128]Kärkkäinen groups these proposals under three headings which broadly parallel the exclusivist, inclusivist and pluralist positions.

to a more coherent, satisfactory trinitarian theology of religions."[129] Kärkkäinen argues that Christian trinitarian faith is incompatible with any form of "normative" pluralism (e.g., the pluralism of John Hick) and that the issue of truth must be taken seriously because Christian truth claims possess a universal intent.[130] In addition, he suggests that greater attention must be paid to the question of what constitutes a legitimate doctrine of the Trinity in the theology of religions.[131] Recent formulations need to be assessed in light of salvation history and the classic creeds.[132] Along the way Kärkkäinen surfaces several problems that arise in recent proposals including severed links between Trinity and Christology, between Trinity and salvation history, and between Trinity and church. He concludes his investigation by identifying several questions that must be answered on the way to an adequate trinitarian theology of religions. What relationship exists between the Son and the Spirit in the economy of salvation? Should pneumatological approaches to the theology of religions replace christological approaches? Among current approaches, which are adequate from a biblical and theological standpoint? Finally, what criteria might be employed to evaluate the adequacy of various proposals?[133]

Although important differences exist among the proposals outlined above, they share one feature in common: an assumption that the doctrine of the Trinity (or, more precisely, a particular construal of this doctrine)[134] constitutes the basis for a positive interpretation of religious diversity from the standpoint of Christian theology.[135] Increasing appeal

---

[129]Kärkkäinen, *Trinity and Religious Pluralism*, p. 164.

[130]Ibid., pp. 165-66.

[131]Ibid., pp. 169-71.

[132]Ibid., p. 170.

[133]Ibid., p. 182.

[134]By referring to "the" doctrine of the Trinity I am not implying that there is one particular systematic understanding of the triune God upon which all Christians agree. In this sense, it might be more accurate to speak about "a" doctrine of the Trinity. By speaking of "the" doctrine of the Trinity I have in mind trinitarian doctrine in contrast to other loci of Christian doctrine (e.g., soteriology, anthropology, etc.). Of course, the classic trinitarian *faith* of the church is confessed in the ancient ecumenical creeds.

[135]In addition to the works discussed previously, a number of other theologians also commend

to trinitarian doctrine in the Christian theology of religions raises a host of questions: Does the doctrine of the Trinity provide a roadmap for interreligious dialogue? Can vestiges of the Trinity be found in non-Christian religious experience? Is it legitimate to appeal to complexity in the Trinity as a basis for multiple religious ends? To what extent can one affirm the presence of conflicting economic manifestations of the triune God in other religions without undermining the unity of the economic Trinity and the immanent Trinity? In light of the fact that the divine persons act with one will in the economy of salvation, to what extent—if any—is it appropriate to ground a theology of religions in an independent economy of the Spirit? These are some of the questions that will be examined in the chapters that follow.

---

the doctrine of the Trinity as an important resource for understanding religious diversity. See Daniel P. Sheridan, "Grounded in the Trinity: Suggestions for a Theology of Relationship to Other Religions," *Thomist* 50 (1986): 260-78; Anthony Kelly, *The Trinity of Love: A Theology of the Christian God*, New Theology (Wilmington, Del.: Michael Glazier, 1989), pp. 228-48; M. Darrol Bryant, "Interfaith Encounter and Dialogue in a Trinitarian Perspective," in *Christianity and the Wider Ecumenism*, ed. Peter C. Phan (New York: Paragon House, 1990), pp. 3-20; Anne Hunt, *Trinity: Nexus of the Mysteries of Christian Faith*, Theology in Global Perspective (Maryknoll, N.Y.: Orbis, 2005), pp. 139-64; Reinhold Bernhardt, "The Real and the Trinitarian God," in *The Myth of Religious Superiority: Multifaith Explorations of Religious Pluralism*, ed. Paul F. Knitter (Maryknoll, N.Y.: Orbis, 2005), pp. 194-210; Peter C. Hodgson, "The Spirit and Religious Pluralism," in *The Myth of Religious Superiority: Multifaith Explorations of Religious Pluralism*, ed. Paul F. Knitter (Maryknoll, N.Y.: Orbis, 2005), pp. 135-50; Harvey G. Cox Jr., "Make Way for the Spirit," in *God's Life in Trinity*, ed. Miroslav Volf and Michael Welker (Minneapolis: Fortress, 2006), pp. 93-100; Daniel L. Migliore, "The Trinity and the Theology of Religions," in *God's Life in Trinity*, ed. Miroslav Volf and Michael Welker (Minneapolis: Fortress, 2006), pp. 101-17; Roger Haight, "Trinity and Religious Pluralism," *Journal of Ecumenical Studies* 44 (2009): 525-40; and Ilia Delio, "Religious Pluralism and the Coincidence of Opposites," *Theological Studies* 70 (2009): 822-44.

2

INTRODUCING THE TRINITARIAN
THEOLOGY OF AUGUSTINE

◆

In the Western church, Augustine of Hippo (354-430) has been recognized as a "Doctor of the Church" (*Doctor Ecclesiae*), that is, a reliable authority whose teaching on the Trinity reflects the teaching of Scripture and creedal expressions of Christian orthodoxy.[1] The purpose of this chapter is to introduce the trinitarian theology of the bishop of Hippo. In the first section of the chapter I will discuss four factors that provide important context for understanding Augustine's trinitarian doctrine. In the second section I will introduce one of the most important sources for Augustine's teaching on the Trinity—*De trinitate*.

CONTEXTUALIZING AUGUSTINE'S TRINITARIAN THEOLOGY

The basic point of reference for the development of Augustine's trinitarian theology is Latin pro-Nicene theology.[2] Pro-Nicene theology is

---

[1]In the Western church, Gregory the Great, Ambrose, Augustine and Jerome were recognized as "Doctors of the Church" (*Doctores Ecclesiae*).

[2]Michel Barnes argues that when Augustine's trinitarian theology is read as a whole in its proper context, we will recognize (as we might expect of Latin theologians writing on the Trinity at this time) that "Augustine's basic frame of reference for understanding the Trinity is the appropriation of Nicaea. That appropriation takes place within a polemical context, and, more-

not merely a simple reassertion of the teaching of Nicaea. It represents an interpretation of Nicaea that emerged in the second half of the fourth century.[3] The pro-Nicene theology on which Augustine is dependent centers on common nature, common power and common operations.[4] In context of a clear distinction between *person* and *nature*, pro-Nicenes affirm that Father, Son and Holy Spirit share the same power, perform the same works and possess the same nature.[5] Representatives of pro-Nicene theology include Basil of Caesarea, Gregory of Nyssa, Gregory of Nazianzus, Hilary of Poitiers, Marius Victorinus and Ambrose of Milan.[6] Augustine's indebtedness to pro-Nicene theology can be seen early in book one of *De trinitate*, where he summarizes "Catholic" teaching on the triune God.[7]

One of the key axioms of pro-Nicene theology is the "inseparable

---

over, involves rearticulating the creed of Nicaea in terms which were not originally part of that text" ("Rereading Augustine's Theology of the Trinity," in *The Trinity: An Interdisciplinary Symposium on the Trinity*, ed. Stephen T. Davis, Daniel Kendall and Gerald O'Collins [New York: Oxford University Press, 1999], p. 154).

[3]"By this term [pro-Nicene] I refer to that *interpretation* of Nicaea and of earlier Nicene theologies which formed the context for the establishment of Catholic orthodoxy under the emperors Theodosius and Gratian through the actions of the councils of Constantinople and Aquileia, through imperial decree, and through the slow mutual recognition of a number of different pro-Nicene parties. This theology is not sufficiently defined by reference to Nicaea alone, but only by reference also to a number of the key principles within which Nicaea was interpreted as teaching a faith in three coordinate divine realities who constitute one nature, power, will and substance" (Lewis Ayres, *Augustine and the Trinity* [Cambridge: Cambridge University Press, 2010], p. 43). Ayres and Barnes have slightly different understandings of the label pro-Nicene (see Michel R. Barnes, "De trinitate VI and VII: Augustine and the Limits of Nicene Orthodoxy," *Augustinian Studies* 39 [2007]: 196 n. 19).

[4]See Michel R. Barnes, "One Nature, One power: Consensus Doctrine in Pro-Nicene Polemic," in *Studia Patristica*, vol. 29, *Historica, Theologica et Philosophica, Critica et Philologica*, ed. Elizabeth A. Livingstone (Louvain: Peeters, 1997), pp. 205-23; and Lewis Ayres, *Nicaea and Its Legacy: An Approach to Fourth-Century Trinitarian Theology* (New York: Oxford University Press, 2004), pp. 236-40. Ayres and Barnes have slightly different understanding of the label pro-Nicene (see Barnes, "De trinitate VI and VII," p. 196 n. 19.

[5]Other elements of pro-Nicene theology include an assumption that there are no degrees of divinity, that the divine persons are distinct yet possess the same nature apart from any ontological hierarchy, and that the generation of the Son by the Father takes place within the being of God and involves no division of being (see Ayres, *Nicaea and Its Legacy*, pp. 236, 434).

[6]Ibid., p. 434.

[7]See Augustine, *De trinitate* 1.7. This passage will be discussed in chap. 4.

operation" of the divine persons.[8] Anti-Nicenes argued that the distinct activity of the divine persons meant that Father, Son and Holy Spirit are separate beings, with the Father being ontologically superior. In response pro-Nicenes like Ambrose and Hilary argued that Scripture demonstrates that all three persons are involved in acts of creation, providence and redemption.[9] Thus, Father, Son and Holy Spirit share one nature. The inseparable action of the divine persons represents one of the fundamental elements of Augustine's trinitarian grammar.[10]

Second, Augustine's teaching on the Trinity arises from substantive engagement with Scripture. Whatever else may have been involved, one thing is clear: the fourth-century battle over the doctrine of God was a battle about how to rightly read and interpret Scripture. In the latter context Augustine contends "for the rightness of saying, believing, understanding that the Father and the Son and the Holy Spirit are of one and the same substance or essence." Hence, his first priority is to "establish by the authority of the holy scriptures whether the faith is in fact like that."[11] In his effort to demonstrate the unity and equality of the Father, Son and Holy Spirit, Augustine discusses numerous biblical texts. The scriptural index to *De trinitate* in volume 50a of *Corpus Christianorum Series Latina* contains over 6,800 biblical citations and allusions.[12] In addition to twenty-seven canonical Old Testament books, citations can be found from every New Testament book except Philemon.

---

[8]"The inseparable operation of the three irreducible persons is a fundamental axiom of those theologies which provide the context for the Council of Constantinople in AD 381 and for the reinterpretation of Nicaea, which came to be the foundation of orthodox or catholic theology at the end of the fourth century" (Lewis Ayres, "The Fundamental Grammar of Augustine's Trinitarian Theology," in *Augustine and His Critics: Essays in Honour of Gerald Bonner*, ed. Robert Dodaro and George Lawless [New York: Routledge, 2000], p. 56; see also Ayres, *Augustine and the Trinity*, pp. 42-71).

[9]It should be noted that the distinction of the divine persons is not lost in inseparable operation. The Father always works *through* the Son and *in* the Holy Spirit. See chap. 4.

[10]Ayres, "Fundamental Grammar of Augustine's Trinitarian Theology," p. 55. Augustine's account of inseparable operation will be discussed in chap. 4.

[11]Ibid.

[12]See *Corpus Christianorum Series Latina* 50A, (Turnholt, Belgium: Brepols, 1968), pp. 601-721.

Third, despite popular claims to the contrary, Augustine's teaching does not stand in sharp contrast to the trinitarian theology of the Cappadocians (Basil of Caesarea, Gregory of Nyssa and Gregory of Nazianzus). Many contemporary narratives of the development of the trinitarian theology proceed from the unwarranted assumption that significant differences exist between early Western approaches (which emphasize divine unity) and Eastern approaches (which emphasize the communion of divine persons).[13] As Orthodox theologian David Hart explains, the idea that from the early centuries the trinitarian theologies of the East and West operate on "contrary logics" is "a particularly tedious, persistent and pernicious falsehood."[14] Although it will eventually "fade away from want of documentary evidence," at the present time "it serves too many interests for theological scholarship to dispense with it too casually."[15] Michel Barnes points out belief in Greek versus Latin paradigms is a modern phenomenon: "only theologians of the last one hundred years have ever thought it was true."[16] Although numerous works arrange their history of trinitarian theology around this paradigm, none express awareness that the truth of this paradigm needs to be demonstrated.[17] Against the East-West paradigm, it is important to recognize that Augustine and Cappadocians share in common all the core elements of pro-Nicene theology discussed earlier (common power, common operations, common nature).[18]

Finally, Augustine's trinitarian doctrine is not static. It develops

---

[13]This problematic assumption can be traced to the work of nineteenth-century Jesuit Théodore de Régnon. Trenchant criticisms of this polarizing paradigm can be found in Michel R. Barnes, "De Régnon Reconsidered," *Augustinian Studies* 26 (1995): 51-79; "Augustine in Contemporary Trinitarian Theology," *Theological Studies* 56 (1995): 237-50; David B. Hart, "The Mirror of the Infinite: Gregory of Nyssa on the *Vestigia Trinitatis*," *Modern Theology* 18 (2002): 541-61; and Ayres, *Nicaea and Its Legacy*, pp. 273-383.

[14]Hart, "Mirror of the Infinite," p. 541.

[15]Ibid.

[16]Barnes, "Augustine in Contemporary Trinitarian Theology," p. 238.

[17]Ibid. See also Barnes, "De Régnon Reconsidered," p. 55.

[18]A case in point is inseparable operation. Augustine and the Cappadocians have virtually identical accounts of the inseparable operation of the Father, Son and Holy Spirit. See chap. 4.

throughout his lifetime.[19] One area where development can be clearly seen is in his explanation of one of the core elements of pro-Nicene theology: unity of operation.[20] Lewis Ayres traces Augustine's explanation of inseparable operation from Augustine's early writings to his mature writings highlighting the development that occurs in the process.[21] Augustine's understanding of divine communion also develops. Ayres suggests that between 410 and 420, Augustine moves "towards a sophisticated account of the divine communion as resulting from the eternal intra-divine acts of the divine three."[22] That Augustine's trinitarian theology develops has at least two implications for contemporary readers. First, we must pay attention to continuities and discontinuities between his statements in one portion of his writings and others. Second, we must attend to *all* his trinitarian writings in order to form judgments about the relative significance of particular concepts he employs.

INTRODUCING *DE TRINITATE*

With this background in mind, we will turn our attention to Augustine's most substantive work on the Trinity—*De trinitate*.[23] This work represents the primary (but not exclusive) source for the "Augustinian" assessment that will be offered in chapters three to five. *De trinitate* was composed over a period of twenty years (c. 400-420) and can be divided into two sections: books 1-7 and 8-15.[24] In the first section, Augustine

---

[19]For a condensed overview of some of the ways Augustine's trinitarian theology develops over time, see Ayres, *Augustine and the Trinity*, pp. 320-25.

[20]Another example of development can be seen in Augustine's pneumatology. For a discussion of how Augustine's pneumatology develops toward the end of his life through polemical engagement with Homoian theologians, see Michel R. Barnes, "Augustine's Last Pneumatology," *Augustinian Studies* 39 (2008): 223-34.

[21]Lewis Ayres, "'Remember That You Are Catholic' (Serm 52.2): Augustine on the Unity of the Triune God," *Journal of Early Christian Studies* 8 (2000): 39-82.

[22]Ayres, *Augustine and the Trinity*, p. 3.

[23]English citations of *De trinitate* will be taken from Augustine, *The Trinity*, trans. Edmund Hill (Brooklyn: New City Press, 1991). To avoid multiplying footnotes, references *to De trinitate* (and other key works) will be placed in the main text. Numbers following the comma in these references are page numbers in *The Trinity*.

[24]Augustine was in the process of writing book 11 when it was pirated. Work stopped for a number of years. At the prompting of others, Augustine eventually completed *De trinitate*

defends a pro-Nicene understanding of trinitarian doctrine from the standpoints of Scripture (bks. 1-4) and logic (bks. 5-7). Augustine explores a wide range of New Testament (bks. 1, 2a) and Old Testament (bks. 2b, 3) texts. In the process of countering Arian exegesis, he develops a sophisticated trinitarian hermeneutic (see chap. 4). Important themes in books 1-4 include the unity and equality of the divine persons, the generation of the Son and procession of the Holy Spirit, the temporal missions of the Son and Spirit, the mediatorial work of Christ, and contemplation of the triune God as the goal of Christian existence. Key themes in books 5-7 include the incomprehensibility of the triune God, a discussion of language used to describe the Trinity (substance, accident and relationship), the identity of the Holy Spirit, and the status of Father, Son and Holy Spirit as "persons."

Augustine's purpose in books 1-7 is not merely apologetic. Luigi Gioia points out that two layers of argument can be discerned in these books: an outer layer focused on exposition of the doctrine of Trinity, and an inner layer focusing on the means by which humans come to know the invisible God (i.e., the incarnation).[25] For example, Augustine's distinction in book 1 between the Son in the "form of a servant" and the Son in the "form of God" (discussed later) does not merely secure a proper understanding of the identity of Christ as the God-man but this distinction also plays a crucial role in what Lewis Ayres has characterized as Augustine's "Christological epistemology."[26] It is through the "form of a servant" that we come to know the triune God who is invisible. Thus, revelation and soteriology are inextricably linked for Augustine.

In the second half of *De trinitate* (bks. 8-15), Augustine searches for reflections of the generation of the Son and procession of the Holy Spirit in the highest functions of the human soul. The concern animat-

---

around 420. For discussion of the dating of *De trinitate* see Ayres, *Augustine and the Trinity*, pp. 118-20.

[25]Luigi Gioia, *The Theological Epistemology of Augustine's* De trinitate (Oxford: Oxford University Press, 2008), pp. 24-39. Gioia's work offers an excellent introduction to *De trinitate*.

[26]See Ayres, *Augustine and the Trinity*, pp. 142-74.

ing books 8-15 is not apologetic (e.g., trying to prove the Trinity apart from Scripture) but theological and, more specifically, epistemological. Augustine wants to lead readers into deeper knowledge and experience of the triune God. These books build on the theme of "contemplation" that was introduced in book 1 of *De trinitate*.

Although a number of proposals have been offered regarding the overarching structure of *De trinitate*, it is perhaps best to see the unity of this work not in terms of some structural feature that unites all the books (e.g., a *chiasmus*, as Edmund Hill proposes) but rather in terms of recurring and developing themes.[27] Although *De trinitate* later tended to circulate in discrete sections (e.g., bks. 5-7 or bks. 8-15), it is clear that Augustine intended this work to be read and understood as a whole.[28]

De trinitate is shaped by a "spiritual quest" to know and understand the God in whom Augustine believes.[29] Psalm 105:3-4 [104:3-4 LXX], with its exhortation to seek God's face, provides the motivation for this journey:

> Glory in his holy name;
> let the hearts of those who seek the LORD rejoice!
> Seek the LORD and his strength;
> seek his presence continually!

Edmund Hill rightly identifies Psalm 105:3-4 as a "theme-setting text for the whole book."[30] Augustine invites his readers to join him in

---

[27]Gioia argues that human knowledge of the Trinity represents the central theme of *De trinitate* (Gioia, *Theological Epistemology*, p. 4).

[28]This reality fuels misreadings of *De trinitate*.

[29]John Cooper suggests that one of the most basic notions in Augustine's writings is that of a "spiritual quest": "After a close study of the eight works in question here, the following thesis is now offered concerning the most basic notions of Augustine's entire thought-world: *That Augustine's basic philosophical-theological notion is a universalization of the particular spiritual journey which he himself experienced.* Stated in his own words this 'elephantine' idea is: 'Thou hast made us for Thyself, and our hearts are restless 'til they rest in thee.' (*Confs.* I, 1, 5.) *Thus, Augustine's basic notion is the concept of the spiritual quest*" (John Cooper, "The Basic Philosophical and Theological Notions of Saint Augustine," *Augustinian Studies* 15 [1984]: 94).

[30]Hill, *Trinity*, p. 91 n. 11. Augustine's use of this scriptural text will be discussed further in chap. 5.

his quest to seek God's face. This quest might further be characterized as "faith seeking understanding."

The redemptive work of Christ plays a crucial role in this quest to know God.[31] Although it would be an overstatement to describe the primary purpose of *De trinitate* as offering a polemic against the possibility of a Neo-Platonic ascent to God,[32] Augustine is clear that the mediatorial work of Christ is necessary in order to contemplate God.[33] Indeed, apart from Christ's "soteriological and epistemological mediation," humans cannot know the invisible God.[34] Christology, soteriology and revelation are inextricably linked in *De trinitate*. This is because the identity of God cannot be separated from questions of how humans are able to know God.[35] Humans come to know and love God "through God," that is to say, through the work of Christ and the Holy Spirit.[36] Conversion plays a crucial role in this process. Rowan Williams rightly notes that "the genius of *De trinitate* is its fusion of speculation and prayer, its presentation of trinitarian theology as, ultimately, nothing other than a teasing out of what it is to be converted and to come to live in Christ."[37]

De trinitate is driven by exegetical and polemical concerns. This judgment runs counter to a tendency in modern scholarship to read *De trinitate* as driven by "speculative" (read: metaphysical) concerns. Although Augustine refers at various points to "Arian" opponents, some scholars have suggested that these references simply constitute a literary device based on the assumption that "Augustine's knowledge of Homoian theology was unsubstantial, formal, or secondhand in character,"

---

[31]It should be noted that Augustine does not distinguish trinitarian concerns from Christology, as is the case in contemporary theology.

[32]Contra John Cavadini, "The Structure and Intention of Augustine's *De trinitate*," *Augustinian Studies* 23 (1992): 103-23.

[33]Gioia, *Theological Epistemology*, pp. 33-34

[34]Ibid., p. 33.

[35]Ibid., p. 3.

[36]Ibid., p. 4.

[37]Rowan Williams, "*De Trinitate*," in *Augustine Through the Ages: An Encyclopedia*, ed. Allan D. Fitzgerald (Grand Rapids: Eerdmans, 1999).

and that his first genuine encounter with Latin Homoian theology did not emerge until 419, when he had virtually finished writing *De trinitate*.[38] Against this view, Michel Barnes demonstrates that Augustine is engaged in polemic against Latin Homoian theologians in the earliest sections in the composition of *De trinitate*. For example, when Augustine refers in Book I to "Those who have affirmed that our Lord Jesus Christ is not God, or is not true God, or is not with the Father the one and only God, or is not truly immortal because he is subject to change" (*De trinitate* 1.9, 70-71), Barnes argues that Augustine is referring to the views of Homoian theologians like Palladius.[39] Moreover, his the-

---

[38]See Michel R. Barnes, "Exegesis and Polemic in Augustine's '*De Trinitate* I,'" *Augustinian Studies* 30 (1999): 43. As Homoian theologians were not present in large numbers in North Africa in the late fourth century, Lewis Ayres believes that Augustine's initial engagement with Homoian theology in *De trinitate* does not reflect direct engagement with these theologians. Nevertheless, even after he engages in debate with representatives of Homoian theology in the early fifth century, "the basic lines of his attack remain the same" (Ayres, *Augustine and the Trinity*, p. 172).

[39]"The three doctrines that Augustine cites at *de Trinitate* 1.9 as representative of his opponents are each attested to in Latin Homoian literature, and fit within the overall Latin Homoian emphasis on the Father as 'true God' due to his unique or exclusive status as *ingenerate*—a theology which has too often been misrecognized as Eunomian. This summary at *de Trinitate* 1.9 by Augustine of his opponents' beliefs resembles a large body of polemical literature which contains similar summaries of both Arian and Homoian doctrines. The oldest such summary, and the most widely distributed one among Latin Nicenes, is Arius's *Letter to Alexander*, which from the late 350s on was well known in the West" (Barnes, "Exegesis and Polemic in Augustine's *De trinitate* I," pp. 45-46). Later in the same essay Barnes also explains, "The Homoian theology Augustine describes in the first books of *de Trinitate* cannot be reduced simply to the theology opposed by Hilary, much less to the theology of Arius. Augustine's opponents represent a change, indeed perhaps a development, in anti-Nicene theology from the theology of Hilary's opponents, and a major development from the theology of Arius. In Book I of Augustine's *de Trinitate* we are dealing with a third generation of anti-Nicene theology, and a second generation of Latin Homoian theology" (ibid., p. 48). The first generation would represent the teachings of Arius. The second generation of anti-Nicene theology differs from the first in that the former treats the visibility and materiality of the Son (in contrast to the invisibility and immateriality of the Father) as the basis for distinguishing the real divinity of the Father (who is "true God") from the Son. Hillary responds to these second-generation anti-Nicenes in his writings. Augustine's opponents represent a third generation of Latin-speaking anti-Nicenes who grounded the visibility and materiality of the Son not in the incarnation but in the Old Testament theophanies. Representatives of third generation anti-Nicene theology include Palladius and Bishop Maximinus. For further discussion of Augustine's Homoian opponents, see Michel R. Barnes, "Anti-Arian Works," in *Augustine Through the Ages: An Encyclopedia*, ed. Allan D. Fitzgerald (Grand Rapids: Eerdmans, 1999).

ology develops through his engagement with his opponents.[40]

At the center of his debate with Homoian theologians was how to rightly read and interpret Scripture. How, Augustine asks, are we to understand biblical texts that speak of the Father as somehow "greater" than the Son (e.g., Jn 14:28; 1 Cor 15:24-28)? The answer is found in a "rule" provided by the apostle Paul in Philippians 2:6-7 (*De trinitate* 1.14, 74). "Who, though he was in the form of God, did not count equality with God a thing to be grasped, but made himself nothing, taking the form of a servant, being born in the likeness of men." On the basis of this text, Augustine explains that we must distinguish the Son in the "form of God" (i.e., deity) from the Son in the "form of a servant" (i.e., humanity) (*De trinitate* 1.22, 82).[41] In the "form of God," he is equal to the Father, while in the "form of a servant" he is "less" than the Father.[42] Problems arise when people confuse these two forms: "This has misled people who are careless about examining or keeping in view the whole range of the scriptures, and they have tried to transfer what is said of Christ Jesus as man to that substance of his which was everlasting before the incarnation and is everlasting still" (*De trinitate*, 1.14, 74). In the form of God, Christ created all things (Jn 1:3), while in the form of a servant he was born of a woman (Gal 4:4). In the form of God, Christ is equal to the Father (Jn 10:30), while in the form of a servant he obeys the Father (Jn 6:38). In the form of a God, Christ is "true God" (1 Jn 5:20), while in the form of a servant he is obedient to the point of death (Phil 2:8). These two "forms" exist in one person— the Son of God (*De trinitate*, 1.28, 86).

Augustine employs this first rule like a battering ram against Ho-

---

[40]"In other words, Augustine's engagement with Homoian theology can be seen to be a moment in which the heart of Augustine's own trinitarian theology is at stake. Augustine's trinitarian theology is at its most distinctive and fundamental level a response to the specific challenge posed by developing Homoian theology" (Barnes, "Exegesis and Polemic in Augustine's *De trinitate* I," p. 52).

[41]For a contemporary defense of Augustine's reading of Phil 2:6-7, see Dennis Jowers, "The Meaning of *Morphe* in Philippians 2:6-7," *Journal of the Evangelical Theological Society* 49 (2006): 739-66.

[42]Distinguishing between the two natures of Christ was a common pro-Nicene strategy.

moian theologians, who argued that the Son is inferior to the Father on the basis of texts like 1 Corinthians 15:24-28. In the form of God, the Son is equal to the Father. Thus, when the Son "hands over" the kingdom to the Father, we should not think that "he deprives himself of it" since "together with the Father he is one God" (*De trinitate*, 1.17, 76). However, in the form of a servant (i.e., as "mediator"), Christ will hand over the kingdom to the Father, that is, he will bring believers into "a direct contemplation of God and the Father" (*De trinitate*, 1.17, 76).[43] Of course, when he brings believers into contemplation of the Father, "he will assuredly bring them to the contemplation of himself" as well (*De trinitate*, 1.18, 79). In Augustine's exegesis of this passage, we see an example of the "two layers" of argument converging. In the outer layer, Augustine uses the distinction between the two "forms" to counter Homoian reading of 1 Corinthians 15:28. However, an inner layer is also present. Commenting on Augustine's reading of 1 Corinthians 15:28, Lewis Ayres explains, "'the man Jesus Christ' has his purpose in leading the just towards contemplation of the Trinity—his incarnate materiality draws us towards his nature as the immaterial and fully divine Son."[44]

In book 2, Augustine points out that the distinction between the Son in the "form of a servant" and the Son in the "form of God" is inadequate to address a number of passages that speak of the Son neither as "less" than the Father nor "equal" to the Father, but rather suggest that the Son is "from" the Father (*De trinitate*, 2.2, 98). Another "rule" must be applied to these texts: "This then is the rule [*regula*] which governs many scriptural texts, intended to show not that one person is less than the other, but only that one is from the other" (*De trinitate*, 2.3, 99).[45] Augustine explicitly cites John 5:19 and John 5:26 as exam-

---

[43]In arguing that contemplation is the outcome of this handing over, Augustine appeals to a variety of biblical texts, including 1 Cor 13:12; 1 Jn 3:2; Ps 5:4; Rom 8:24-25; Mt 5:8. "Contemplation" is a major theme in *De trinitate*.

[44]Ayres, *Augustine and the Trinity*, p. 147.

[45]Commenting on this rule, Ayres explains, "Augustine's new rule does not teach that the texts which it governs reveal only *that* the Son is from the Father, but also *how* the Son is from the

ples of this second rule. Commenting on these texts, Augustine explains, "So the reason for these statements can only be that the life of the Son is unchanging like the Father's, and yet is from the Father [v. 26]; and that the work of Father and Son is indivisible, and yet the Son's working is from the Father just as he himself is from the Father [v. 19]; and the way in which the Son sees the Father is simply by being the Son" (*De trinitate*, 2.3, 99). This second rule is central not only to Augustine's reading of John 5 but also the numerous "sending" texts scattered throughout the Gospel of John. It also plays an important role in his exposition of texts regarding the Holy Spirit. For example, the reason the Spirit does not speak from himself (Jn 16:13-14) is because the Spirit is not, so to speak, from himself. The reason the Spirit glorifies the Son is because he receives from the Son (and the Father). Augustine's explanation of this second rule represents one of his distinctive contributions to the development of Latin pro-Nicene trinitarian hermeneutics.[46]

Combining these two rules, New Testament references to Christ can be grouped into three categories: (1) texts that refer to Son in the "form of God," in which he is equal to the Father (e.g., Jn 10:30; Phil 2:6); (2) texts that refer to the Son in the "form of a servant," in which he is "less" than the Father (e.g., Jn 14:28); and (3) texts that suggest the Son is "from" the Father (e.g., Jn 5:19, 26) (*De trinitate*, 2.3, 98).

Finally, *De trinitate* is neither Augustine's *only* word about the Trinity nor his *final* word about the Trinity.[47] Awareness of his other trinitarian writings is important for determining the relative significance of themes encountered in *De trinitate*. By attending exclusively to *De trinitate*, some scholars have misinterpreted the significance of elements of Augustine's theology. For example, despite the prominent role played

---

Father. The second rule necessarily operates against the background of Augustine's Nicene insistence that each of the divine three possesses the attributes of divinity" (*Augustine and the Trinity*, p. 179).

[46]Augustine was not the first to recognize that Scripture speaks of Christ in this way. His unique contribution relates to his exposition of this foundational hermeneutical principle.

[47]Barnes, "Augustine's Last Pneumatology," p. 223.

by the triad of "memory, understanding and will" in *De trinitate*, Lewis Ayres argues on the basis of an examination of Augustine's other trinitarian writings that this triad should *not* be seen as a central feature of Augustine's trinitarian thought.[48] Michel Barnes concurs with the judgment of Ayres that the triad of memory, understanding and will is not a central feature of Augustine's trinitarian theology. Barnes argues that the most important themes in Augustine's trinitarian theology include (1) the doctrine of God's immaterial nature, (2) inseparable operations, and (3) the notion that theological language is designed to purify our ideas about God.[49]

It is on the basis of the depth and vitality of Augustine's trinitarian theology that I will offer an Augustinian assessment of the role of trinitarian doctrine in the Christian theology of religions in the chapters that follow.[50] In the process of evaluating these proposals and discerning proper use(s) for the doctrine of the Trinity, I will explore several key themes in Augustine's theology, including the relationship between God *in se* and God *pro nobis* (chap. 3), divine relations among the divine persons (both intratrinitarian and economic) (chap. 4), as well as Augustine's search for reflections of the triune God in the functioning of the human soul (chap. 5). The order in which these themes are discussed in chapters three to five follows the overall structure of *De trinitate*. Chapter three will draw extensively on books 1-4. Chapter four will engage books 5-7 (as well as 1-4). Chapter five will draw upon books 8-15. Hence these chapters indirectly offer commentary on the main movements of *De trinitate*.

---

[48]Ayres, *Augustine and the Trinity*, pp. 308-9.

[49]See Michel R. Barnes, "The Logic of Augustine's Trinitarian Theology," unpublished paper presented at the Aquinas the Augustinian Conference, at Ave Maria University in Naples, Florida, on February 4, 2005, p. 5.

[50]My assessment will draw exclusively on the theology of Augustine and not later interpreters of Augustine such as Thomas Aquinas. See the introduction.

3

THE ECONOMIC TRINITY AND
THE IMMANENT TRINITY IN THE
THEOLOGY OF RELIGIONS

◆

Since the patristic period, Christian theologians have drawn an important distinction between God in himself (God *in se*) and God in relation to the world (God *pro nobis*). For patristic theologians (writing in Greek) this distinction was framed in terms of *theologia* (theology) and *oikonomia* (economy).[1] In contemporary theology a distinction between God in himself and God in relation to the world has been framed in terms of the *immanent* Trinity and the *economic* Trinity.[2] The latter denotes God's self-revelation in creation, providence and redemption, while the former refers to the intratrinitarian life of the three divine persons apart from creation and redemption. Although much current debate centers on the God-world relationship,[3] assumptions about the

---

[1]*Theologia* was used to denote to the mystery of God while *oikonomia* was used to describe God's salvific plan. Although the term *oikonomia* plays a relatively minor role in the New Testament (cf. Eph 1:10; 3:2; Col 1:25), it became a key term in patristic thought. *Oikonomia* (and its Latin equivalents) are used in a complex variety of ways in patristic theology.

[2]One of the disadvantages of speaking of the "economic Trinity" and the "immanent Trinity" is that this language may offer the mistaken impression that there are two trinities. *Economic* and *immanent* simply represent two different ways of conceptualizing the triune God. Although it might be more accurate to speak of the "the Triune God from the standpoint of the economy" or the "Triune God from an immanent perspective," such language is awkward and cumbersome. Despite its limitations, I shall retain the language of the immanent Trinity and the economic Trinity.

[3]Karl Rahner's axiom "The 'economic' Trinity is the 'immanent' Trinity and the 'immanent' Trinity is the 'economic' Trinity" constitutes a focal point for much contemporary debate (Karl Rahner, *The Trinity*, trans. Joseph Donceel [New York: Crossroad, 1999], p. 22). For a discus-

relationship of the economic Trinity and the immanent Trinity also play an important role in a Christian theology of religions. The purpose of this chapter is to offer an Augustinian assessment of the relationship between the economic Trinity and the immanent Trinity in S. Mark Heim's trinitarian theology of "religious ends." First, I will outline Heim's proposal. Then, drawing principally on books 1-4 of *De trinitate*, I will develop an Augustinian grammar for understanding the relationship between the economic Trinity and the immanent Trinity. Finally, I will evaluate Heim's proposal on the basis of this grammar, arguing that Heim gains traction only by severing the immanent Trinity from the economic Trinity.

S. MARK HEIM'S TRINITARIAN THEOLOGY OF RELIGIOUS ENDS

In his book *The Depth of the Riches: A Trinitarian Theology of Religious Ends*, Heim suggests that the debate over the theology of religions proceeds on "a largely undefended assumption that there is and can only be one religious end, one actual religious fulfillment."[4] A more fruitful approach to religious diversity involves recognizing the pos-

---

sion of the Rahner's axiom and its implications for contemporary theology, see Fred Sanders, *The Image of the Immanent Trinity: Rahner's Rule and the Theological Interpretation of Scripture*, Issues in Systematic Theology (New York: Peter Lang, 2005); Dennis W. Jowers, *Karl Rahner's Trinitarian Axiom: "The Economic Trinity is the Immanent Trinity and Vice Versa"* (Lewiston, N.Y.: Edwin Mellen Press, 2006). Broadly speaking, Rahner's axiom (frequently called "Rahner's rule") has evoked two responses. One group of theologians follows Rahner in emphasizing the "identity" of the economic Trinity and the immanent Trinity—in some cases pushing this identity to the point that the latter is collapsed into the former. Proponents of this view include Catherine LaCugna, Jürgen Moltmann, Robert Jenson, Eberhard Jüngel and Wolfhart Pannenberg. A second group of theologians insists that Rahner's rule does not maintain an adequate distinction between the economic Trinity and the immanent Trinity. Proponents of this view include Paul Molnar, Walter Kasper, Thomas Weinandy, Thomas Torrance, David Coffey and Hans Urs von Balthasar. These theologians are willing to affirm, at least in a qualified way, the first half of Rahner's axiom ("the economic Trinity is the immanent Trinity") but often reject, or significantly qualify, the second half ("the immanent Trinity is the economic Trinity") in order to protect the freedom and transcendence of God.

[4]S. Mark Heim, *The Depth of the Riches: A Trinitarian Theology of Religious Ends*, Sacra Doctrina (Grand Rapids: Eerdmans, 2001), p. 17. A condensed summary of his proposal can also be found in S. Mark Heim, "God's Diversity: A Trinitarian View of Religious Pluralism," *Christian Century* 118 (2001): 14-18.

sibility of multiple "religious ends." Christian salvation—involving a relation of communion with God—constitutes only one possible end. Other ends exist, and while they are distinct from "salvation," they are quite real. On the one hand, "we may say that another religion is a true and valid path to the religious fulfillment it seeks."[5] The Buddhist end (*nirvana*) can be achieved only by following the Buddhist path to liberation. At the same time, "we may say what the book of Acts says of Jesus Christ, that 'there is salvation in no one else, for there is no other name under heaven given among mortals by which we must be saved' (Acts 4:12)."[6]

We might ask, "If the notion of multiple ends is so plausible, why has it not been more widely embraced?" The possibility of multiple religious ends is frequently dismissed because of its perceived association with polytheism. Although an affirmation of multiple religious referents may have seemed plausible in past contexts (e.g., the first-century Greco-Roman world), it is no longer plausible today. Our contemporary world is shaped by a "monotheistic consciousness," which inclines us to believe that there can be only one religious ultimate.[7] One "ultimate" seems to imply only one "end." A "monotheistic consciousness," however, need not rule out the possibility of multiple ends if they were grounded in differing ways of relating to the same divine ultimate reality.[8]

Although he offers several arguments in support of his proposal,[9] Heim's notion of multiple religious ends is ultimately grounded in his understanding of Trinity: "Trinity provides a particular ground for af-

---

[5]Heim, *Depth of the Riches*, pp. 31-32.
[6]Ibid., p. 32.
[7]Ibid., p. 33.
[8]Ibid., p. 34.
[9]Heim offers at least four arguments in support of his proposal. First, drawing on the work of Jerome Gellman, he argues that a "determinate view of the religious ultimate" is not inconsistent with a wide variety of religious experiences. Second, he claims that while emphasizing "salvation" and "damnation," the New Testament is silent about alternative ends. It may, therefore, be possible that other human conditions might subsist within these ends. Third, he appeals to the notion of "plenitude." Finally, he appeals to the doctrine of the Trinity. The latter is by far the most significant component of his argument for multiple ends.

firming the truth and reality of what is different. Trinitarian conviction rules out the view that among all the possible claimed manifestations of God, one narrow strand alone is authentic."[10] Because there is an "irreducible variety" in what is most important (the Trinity), Christians are able to affirm the legitimacy of other religions. This is because the Trinity offers a universal description of God and the world.[11] How does the Trinity ground multiple religious ends? According to Heim, the immanent life of the triune God is "complex." This complexity constitutes the basis for multiple ends: "The complex nature of God holds out the possibility of a variety of distinct relations with God. That variety is the basis for truly different religious ends."[12] One may wonder what Heim has in mind when he refers to the "complex nature of God." This brings us to the heart of his attempt to relate the Trinity and religious diversity. Three terms play a critical role in his proposal: *dimensions*, *relations* and *ends*. The key to understanding his proposal is apprehending the interrelationships among these terms. Notice the way these terms are linked in the following summary:

> The distinctive religious *ends* of various traditions correspond to *relations* with God constituted by limitation or intensification within a particular *dimension* of the trinitarian life. This provides the basis both to affirm the reality of these religious *ends* and to distinguish them from salvation.[13]

Thus, to understand his proposal we must first attempt to understand what Heim means by *dimensions*. Then we will examine the *relations* and finally *ends*.

Three dimensions of the divine life. Building on the work of Ninian Smart and Steven Konstantine,[14] Heim claims that the divine life of

---

[10]Heim, *Depth of the Riches*, p. 127.
[11]Ibid.
[12]Ibid., p. 179 (italics added).
[13]Ibid., pp. 167-68 (italics added).
[14]Ninian Smart and Stephen Konstantine, *Christian Systematic Theology in World Context* (Minneapolis: Fortress, 1991). To a lesser degree, Heim also draws on the work of Raimundo Panikkar.

the triune God is characterized by three dimensions: impersonal, personal and communion. These dimensions arise from the complex life of three irreducible persons who live in perfect communion.[15] One of his favorite images for describing these dimensions comes from the world of broadcasting.[16] Heim likens the Trinity to a transmitter, which because of its complexity is able to send and receive signals on several frequencies. By tuning into one of these frequencies, humans encounter differing aspects of God which, in turn, lead to differing ends.[17] Christians have mistakenly assumed that the triune God merely broadcasts (and receives) signals on one frequency. This is not true. God's complex nature allows him to send and receive on a variety of wavelengths.

The impersonal "dimension" represents the infinite divine life as it circulates among the persons.[18] Economically, this dimension is expressed in divine manifestations through wind, fire and other displays of raw power. Divine impersonality can be perceived in two ways. First, this exchange among the persons can be experienced as a kind of "flux." This would give rise to the perception that "all is changing and impermanent: all is arising. . . . The only thing that could be more fundamental would be the cessation of such arising: something like what Buddhism calls *nirvana*."[19] Heim refers to this as the experience of "no self." Second, divine impersonality can be perceived as "self without relation." "If there were but one absolute self, then the flux and impermanence humans perceive as a dimension of the divine presence could

---

[15]According to Heim, a social understanding of the Trinity offers the most adequate description of God (see Heim, *Depth of the Riches*, pp. 168-81). Heim draws heavily on the social trinitarianism of John Zizioulas; however, because the work of Smart and Konstantine is more integral to the substance of proposal than that of Zizioulas, I have chosen not to discuss his engagement with Zizioulas.

[16]Heim, *Depth of the Riches*, p. 179. This image is also employed extensively in Heim, "God's Diversity," pp. 14-18.

[17]In his analogy the frequencies correspond to the three dimensions: "The polyphony of the three trinitarian persons is a single divine life that manifests three frequencies analogous to those we have just described" (Heim, "God's Diversity," p. 14).

[18]*Depth of the Riches*, p. 185.

[19]Ibid., p. 187.

be taken as the natural inner reality of that self."[20] This would correspond to Advaita Vedanta Hindu thought. In sum, divine impersonality can be perceived either in terms of God's withdrawal from the world or God's identity (immanence) with the world.

A second dimension involves God's personal involvement in the world. Just as the divine persons encounter one another as unique persons, so humans encounter God as a "thou." Through this dimension humans "seek God's presence, hear God's word, see God's acts, obey or disobey God's commandments, and offer praise or petition."[21] This "personal" dimension is characteristic not only of Christianity but also of Judaism and Islam.

A third dimension involves communion. Encountering others as persons is not the same as experiencing communion with them. Communion involves a "mutual indwelling, in which the distinct persons are not confused or identified but are enriched by their participation in each other's inner life."[22] These three dimensions of divine life constitute a "seamless unity in the communion of the three persons" and relations arising from them are "irreducible."[23] Furthermore, through a relation with any of these dimensions, one encounters all three persons of the Trinity—not merely one of the divine persons.

Three relations. Relations among human beings can take a variety of forms. They may be impersonal (e.g., blood transfusion), personal (e.g., giving directions to a stranger) or involve communion (e.g., sharing one's life with another person).[24] Similar types of relations obtain between humans and God. By tuning into specific frequencies (dimensions) of the divine life, Heim claims that humans are able to experience three types of relations with God: (1) "impersonal identity," (2) "iconographic encounter" and (3) "personal communion."[25]

---

[20]Ibid., p. 189.
[21]Ibid., pp. 192-93.
[22]Ibid., p. 196.
[23]Ibid., p. 197.
[24]Ibid., p. 184.
[25]"My contention is that the life of the Trinity manifests three dimensions analogous to the

Impersonal identity involves a relation with the impersonal dimension of God's life and exists in two forms. The first variation, being apophatic, "is grounded in the emptiness by which each of the divine persons makes space for the others."[26] The second variation, which is unitive, "is grounded in the coinherence or complete immanence of each of the divine persons in the others."[27] In terms of God's economic interaction with creation, the first variation involves God's withdrawal from (or transcendence over) creation—a withdrawal that enables creation to possess its own integrity. In economic terms the second variation involves God's immanence in the form of his sustaining presence: "This constant divine activity reveals a universal immanence of God in every creature. It reflects the impersonal mutual indwelling of the three triune persons."[28]

The "iconographic encounter" is grounded in the interpersonal encounter among the three divine persons. Each encounters the other as a unique character. In a parallel way, humans encounter God as a "distinct other." As with the first relation, two variations exist. In the first variation, one encounters the divine life as a "law, an order or structure."[29] An example of this would be the Buddhist *dharma*. A second variation centers on God as a personal being. Here one experiences an "I-thou" relationship with God. This is characteristic of Christianity. A third type of relation, "personal communion," derives from the *"perichoresis* or mutual communion of the three divine persons."[30] Each of these dimensions, and their corresponding relations, possesses its own integrity and might be described as "co-equal" in trinitarian terms.[31]

Multiple religious ends. When a relation with God is pursued through one of the three dimensions, the result is a distinctive religious

---

three I have described, and *that relation with God can be tuned or concentrated in one of these channels*, with distinctive religious results" (Heim, *Depth of the Riches*, p. 185 [italics added]).
[26]Ibid., p. 210.
[27]Ibid.
[28]Ibid.
[29]Ibid., p. 211.
[30]Ibid.
[31]Ibid., p. 167.

end.[32] In this context, four types of human destiny are possible: (1) salvation (communion with the triune God), (2) alternative religious ends (which arise in response to an economic manifestation of a dimension of the triune life), (3) nonreligious human destinies (which result from fixation on some created good), and (4) negation of the created self.[33] Alternative religious ends are rooted in "authentic revelation *of* the triune God, but not revelation of God *as* triune."[34]

Heim offers two concrete examples of alternate ends—one from Advaita Vedanta Hinduism and a second from Islam. The religious end pursued within the Vedanta tradition is *moksha*, or liberation. This end is achieved through the realization of oneness with *Brahman*. Heim claims that this end involves a real relation with the triune God that is "tuned in" to the first dimension of divine life:

> Thus, I as a Christian do not deny that a Hindu may actually realize identity with the divine, with absolute *Brahman*. I regard this as in fact identity with the underlying immanence of the triune God. Real though a relation of immanence may be between creator and creature, this kind of identification in such pure form is achieved through a constriction, a limitation of both human reality and of God. The identity rests finally on the contact between an aspect of the human and an aspect of the divine.[35]

In contrast, Islam identifies with the "second dimension of divine life: the collective 'I' of the Trinity, the agent-God who reveals truth, ordains the course of the world's life, and calls humans to obedience."[36] Despite its similarities to Christianity, Islam articulates an end that must be distinguished from Christian salvation.[37] The religious end sought by Muslims involves a transformation of the human person in

---

[32]"If pursued consistently and exclusively, relation through any one of these dimensions results in its own distinctive religious end or fulfillment. The 'one way' to salvation, and the 'many ways' to religious ends are alike rooted in the Trinity" (ibid., p. 209).

[33]Ibid., pp. 272-73.

[34]Ibid., p. 275.

[35]Ibid., p. 229.

[36]Ibid., p. 230.

[37]Ibid., p. 231.

relation to the Creator. The primary means to this religious end is "surrender" or "submission" expressed through observance of the five pillars and adherence to *shari'a*. For Muslims, "The triune God acts with one purpose, one will, and one economy in relation to creation."[38] Humans must respond by aligning themselves with God's will and purpose. The Muslim end arises from focusing on the personal dimension of the divine life to the exclusion of the impersonal and communal dimensions.[39]

Plenitude and multiple ends. In response to his proposal, we might ask, "Why would God *want* multiple ends?" Anticipating this question, Heim offers an additional argument for multiple ends that draws upon the notion of divine plenitude. *Plenitude*, according to Heim, "is a qualitative description of the divine life as triune."[40] Economically, this fullness is expressed in everything God has created.[41] Multiple religious ends can be viewed as an expression of divine plenitude within creation: "A plenitude of religious ends is a reflection of the goodness and the saving will of God, applied in relation to free persons who seek something other than communion with the triune God. Every relation with God that is sought is fulfilled. Everything is offered. Nothing is denied."[42]

THE ECONOMIC TRINITY AND THE IMMANENT TRINITY IN *DE TRINITATE*

In my Augustinian assessment to follow, I will argue that the trinitarian problems in Heim's proposal center on the relationship of the immanent Trinity to the economic Trinity. To lay the groundwork for this critique, we need to explore the relationship between the economic Trinity and the immanent Trinity in *De trinitate*. Although it may seem anachronistic to consider how he relates the economic and the imma-

---

[38]Ibid., p. 233.
[39]Ibid.
[40]Ibid., p. 253.
[41]Ibid.
[42]Ibid., pp. 255-56.

nent Trinity, a distinction between God *in se* and God *pro nobis* plays an important role in Augustine's theology. For example, at the beginning of *De trinitate* he offers a compact summary of Latin pro-Nicene teaching on the Trinity that is structured around a distinction between God in himself and God in relation to creation (*De trinitate* 1.7, 69-70).[43] First, Augustine summarizes pro-Nicene teaching on the divine persons in their unity and distinction apart from creation (immanent Trinity). Then, he summarizes pro-Nicene teaching about divine persons in their unity and distinction in the economy of salvation (economic Trinity).

The clearest window into the relationship between the economic and the immanent Trinity can be found in Augustine's discussion of the temporal missions of the Son and the Holy Spirit. The divine missions represent one of the key themes in *De trinitate*.[44] At least two factors contribute to the centrality of this theme. First, *De trinitate* is shaped by a quest to know and understand God. In this context, Augustine wants to invite his readers to "contemplate" the Trinity. It is precisely through the temporal missions that human beings come to "contemplate" the triune God.[45] Second, discussion of the divine missions was necessitated by Augustine's Homoian opponents who argued that the "sendings" of the Son and Spirit reveal their ontological inferiority to the Father.[46] Augustine labors to show that *sending* implies no inferiority to the Father on the part of the Son and Spirit. He accomplishes this by arguing that the temporal missions of the Son and Spirit simply reveal that they proceed eternally from the Father:

---

[43]This summary will be discussed in chap. 4.

[44]The missions of the Son and Spirit are discussed in detail in chap. 4.

[45]Ayres describes this as Augustine's "Christological epistemology" (see Ayres, *Augustine and the Trinity*, pp. 142-74).

[46]"Refuted here, they turn to another axiom: 'The one who sends is greater than the one sent.' So the Father is greater than the Son, who is constantly presenting himself as sent by the Father; he is also greater than the Holy Spirit, of whom Jesus said, *whom the Father will send in my name* (Jn 14:26). And the Holy Spirit is less than either, since besides the Father sending him, as mentioned, the Son sends him too, saying as he does, *But if I go away I will send him to you* (Jn 16:7)" (Augustine, *De trinitate* 2.7, 101).

> If however the reason why the Son is said to have been sent by the Father
> is simply that one is the Father and the other the Son, then there is noth-
> ing at all to stop us from believing that the Son is equal to the Father and
> consubstantial and co-eternal, and yet that the Son is sent by the Father.
> Not because one is greater and the other less, but because one is the Father
> and the other the Son. (*De trinitate* 4.27, 172)

A distinction between the eternal *relations* of the Son and Spirit and
their temporal *missions* plays an explicit role in Augustine's response.
Notice how he carefully distinguishes the generation of the Son from
the sending of the Son: "Just as the Father, then, begot and the Son was
begotten, so the Father sent and the Son was sent. . . . And just as being
born means for the Son his being from the Father, so his being sent
means his being known to be from him" (*De trinitate* 4.29, 174). In the
first sentence, the eternal generation of the Son (immanent Trinity) is
expressed in the language of "was begotten" while the temporal mission
of the Son (economic Trinity) is expressed in the phrase "being sent."
The second sentence, while formally parallel to the first, makes the additional claim that the temporal sending of the Son was explicitly designed to *reveal* his eternal relation to the Father (i.e., generation). Augustine makes a parallel point regarding the Holy Spirit: "And just as
for the Holy Spirit his being the gift of God means his proceeding from
the Father, so his being sent means his being known to proceed from
him" (*De trinitate* 4.29, 174). The eternal procession of the Spirit (immanent Trinity) is expressed in the language of "being gift of God"
while the temporal mission of the Spirit (economic Trinity) is expressed
in the phrase "being sent."[47]

It is helpful to consider Augustine's distinction between generation/
procession and mission both from ontological and epistemological perspectives. From an *ontological* perspective, generation/procession constitutes the foundation for sending. The Son does not become Son by
being sent into the world. To the contrary, the Son is constituted as Son

---

[47]The generation of the Son and procession of the Holy Spirit will be discussed in chap. 4.

by virtue of his relation to the Father—that is, eternal generation ("being born"). Similarly, the Holy Spirit does not become Spirit by being sent; rather, the Holy Spirit is constituted by proceeding from the Father and the Son ("being the gift of God").

From an *epistemological* perspective, the order is reversed: the temporal missions constitute the epistemic means by which the generation of the Son and procession of the Holy Spirit are known. Augustine reminds his readers that the sending of the Son reveals his eternal generation by the Father, while sending of the Spirit reveals his eternal procession from the Father and Son. Because the missions merely reveal eternal relations, there is no reason to conclude that sending implies inferiority on the part of the one sent in the case of the Son and Holy Spirit (*De trinitate* 4.32, 176-77).

Another window into the distinction Augustine draws between the economic Trinity (temporal sending) and the immanent Trinity (eternal relations) can be seen in his discussion of the Holy Spirit as "Gift" (*donum*). Inasmuch as the Holy Spirit only becomes "Gift" when he is given in time (a point emphasized in the New Testament), employing gift language may run the risk of potentially undermining the Spirit's equality with the Father and Son. Augustine, however, averts this problem by explaining that the Holy Spirit does not become "Gift" by being given:

> We should not be disturbed at the Holy Spirit, although he is coeternal with the Father and the Son, being said to be something from a point of time, like this name we have just used of "donation" [*donatum*]. The Spirit, to make myself clear, is everlastingly gift [*donum*], but donation [*donatum*] only from a point of time. (*De trinitate* 5.17, 200)

Augustine draws a distinction between a gift in itself (*donum*) and a gift as a thing given (*donatum*) with the former constituting the basis for the latter. Spirit can exist as a "Gift" in time (economic Trinity) because the Spirit is "Gift" from all eternity (immanent Trinity).[48]

---

[48]Thomas Aquinas will build on this explanation, suggesting that the Holy Spirit is rightly

As Edmund Hill rightly notes, Augustine's distinction between the eternal relations of the persons and their temporal missions represented an improvement over an earlier generation of economic theologians: "Whereas Tertullian had been constrained to say that the economy *constitutes* the mystery of God," Augustine claimed "that the economy (the missions) reveals the eternal mystery of God."[49] Table 3.1 summarizes the distinction Augustine draws between temporal missions of the Son and Spirit, and their eternal relations in *De trinitate*.

Table 3.1. Distinction Between Mission and Generation/Procession

Mission (Sending)	Generation/Procession
Temporal	Eternal
Sending of the Son	Eternal generation of the Son by the Father
Giving of the Spirit	Eternal procession of the Spirit from the Father and the Son
Visible	Invisible
Represents the *epistemic* means through which the generation of the Son and procession of the Holy Spirit are known	Constitutes the *ontological* basis for the temporal sending of the Son and the Spirit
Economic Trinity	Immanent Trinity

Although Augustine carefully distinguishes the economic from the immanent Trinity, the later and former remain inextricably linked in such a way that the missions of the Son and Spirit represent a kind of temporal expression of their eternal relations. Augustine's claim that the temporal missions *reveal* the eternal generation of the Son and the procession of the Spirit (necessarily) assumes a high degree of continuity between God in himself and God for us; otherwise the missions could not reveal the eternal relations. Notice how the following statement regarding the equality of the Son to the Father assumes a close continuity between the economic and the immanent Trinity: "So the Word of God is sent by him whose Word he is; sent by him he is born

called "Gift" from all eternity because of an aptitude for being given (see Thomas Aquinas, *Summa Theologiae* Ia, q.38, a.1, ad. 4).
[49]Hill, *Trinity*, p. 48.

of. The begetter sends, what is begotten is sent" (*De trinitate* 4.28, 173). It is most fitting that the Son was sent because the Son is *from* the Father. Another window into the unity of the economic and the immanent Trinity can be seen in Augustine's account of trinitarian agency.[50] Just as the Father and Son are inseparable (immanent Trinity), so the Father and Son act inseparably (economic Trinity) in creation, providence and redemption (*De trinitate* 1.7, 69-70).

Augustine's account of the relationship between the economic and the immanent Trinity can be summarized in the following points:

P1. From an epistemological perspective, Scripture constitutes the sole foundation for our knowledge of the triunity of God. It is through God's self-revelation in the economy of salvation that we have knowledge of the immanent Trinity.

P2. An important distinction must be drawn between the economic and the immanent Trinity. Although the economic Trinity reveals the immanent Trinity, the latter cannot be reduced to the former.

P3. As a revelation of the triune God in time, the economic Trinity reveals and closely reflects the immanent Trinity.

P4. From an ontological perspective, the immanent Trinity (God *in se*) constitutes the foundation for the economic Trinity.

I will return to these four points when I evaluate Heim's proposal.

Before offering an Augustinian evaluation of Heim's proposal, it will helpful briefly to examine the work of David Coffey,[51] which not only sheds further light on the relationship between the economic and the

---

[50]Augustine's account of divine operations will be discussed in chap. 4.

[51]David Coffey, *Deus Trinitas: The Doctrine of the Triune God* (New York: Oxford, 1999), pp. 16-17. According to Coffey, one of the weaknesses of Rahner's axiom is that it "does not tell us which perspective [economic or immanent] is the more fundamental, nor does it throw light on the order of our knowledge of the Trinity" (ibid., pp. 14-15). Coffey addresses this lacuna by distinguishing "epistemological" and "ontological" orders. From an epistemological perspective God's self-revelation in the economy of salvation constitutes the foundation for our knowledge of the immanent Trinity. From an ontological perspective the immanent Trinity constitutes the foundation for the economic Trinity.

immanent Trinity but will also frame my Augustinian critique of Heim.[52] Coffey suggests that three steps can be distinguished in our knowledge of the triunity of God. In the first step, one encounters the self-revelation of the triune God in the economy of salvation recorded in Scripture. Coffey refers to this as the "biblical Trinity."[53] By biblical Trinity Coffey does *not* mean a biblical account of the Trinity over and against a nonbiblical one, but simply the biblical revelation of the triune God recorded in Scripture.[54] In the second step, one reflects upon what must be true regarding being and nature of the divine persons on the basis of God's self-revelation in Scripture. The outcome of this reflection represents a doctrine of the immanent Trinity. In the third and final step, one articulates a systematic conceptualization of the triune God in the economy of salvation—a doctrine of the economic Trinity.[55]

HEIM'S TRINITARIAN THEOLOGY OF RELIGIOUS ENDS: AN AUGUSTINIAN EVALUATION

In the discussion that follows I will argue that the trinitarian problems in Heim's proposal center on the relationship between the economic

---

[52]Coffey, of course, does not address Heim's proposal.

[53]According to Coffey, the New Testament presents what would best be described as a "functional" theology. In this context he denies that the New Testament (even in the Gospel of John) affirms an ontological (metaphysical) incarnation (see Coffey, *Deus Trinitas*, pp. 12-15). In making this move Coffey parts company with Augustine and classical orthodoxy. Coffey's claims notwithstanding, there are good reasons to believe the New Testament affirms an ontological incarnation. For example, regarding the claim that the Son is *homoousios* with the Father see, David S. Yeago, "The New Testament and the *Nicene* Dogma: A Contribution to the Recovery of Theological Exegesis," *Pro Ecclesia* 3 (1994): 152-64.

[54]Coffey asserts that the New Testament never "penetrate[s] to the level of the immanent Trinity" (Coffey, *Deus Trinitas*, p. 15). Although the New Testament certainly does not contain a developed *doctrine* of the immanent Trinity, it does make statements about the immanent life of the divine persons (e.g., biblical texts affirming the equality of the divine persons). Following Augustine and the rest of the classic tradition, I would differ with Coffey in seeing the biblical witness penetrating to the level of the immanent Trinity even though Scripture does not provide a ready-made *doctrine* of the immanent Trinity.

[55]In this third step Coffey explains that we make two simultaneous affirmations: first, the immanent Trinity, which because of divine transcendence must exist in its own right, and second, the economic Trinity, that is, this same Trinity involved in the divine plan of salvation through the missions of the Son and of the Holy Spirit (Coffey, *Deus Trinitas*, p. 24).

and the immanent Trinity.[56] More specifically, I will demonstrate that
the breakdown in Heim's trinitarian grammar occurs in the second and
third steps of the "epistemic order" outlined earlier. In step two, Heim
articulates a speculative understanding of the immanent Trinity that
has little basis in Scripture. Then, in step three, he outlines a conception of the economic Trinity that includes "economies" of divine activity that bypass the temporal missions of the Son and the Spirit as revealed in Scripture. Heim's plurality of ends necessitates a plurality of
economies.

I will begin by summarizing Heim's understanding of the relationship between the economic and the immanent Trinity. In his proposal,
Heim draws a distinction between the ontological and the economic
Trinity.[57] The latter denotes "an understanding of the triune persons as
varying external faces of God's action in the world" while the former
refers to "the actual triune persons whose communion in God is the
divine life itself."[58] Although he insists that a distinction must be drawn
between the ontological and the economic Trinity, Heim also affirms
that the economic activity of the triune God closely corresponds to and
reflects God's inner nature: "Christian belief that God is ontologically
triune is belief that God's manifestation to us is shaped by God's true,
deepest character."[59] This can be seen most clearly in the case of Christian salvation: "Salvation as a relation of deep communion with God
makes sense because God's nature itself has the character of
communion."[60] Underlying the latter statement is an assumption that
the economic activity of the triune God must closely correspond to and
reflect the immanent Trinity. From an ontological perspective Heim
insists that the ontological (i.e., immanent) Trinity constitutes the

---

[56]This is not to suggest that the problems with Heim's proposal are exclusively trinitarian. I
  could also raise questions regarding the ontological coherence of multiple religious ends. My
  critique will center exclusively on the trinitarian content of his proposal.
[57]Heim, *Depth of the Riches*, pp. 59-61, 126-33.
[58]Ibid., p. 126.
[59]Ibid., p. 61.
[60]Ibid., p. 59.

ground for the economic Trinity.[61] However, the ultimate purpose of trinitarian reflection is not to offer a description of God's inner life but simply to narrate "the various ways God acts in the world, and the various ways we experience God's presence."[62]

Four assumptions shape Heim's trinitarian grammar:

A1. God's self-revelation through the person and work of Christ constitutes the epistemic basis for our knowledge of the triunity of God.

A2. An important distinction must be drawn between the economic Trinity and the ontological (immanent) Trinity.

A3. The economic Trinity closely corresponds to and reflects the ontological (immanent) Trinity. *Trinity* does not merely describe an external representation of God. *Trinity* describes something that is ontologically true about God's nature.

A4. From an ontological perspective the immanent Trinity constitutes the ground for the economic Trinity.

So far Heim's grammar appears to be perfectly consistent with our Augustinian grammar: A1 corresponds to P1, A2 to P2, A3 to P3 and A4 to P4. In the case of the Christian religious end (salvation), Heim's trinitarian grammar functions perfectly. The inherent relationality of salvation reflects the relationality of the divine life of the triune God. A problem, however, arises for Heim's trinitarian grammar in the case of other religious ends. According to A3, a close correspondence must exist between the economic activity of the triune God and the immanent life of the triune God. In the case of Christian salvation a close correspondence obtains; however, what about other religious ends? How, for example, does the Hindu end (*moksha*), which involves release

---

[61]"The affirmation that the economic Trinity (an understanding of the triune persons as varying external faces of God's action in the world) is *grounded* in the ontological Trinity (the actual triune persons whose communion in God is the divine life itself) implies that not all representations of God are mere projections. Relational images of God express something true of God's true nature" (ibid., p. 126 [italics added]).

[62]Ibid., p. 180.

from the endless cycle of birth, death and rebirth, closely correspond to and reflect the immanent life of the triune God? Heim faces a dilemma. On the one hand, he insists that the economic activity of the triune God closely corresponds to and reflects God's true nature (A3). On the other hand, he affirms the existence of multiple religious ends, which involves great economic diversity. How can these be reconciled?

One alternative might be the follow the lead of pluralists like John Hick and drop A3; however, if A3 is dropped, we can no longer claim that the Christian end (salvation) corresponds to and reflects God's triune nature. Furthermore, we must also surrender the claim that *Trinity* describes something that is ontologically true about God. Ultimately, a denial of A3 would lead us to a position in which all religions are conceived as economic responses to some indeterminate immanent divine reality (as Hick does). Heim clearly does not want to surrender A3. Thus, rather than dropping A3, he simply adds another premise into his trinitarian "grammar":

A5. The immanent life of the triune God is complex.

Positing complexity in the inner life of God (A5) constitutes Heim's solution to the dilemma of how, on the one hand, he can affirm that God's economic activity closely corresponds to and reflects God's nature and how, on the other, he can affirm that the economic activity of the triune God is incredibly diverse.

What constitutes complexity in the divine life of the triune God? As I noted in A4, the immanent (or ontological) Trinity represents the constitutive basis for alternative religious ends. How then does Heim conceive of the immanent Trinity? Heim claims that God is a communion of three divine persons: "God's personal reality is complex: God is 'made up' of personal communion-in-difference."[63] In this statement it may sound as if all Heim means by *complex* is that the divine life is merely constituted by three persons; however, as his proposal unfolds it becomes clear that the primary referent of complexity is not the divine

---

[63]Ibid., p. 62.

persons but the three dimensions of divine life, which "are a feature of the triune God's integral reality."[64]

Speculative account of the immanent Trinity. Having examined Heim's trinitarian grammar, we will turn our attention to the first major trinitarian problem with his proposal. Earlier I suggested that three phases of discovery may be distinguished: (1) biblical Trinity, (2) immanent Trinity, and (3) economic Trinity. These are summarized in table 3.2.

Table 3.2. Trinity: Biblical, Immanent and Economic

Biblical Trinity	Immanent Trinity	Economic Trinity
Revelation of the triunity of God in the economy of salvation recorded in Scripture	Conceptualization of the being and nature of the divine persons on the basis of God's self-revelation in Scripture	Conceptualization of the salvific action of the triune God in the economy of salvation

Thus, the biblical Trinity constitutes the epistemic foundation for our knowledge of the triunity of God (P1)—a point Heim affirms (A1). Inasmuch as the knowledge of the Trinity can be gained only *through* the economy of salvation revealed in Scripture, any conceptualization of the Trinity (immanent or economic) must possess a clear basis in the biblical Trinity. Thus, what Augustine affirmed regarding his own proposal applies equally to Heim's: "But first we must establish by the authority of the holy scriptures whether the faith is in fact like that" (*De trinitate* 1.4, 67). In light of table 3.2, we must ask, What constitutes the revelatory basis for Heim's claim that the inner life of the triune God is constituted by three dimensions? This is illustrated in table 3.3 by inserting Heim's accounts of the immanent and the economic Trinity.

Although Heim would insist that the triune God as revealed in Christian Scripture constitutes the basis for his proposal,[65] there are

---

[64]Ibid., p. 197.
[65]"By 'Trinity' I do not mean to refer to a generic and symbolic scheme of abstract threeness. With such a minimalist pattern, one can run merrily through the religions gathering 'trinities,' from the *Brahma-Shiva-Vishnu* triumvirate of Hinduism to the *trikay* or 'three bodies' doc-

Table 3.3. Trinity in Heim's Proposal

Biblical Trinity	Immanent Trinity	Economic Trinity
???	Three dimensions of the divine life: • Impersonal • Personal • Communion	Three types of relations: • Impersonal identity • Iconographic encounter • Personal communion

good reasons to question this claim. To make this criticism more concrete, it will be helpful to explore a specific example. According to Heim, the impersonal dimension involves the "radical immanence and the radical emptiness, by which the divine persons indwell each other and make way for the others to indwell them."[66] What constitutes the foundation in the biblical Trinity for this claim? Heim explains that an "impersonal" dimension can be seen in God's economic interactions—particularly in the Old Testament. It will be helpful to quote him at length:

> In the biblical tradition, we find clear indications of relation with God tuned into this wavelength. There is a very real note in Scripture that highlights an impersonal side of the divine. In the Old Testament the holiness of God and the direct presence of God frequently have this character, like a fire in the presence of which everything mortal is consumed. Theophanies, or even the continuing presence of God that rests in the ark of the tabernacle as its travels with the people of Israel, have this quality. Humans exposed to this presence are in great danger, in a purely "chemical" and impersonal sense, quite apart from any specific intention on God's part. It is as if a creature stepped into a circuit where unimaginable current was being exchanged. The raw divine life is a "consuming fire," and accounts of those who encounter it (Moses or Job, for instance) trade strongly on the language of impersonal forces like fire or wind. This divine power

---

trine of Buddhism. I am speaking of the reality of God as presented in the doctrine of the Christian church, which presupposes the incarnation of the Word as crucial revelation and act of God" (ibid., p. 130).

[66]Ibid., p. 185.

or force might be viewed as something like an electrical charge or field, generated by the constant interchange of the three divine persons with each other.[67]

There are at least three problems with this argument. First, these apparently "impersonal" divine manifestations represent one aspect of a fundamentally "personal" self-revelation. It is the God of Abraham, Isaac and Jacob who *speaks* to Moses from the "burning bush." To sever an impersonal aspect from the personal and make it stand alone is unwarranted. Second, no epistemic warrant exists for assuming that a particular created form (e.g., fire) *necessarily* reveals something about the immanent nature of the triune God. In his discussion of the Old Testament theophanies Augustine points out that God appeared to humans through a variety of "created objects" (*De trinitate* 3.22, 140). He insists that these Old Testament theophanies did not manifest God's immanent nature: "All these visions, however, were produced through the changeable creation subject to the changeless God, and they did not manifest God *as he is in himself,* but in a symbolic manner as times and circumstances required"(*De trinitate* 2.32, 120, italics added). Thus, to draw necessary inferences about the immanent life of the triune God based on the nature of a particular created representation (e.g., pillar of cloud, burning bush, fire and smoke, etc.) is unwarranted.[68] Third, what is being (indirectly) manifested in these theophanies is not a "dimension of the divine life" but the divine persons.[69]

The primary source for Heim's claim that the immanent life of the triune God is characterized by three dimensions is not God's self-

---

[67]Ibid., pp. 185-86.

[68]Augustine draws a clear distinction between the created medium of manifestation and the persons in such a way that the nature of the former does not entail any necessary assumptions about the nature of the latter. This ties into a larger investigation in bks. 2-4 as to which of the divine persons was manifest in the theophanies. He argues that the matter is ambiguous. His opponents argued for the ontological inferiority of the Son on the ground that the Son is the "visible" member of the Trinity. Augustine inductively builds a biblical case against this view by examining the major theophanies and arguing that it is not clear which of the divine persons is revealed.

[69]It is almost as if Heim is searching for theophanies of the "dimensions" in his reading of the Old Testament.

revelation in Scripture but Smart and Konstantine's *Christian Systematic Theology in World Context*. The fact that Heim appropriates this
concept from Smart and Konstantine is not in itself problematic. It
simply pushes the same question back one level. What constitutes the
basis for Smart and Konstantine's claim? Smart and Konstantine claim
that the social Trinity—constituted by three dimensions—represents
the ultimate referent of all religious experience. Their proposal starts
with a particular construal of the immanent Trinity and then attempts
to explain all economic activity of the triune God among other religions on the basis of this speculative description. Although they affirm
that the social Trinity constitutes the ultimate divine reality, they are
quite skeptical regarding the epistemic foundation on which this doctrine ultimately rests. The three dimensions that characterize the divine life are simply asserted.[70]

Thus, from an Augustinian perspective, what makes their proposal
most problematic is not their preference for a social understanding of
Trinity over and against a (so-called) psychological approach but the
way that their proposal explicitly abandons Scripture as the epistemic
foundation for human knowledge of the triunity of God (thus undermining P1). According to Smart and Konstantine: "The liberal-
academic solvents have gnawed away the rusts of Biblical certainty. It
therefore seems nonsense to pretend that the Bible has doctrinal or narrative authority."[71] By rejecting the authority of Scripture, they reject
the epistemic basis for a Christian doctrine of the Trinity.[72] While
Heim may not intend to nullify scriptural authority as a starting point
for his theological considerations, by following a methodological path
parallel to that of Smart and Konstantine, his theological conclusions

---

[70]Smart and Konstantine, *Christian Systematic Theology*, p. 174.
[71]Ibid., p. 47.
[72]As an alternative to Scripture, Smart and Konstantine attempt to ground their trinitarian
doctrine in the liturgical life and experience of the church. Apart from scriptural authority, we
cannot help but ask why the religious experience of one particular group (early Christians)
should be epistemically privileged over the religious experiences of other groups (Hindus,
Buddhists, etc.) in formulating an understanding of the religious ultimate.

represent a speculative account of the immanent Trinity that is inadequately rooted in Scripture.

In contrast to Heim, Augustine was quite cautious in speculating about the immanent Trinity. In his introduction to book 5, Augustine explains that "when we think about God the trinity we are aware that our thoughts are quite inadequate to their object, and incapable of grasping him as he is" (*De trinitate* 5.1, 189). Although we should always be praising God, "yet no words of ours are capable of expressing him" (*De trinitate* 5.1, 189). Whatever we say about God's unchanging and invisible nature cannot be measured by material things. From an Augustinian standpoint, Heim simply claims to know too much about the interior life of God.

From the immanent to the economic Trinity. A second trinitarian problem involves the way that Heim's proposal moves from the immanent Trinity to the economic Trinity. To better understand the nature of this problem, we must examine Heim's account of the economic Trinity. According to Heim, three "relations" characterize the economic activity of the triune God: (1) impersonal identity, (2) iconographic encounter, and (3) personal communion. These relations represent three faces of the triune God in the economy of salvation. Heim insists that relations with God through all three dimensions are real relations with the triune God.[73] These real relations constitute the economic means through which alternative religious ends (e.g., moksha, nirvana, etc.) are realized.

To say that other ends are part of God's economy implies that they are *willed* by God.[74] Thus Heim's proposal entails the assumption that

---

[73]"It is important to make the point that relations with God in *all* three dimensions we have described are real relations with God. They are not relations with something else (idols) or with false gods. What humans find in such relations is truly there. These are all relations with the God who is triune, though some may refine and restrict their relationship with the triunity of God. They are not relations to only one divine person rather than to others, since given God's nature and the communion of persons that is not possible. An isolated relation with one person of the Trinity is something that exists only in abstraction. In each case it is God in God's triune nature we meet" (Heim, *Depth of the Riches*, p. 199).

[74]"All of God's manifestation in the world is economic in the sense of being an outward expres-

the triune God actively *wills* alternative religious ends: "The triune God is party to the realization of alternate religious ends. They are not simply the actualization of innate human capacities; they are distinct relations with aspects of the triune life. A particular grace of God is operative in them."[75] It is crucial to recognize the implications of this affirmation: alongside God's economy of salvation in Christ, other economies of divine activity exist. Through these economies of divine activity, the triune God is directing men and women to ends other than communion with the Father, Son and Holy Spirit. We cannot call these "economies of salvation" because Christian salvation does not represent their ultimate goal. Within Heim's proposal there is an economy of salvation (the Christian end), an economy of *nirvana* (the Buddhist end), an economy of *moksha* (the Hindu end), and so on.[76] From a trinitarian standpoint, we might say that alongside the mission of the Son and the Spirit to restore men and women to communion with the triune God, other economic missions exist, through which men and women are directed to ends other than salvation.

What epistemic warrant exists for positing economies of divine activity that bypass the mission of the Son and the Spirit to restore men and women to communion with the triune God—particularly, when this represents the only divine mission revealed in Scripture? In book 4 of *De trinitate* Augustine explains that the "sendings" of the Son and Spirit have as their goal restoring fallen humans into a relationship of communion with the triune God. Mission constitutes a central link between the divine persons (immanent Trinity) and the economy of salvation (economic Trinity). By positing economies of divine activity that effectively bypass the work of Christ, Heim implicitly severs this

---

sion of God's purpose" (ibid., pp. 125-26).

[75]Ibid., p. 275.

[76]From an economic standpoint, a significant difference exists between the role of Christ in the Christian end (salvation) and the role of Christ in other ends. In the former, Christ represents not only the constitutive *means* of salvation but also the constitutive *end* of salvation; in the case of alternative ends, however, Christ represents a constitutive means but *not* a constitutive end—a point Heim recognizes and affirms (ibid., p. 288).

link. No biblical warrant exists for positing (additional) economies of divine activity that bypass (or constitute an alternative) to this one economy of salvation effected in Christ. On the basis of a speculative understanding of the immanent Trinity (step 2), Heim outlines an account of the economic Trinity (step 3) that ultimately undermines the economy of salvation revealed in Scripture.

A Trinity of dimensions replaces the Trinity of persons. At the level of the immanent Trinity, Heim's proposal ultimately employs two trinities. The first (Father, Son and Holy Spirit) is the Trinity of Christian confession; however, this is not the "trinity" that does the real work in Heim's project. Multiple religious ends ultimately rest on a different trinity—a trinity of "three dimensions" (impersonal, personal and communion). These immanent dimensions lead to three kinds of irreducible economic relations (impersonal identity, iconographic encounter and personal communion), which ultimately constitute the basis for multiple religious ends.[77] Heim subtly substitutes the "dimensions" for the divine "persons," effectively creating an alternate trinity.

His substitution of dimensions for persons can be seen most clearly in the application of language to these dimensions that is normally applied to the divine persons. Heim asserts that only three dimensions exist. Why three? Why not two, four or even ten? Is it merely coincidental that there also happen to be three divine persons? Second, Heim suggests that "each of the dimensions is granted co-equality with the others."[78] Here Heim intentionally applies the language of coequality to the dimensions; yet this language applies only to the trinitarian persons. Third, he speaks about the irreducible nature of the relations cor-

---

[77]That "dimensions" are immanent and "relations" economic can be seen in the following quotation: "I am suggesting that there are four broad types of human destiny. There is salvation, that communion through Christ with God and with others that unites an unlimited diversity of persons and opens each to wider participation in the triune life. Second, we have alternative religious ends, the distinctive human fulfillments of various religious traditions. Each of these grasps some dimension of the triune life and its economic manifestation, and makes it the ground for a definitive human end" (ibid., p. 272).

[78]Ibid., p. 213.

responding to these dimensions.[79] Irreducibility, however, only applies to the divine persons. The Father is not the Son and the Son is the not the Father. Finally, he avers that individuals experience relations with these dimensions in such a way that the dimensions effectively displace the divine persons. From an Augustinian perspective this substitution of dimensions for the trinitarian persons is deeply problematic. For Augustine all legitimate predication about God is of two types: statements of substance (*substantia*) and statements of relationship (*relatio*). Even if we were to grant the possibility that such dimensions existed, Augustine would rightly argue that it is fundamentally inappropriate to apply relationship language to these dimensions because they constitute substantive predications.[80] Furthermore, Augustine would insist that individuals experience a relationship with the trinitarian persons, not merely with an aspect or dimension of God's nature. Ultimately Heim's immanent "trinity of dimensions" has subtly replaced the Trinity of persons.

IMPLICATIONS FOR THE CHRISTIAN THEOLOGY OF RELIGIONS

In her controversial book *God for Us: The Trinity and Christian Life*, Catherine LaCugna argues that Christian theology went astray when its reflection on the life of the triune God (*theologia*) was severed from the economy of salvation (*oikonomia*).[81] According to LaCugna, increasing preoccupation with the inner life of God, a trajectory established by the Council of Nicaea, ultimately led to the defeat of trinitarian doctrine, rendering it irrelevant to the Christian life. Although LaCugna's historical and theological analysis is flawed,[82] her under-

---

[79]"If God is Trinity, these dimensions of the divine life are a seamless unity in the communion of the three persons. The various relations with God we have outlined are irreducible. If God is Trinity, then no one of these need be or can be eliminated in favor of the others" (ibid., p. 197).

[80]See Augustine, *De trinitate* 5, 189-201.

[81]Catherine Mowry LaCugna, *God for Us: The Trinity and Christian Life* (San Francisco: HarperSanFrancisco, 1992).

[82]See Thomas Weinandy, "The Immanent and Economic Trinity," *Thomist* 57 (1993): 655-66;

lying concern regarding the danger of *theologia* becoming severed from *oikonomia* is, nonetheless, quite legitimate. Our analysis of Heim's proposal demonstrates that LaCugna was right to be concerned about the danger of severing *theologia* and *oikonomia*. We must note, however, that it is not simply by articulating a doctrine of the immanent Trinity (God *in se*) that one severs *theologia* from *oikonomia*, as LaCugna would have us believe. Heim errs *not* because the immanent Trinity constitutes the ontological basis for his proposal; rather, he errs because he offers a speculative account of the immanent Trinity that is without support in God's self-revelation in Scripture and then uses this speculative account to develop a doctrine of the economic Trinity that ultimately undermines the *oikonomia* revealed in Scripture. From an Augustinian perspective, Heim's trinitarian grammar ultimately fails to maintain Scripture as the epistemological foundation of our knowledge of the triunity of God. With reference to LaCugna, we might say that it is by articulating an account of the immanent (and the economic) Trinity that has little epistemic foundation in God's self-revelation in Scripture that one severs *theologia* from *oikonomia*.

Perhaps the clearest example of severing the economic and the immanent Trinity can be seen in the case of pluralist theologies of religion. For example, John Hick asserts that all religions are culturally conditioned yet authentic responses to an indeterminate divine ultimate reality, which he calls "the Real."[83] The Real in itself cannot be known; it can only be perceived and experienced in a variety of economic faces through various religious traditions. From a trinitarian perspective Hick's proposal entails a complete severing of the economic and the immanent Trinity. An immanent Real, which in principle cannot be known, expresses itself through an unending number of economic faces (some of which greatly contradict one another). Although

---

and Paul Molnar, *Divine Freedom and the Doctrine of the Immanent Trinity: In Dialogue with Karl Barth and Contemporary Theology* (Edinburgh: T & T Clark, 2002).

[83]John Hick, *An Interpretation of Religion: Human Responses to the Transcendent* (New Haven, Conn.: Yale University Press, 1989), pp. 233-51.

Heim's proposal differs substantively from Hick's, it faces a problem similar to Hick's inasmuch as both sever the economic and the immanent Trinity.

Just as reflection on the relationship between the economic and the immanent Trinity has brought sharply into focus the problems regarding certain accounts of the God-world relationship, greater attention to the relationship between the economic and the immanent Trinity could also help clarify problems in the trinitarian theology of religions. Ironically, much appropriation of the doctrine of the Trinity within the theology of religions moves in a direction that is at odds with the modern trinitarian revival. One distinctive feature of the modern trinitarian movement is an attempt to reconnect Trinity and history, Trinity and salvation, Trinity and Christian living—in short, *theologia* and *oikonomia*. Ironically, in their attempts to make the doctrine of the Trinity relevant to other religions, theologians such as Heim move in a direction at odds with this movement by implicitly severing the economic and the immanent Trinity.

4

DIVINE RELATIONS IN THE
THEOLOGY OF RELIGIONS

◆

Assumptions regarding the relations among the divine persons play
an important role in two recent proposals: Amos Yong's pneumatological theology of religions and Jacques Dupuis's Christian theology of
religious pluralism.[1] On the basis of a particular understanding of the
relationship of the Spirit to the Son, Yong argues that the Holy Spirit
is present and active in non-Christian religions, acting in an economy
of salvation distinct from that of the Son. Similarly, on the basis of a
particular construal of the Father-Son relationship, Dupuis argues that

---

[1]The relations among the divine persons have been the subject of extensive debate in contemporary theology. Divine *personhood* represents an excellent case in point. On the one hand, Karl
Barth and Karl Rahner both argue that a modern (post-Enlightenment) concept of "person"
should not be applied to Father, Son and Holy Spirit. Other theologians (who tend to be quite
critical of the Augustinian tradition) commend social understandings of the Trinity that not
only apply a modern concept of person to the divine hypostases but also present the perichoretic
unity of the Father, Son and Holy Spirit as a model for human relationships. In addition to
divine personhood, the relation of the Son to the Holy Spirit has also received attention. Advocates of Spirit Christology insist that theologians have not paid adequate attention to the
radical dependence of Jesus Christ on the Spirit during his earthly life and ministry. On ecumenical grounds there has been a growing consensus that the *filioque* clause should not have
been unilaterally inserted into the Nicene-Constantinopolitan Creed by the Western church.
Moreover, in response to criticisms by the Orthodox theologians, some Western theologians
have abandoned the Augustinian position that the Spirit proceeds from the Father and the
Son.

Jesus Christ is not "absolute" Savior and that Christian salvation is mediated through non-Christian religious traditions. Whereas Yong's proposal builds on trinitarian *pneumatology,* Dupuis's proposal builds on trinitarian *Christology.* The purpose of this chapter is to offer an Augustinian assessment of the trinitarian theology that informs the proposals of Yong and Dupuis. Readers will want to pay careful attention to the relationship of the Spirit to Son in Yong's proposal as well as the relationship of the Son to the Father in Dupuis's proposal. This chapter will follow the same pattern as chapter three. First, I will outline their proposals. Then, I will explore Augustine's teaching on the divine relations. Finally, I will offer an Augustinian critique.

AMOS YONG'S PNEUMATOLOGICAL THEOLOGY OF RELIGIONS

In *Discerning the Spirit(s)* Amos Yong, a Pentecostal theologian, attempts to develop a Pentecostal-charismatic theology of religions.[2] While affirming that christological questions play an important role in any attempt to formulate a viable theology of religions, Yong suggests that pneumatology may provide the key to moving beyond what he calls the christological impasse, that is, "the almost irreconcilable axioms of God's universal salvific will and the historical particularity of Jesus of Nazareth as Savior of all persons."[3] The metaphysical basis for Yong's proposal is the universal presence of the Holy Spirit. According to Yong, the Holy Spirit is present and active among non-Christian religions, and Christians must learn to discern the Spirit's presence.

The foundational pneumatology Yong develops in *Discerning the Spirit(s)* is predicated on a trinitarian distinction between an economy of the Word and an economy of the Spirit: "The entire objective of shifting to a pneumatological framework in order to understand non-Christian faiths is premised upon the recognition that there is a dis-

---

[2]Amos Yong, *Discerning the Spirit(s): A Pentecostal-Charismatic Contribution to a Christian Theology of Religions* (Sheffield, U.K.: Sheffield Academic Press, 2000).
[3]Ibid., p. 94.

tinction between the economy of the Son and that of the Spirit relative to the redemption of the world."[4] Although he acknowledges that the economies of the Son and Spirit are "mutually related," Yong emphasizes their autonomy and distinction.[5] That they are distinct can be seen in the fact that they converge only eschatologically.[6]

It would not be an overstatement to say that a distinction between the economy of Son and economy of the Spirit constitutes the trinitarian key to Yong's proposal: "Recognition of the procession or mission of the Holy Spirit into the world relative to, yet distinct from that of the Son provides the theological space that is greatly needed at the present time for reflection on the place of the religions in the economy of the Spirit."[7] On the basis of this distinct economy of the Spirit, Yong affirms the presence and activity of the Holy Spirit among non-Christian religions and justifies the use of non-christological criteria for discerning the presence of the Spirit.

In arguing for a "distinct economy" of the Spirit, Yong builds on the work of Georges Khodr. In addition to adopting Khodr's distinction between the economies of the Word and Spirit, Yong also follows Khodr in justifying this distinction by appealing to Irenaeus's image of the "two hands" and denying any economic subordination of the Spirit to the Son.[8] The latter point can be seen in Yong's discussion of the *filioque* clause. Yong approvingly cites Orthodox concerns that the *filioque* leads to subordination of the Spirit to the Son—a subordination which, in the judgment of Yong, buttresses ecclesiocentrism in the Western church: "In

---

[4]Ibid., p. 61. Although in the immediate context Yong is describing the proposal of Georges Khodr, it is clear that he embraces this assumption as well.

[5]Ibid., p. 69.

[6]Ibid., p. 132.

[7]Ibid., p. 70. Similarly, Yong elsewhere notes, "The gain in this approach is that the recognition of the procession or mission of the Holy Spirit into the world as related to and yet distinct from that of the Son provides the theological space that is greatly needed at the present time because while the person of Jesus Christ is a historical symbol of God's reality in the world, the Holy Spirit is *par excellence* the symbol of divine presence and activity in the cosmic realm" (ibid., p. 29).

[8]Yong's reading of Khodr has been influenced by Paul Knitter (see Paul F. Knitter, "A New Pentecost? A Pneumatological Theology of Religions," *Current Dialogue* 19 [1991]: 32-41).

short, failure to differentiate between the two economies inevitably risks the subordination of the mission of the Spirit to that of the Son and ultimately to an ecclesiological definition of soteriology."[9]

Having established this framework, Yong turns to the problem of criteria for discerning this presence of the Spirit: "The goal of a pneumatological approach to the religions is to find sufficient analogues in other traditions to the Christian doctrine of the Holy Spirit such that we are put in a position to pursue the comparative task and affirm or deny the Spirit's presence or activity."[10] Previous pneumatological approaches floundered because they were unable to identify non-christological criteria for discerning the Spirit's presence. Although christological criteria are clearly useful in certain contexts, they are not particularly helpful outside the church.[11] Because the Spirit acts in an economy distinct from that of the Son, we should be able to identify aspects of the Spirit's work that are not "constrained" by the Son.[12] To this end, Yong outlines a three-tiered process for discerning the work of the Spirit among adherents of other religions. At the first level ("phenomenological-experiential") one compares the religious experiences of adherents of other religions with Pentecostals looking for phenomenological similarities. On the second level ("moral-ethical") one looks for "concrete signs that follow claims of experiencing the transcendent."[13] Evidence of the Spirit's activity on this level includes lives being made whole and mending of communal relationships.[14] At the third level ("theological-soteriological") one must tackle the difficult question of the reference of the religious symbols in non-Christian religions: "To what transcendental reality, if any, do religious symbols refer?"[15]

In addition to "divine presence" (i.e., the Holy Spirit), a foundational

---

[9]Yong, *Discerning the Spirit(s)*, p. 64.
[10]Ibid., p. 143.
[11]Ibid., p. 137.
[12]Ibid., p. 136.
[13]Ibid., p. 251.
[14]Ibid., p. 253.
[15]Ibid., p. 254.

pneumatology must also account for "divine absence." In the Christian tradition divine absence has been traditionally understood in terms of the demonic. The demonic can be understood as a contrast symbol to that of the Holy Spirit.[16] Whereas the Holy Spirit "points to the idea of law or legality, rationality, relationality, and processive continuity culminating in the eschaton," the demonic "sets in motion force fields or habits of chaos, irrationality, isolation or alienation, and stagnation."[17] Thus, Yong's theology of religions is able to account both for the "transformative" nature of religious experience as well negative elements.

Pentecostals must learn to discern the presence of the Spirit (or spirits) in other religions by cultivating a "pneumatological imagination" informed by the three elements previously outlined. When the Spirit's presence is discerned, we may recognize a non-Christian religion "as salvific in the Christian sense."[18] As a test case for his proposal, Yong investigates the possibility of discerning the Spirit's presence within Umbanda (an Afro-Brazilian tradition). Traditionally, Pentecostals have dismissed Umbanda as demonically inspired; however, Yong believes that evidence of the Spirit's presence among the Umbanda can be seen in "the movement toward personal authenticity in the lives of individuals and toward social solidarity."[19] Moreover, through a dialogue with the Umbanda, Pentecostals could grow in at least three areas: (1) understanding the diversity of religious experience in responses to the transcendent, (2) gaining a broader theology of community and healing, and (3) recognizing that the lines between the divine and the demonic are not as sharp as Pentecostals often assume.[20] Adherents of Umbanda could learn from Pentecostals in three areas: (1) discerning the spirit world, (2) a proper understanding of healing, and (3) greater understanding of the battle against Exú spirits.[21]

---

[16]Ibid., p. 131.
[17]Ibid.
[18]Ibid., p. 312.
[19]Ibid., p. 279.
[20]Ibid., p. 288.
[21]Ibid., p. 297.

Although there is good reason to believe the Spirit is present and active in other religions, Yong explains that confirmation of the Spirit's presence can come only through concrete engagement. Christians should not merely view non-Christian religions in terms of *praeparatio evangelica*. Although religions can function this way, "to understand indigenous traditions *solely* on these terms leads to the kind of restrictive christological quests that continue to denigrate the Holy Spirit as having less-than-equal status as a trinitarian member."[22] If the Holy Spirit is genuinely at work in other religions, Christians must acknowledge this and be willing to learn from adherents of other religions:

> The possible presence and activity of the Spirit in other traditions means the possible existence of theological insights in other traditions that may have a positive impact on Christian theology. To deny the latter possibility is to lapse to an extremely anemic pneumatology even on biblical grounds.[23]

Furthermore, Christian theologians must also acknowledge the possibility that "other canonical traditions may also be divinely inspired in some way."[24] None of this undermines the gospel mission of the church. On the contrary, it invigorates it.

JACQUES DUPUIS'S CHRISTIAN THEOLOGY OF RELIGIOUS PLURALISM

In *Toward a Christian Theology of Religious Pluralism* Jacques Dupuis, a Catholic theologian, argues on trinitarian grounds that non-Christian religions mediate God's saving grace.[25] Because the triune God constitutes the ultimate source of all genuine religious experience, different religions are able to convey differing—yet legitimate—insights into this divine ultimate reality.[26]

---

[22]Ibid., p. 320.

[23]Ibid., p. 317.

[24]Ibid., pp. 317-18.

[25]Jacques Dupuis, *Toward a Christian Theology of Religious Pluralism* (Maryknoll, N.Y.: Orbis, 1997).

[26]Ibid., p. 279.

It will be helpful to locate Dupuis's work in the context of contemporary Catholic approaches to religious diversity. Although Vatican II clearly affirmed that non-Christian religions are, in some sense, to be viewed positively and that individuals who have never heard the gospel can experience salvation apart from the witness of the church, conciliar bishops were silent regarding the means through which salvific grace is mediated apart from the church.[27] Silence on this question has led to two conflicting positions among Catholics, which can be summarized as follows: (P1) Although salvation is available outside the church, it is not mediated through non-Christian religions.[28] (P2) Salvation is not only available outside the church but it is also mediated through non-Christian religions in such a way that non-Christian religions in some sense constitute means of salvation.[29] Dupuis embraces a form of P2.

Although Jesus Christ is the universal Savior of humankind, Dupuis maintains that Christ should not be viewed as "absolute" Savior. Absoluteness can be attributed only to God the Father. Jesus Christ is Savior in the derivative sense that "the world and humankind find salvation in and through him."[30] Thus, rather than speaking of Jesus Christ as absolute Savior, Dupuis suggests it would be better to speak of Jesus Christ as *constitutive* Savior.[31] By insisting that Jesus Christ is constitutive savior, Dupuis wants to open the door to other saviors who somehow participate in the universal mediation of Christ. Although we cannot sever the "universality of Jesus-the-Christ" from the "particularity of Jesus of Nazareth," we must recognize that God's saving action is not limited to the Christ event.[32] On the contrary, the two hands of God, the Word and the Spirit, are universally present and active in non-Christian religions. A "distinct action" of the nonincarnate Logos con-

---

[27]See Miikka Ruokanen, *The Catholic Doctrine of Non-Christian Religions According to the Second Vatican Council* (New York: E. J. Brill, 1992).

[28]Catholic proponents of P1 would include Gavin D'Costa and Joseph DiNoia.

[29]Catholic proponents of P2 would include Karl Rahner, Paul Knitter, Hans Küng and Raimundo Panikkar.

[30]Dupuis, *Toward a Christian Theology of Religious Pluralism*, p. 293.

[31]Ibid., p. 283.

[32]Ibid., p. 298.

tinues following Christ's resurrection.[33] Furthermore, the Spirit is also universally active following the incarnation. For example, as the result of the Spirit's inspiration, revelation can be encountered in the sacred writings of non-Christian religions. Thus, sacred scriptures such as the Qur'an can be viewed as containing the "word of God."[34]

According to Dupuis, the Word and the Spirit work together in a single economy of salvation that is both singular and complex. Regarding the unity of this economy, Dupuis is critical of theologians such as Paul Knitter who sharply distinguish the economy of the Christ event from the economy of the Spirit, with the result that two separate economies of salvation emerge. Dupuis insists that the action of the second and third persons of the Trinity, while distinct, should not be separated in this way. Moreover, while singular, the economy of salvation is also complex, in that it extends beyond the Hebrew-Christian tradition. "Salvation-revelation" exists in other traditions. Evidence for the latter can be found in a proper understanding of God's covenants with humankind and recognition of the fruit of the Spirit in other traditions. Earlier universal covenants, including the Noahic and Mosaic covenants, have continuing and abiding force. Just as the Mosaic covenant has not been annulled by the Christ event, neither was the covenant with Noah annulled by the Christ event. Furthermore, the fruit of the Spirit among followers of other religious traditions "testifies to God's saving and revealing action among them through their history."[35]

Building on the foundation of Karl Rahner, Dupuis claims that non-Christian religions constitute "channels of salvation" through which efficacious grace is mediated to their adherents. Salvation, therefore, does not reach human beings in spite of their religious traditions but in

---

[33]Ibid., p. 299.

[34]Recognizing the Qur'an contains the "word of God" does not entail the affirmation that *all* of its contents are inspired: "Christian theologians who admit this, let us observe, are aware that the Qur'an in its entirety cannot be regarded as the authentic word of God. Error is not absent from it. But this does not prevent the divine truth it contains from being the word of God uttered through the prophet" (ibid., p. 245).

[35]Ibid., p. 220.

and through them.[36] For example, the worship of images may constitute a means of grace for Hindus: "The worship of sacred images can be the sacramental sign in and through which the devotee responds to the offer of divine grace; it can mediate secretly the grace offered by God in Jesus Christ and express the human response to God's gratuitous gift in him."[37] Even if we were to grant in principle that saving grace is mediated through non-Christian religions, how can we be certain that adherents of non-Christian religions are experiencing divine grace? Dupuis explains that certain "saving values" (e.g., presence of radical *agape*) serve as the basis for affirming the presence of saving grace.[38]

Finally, Dupuis claims that non-Christian religions share in the reign of God. Although they are not members of the church, adherents of other religious traditions are authentic members of the kingdom who contribute to its growth and development.[39] Moreover, in the eschaton they will share in its fullness. In light of these and other factors, religious pluralism should not be viewed with suspicion but welcomed with open arms recognizing that "God has manifested himself to humankind in manifold ways."[40]

AUGUSTINE ON THE RELATIONS OF THE DIVINE PERSONS

Having examined the proposals of Yong and Dupuis, we will turn to Augustine's teaching on the relations of the divine persons. In the Augustinian critique to be offered later in this chapter, I will argue that Yong's pneumatological theology of religions (trinitarian pneumatol-

---

[36]"Can other religions contain and signify, in some way, the presence of God to human beings in Jesus Christ? Does God become present to them in the very practice of their religion? It is necessary to admit this. Indeed, their own religious practice is the reality that gives expression to their experience of God and of the mystery of Christ. It is the visible element, the sign, the sacrament of that experience. This practice expresses, bears, supports and contains, as it were, their encounter with God in Jesus Christ" (ibid. p., 319).

[37]Ibid., p. 303.

[38]Ibid., p. 325.

[39]Ibid., p. 345.

[40]Ibid., p. 386.

ogy) and Dupuis's Christian theology of religious pluralism (trinitarian Christology) gain momentum only by employing deficient accounts of the relations among the Father, Son and Holy Spirit. To understand how these problems emerge we need to examine Augustine's teaching on the divine relations in some detail. I will explore Augustine's teaching on the divine relations under the four headings introduced in the following paragraph.

In book 1 of *De trinitate*, Augustine offers a helpful summary of (Latin) pro-Nicene teaching on the Trinity. His summary contains four themes arranged in chiastic form.[41]

A Inseparable equality of the divine persons in one substance

B Real distinctions between the divine persons

B' Distinction of persons in the economy of salvation

A' Inseparable action of the divine persons in the economy of salvation

It will be helpful to quote Augustine at length:

[A] The purpose of all the Catholic commentators I have been able to read on the divine books of both testaments, who have written before me on the trinity which God is,[42] has been to teach that according to the scriptures Father and Son and Holy Spirit in the inseparable equality of one substance present a divine unity; and therefore there are not three gods but one God; [B] although indeed the Father has begotten the Son, and therefore he who is the Father is not the Son; and the Son is begotten by the Father, and therefore he who is the Son is not the Father; and the Holy Spirit is neither the Father nor the Son, but only the Spirit of the Father and of the Son, himself coequal to the Father and

---

[41]There are no headings in Augustine's summary. These headings are my own.

[42]Notice in this summary how Augustine speaks about the "Trinity which God is" (*de trinitate quae Deus est*). This phrase is not used by any of Augustine's predecessors and represents an important alternative to merely affirming the Father as *Deus* (see Lewis Ayres, *Augustine and the Trinity* [Cambridge: Cambridge University Press, 2010], p. 100). Augustine may also be the first Latin to speak about "the only true God" (cf. Jn 17:3) as Trinity and not merely Father (ibid., p. 103).

the Son, and belonging to the threefold unity. [B'] It was not however this same three (their teaching continues) that was born of the virgin Mary, crucified and buried under Pontius Pilate, rose again on the third day and ascended into heaven, but the Son alone. Nor was it this same three that came down upon Jesus in the form of a dove at his baptism, or came down on the day of Pentecost after the Lord's ascension, with a roaring sound from heaven as though a violent gust were rushing down, and in divided tongues as of fire, but the Holy Spirit alone. Nor was it this same three that spoke from heaven, *You are my Son*, either at his baptism by John (Mk 1:11), or on the mountain when the three disciples were with him (Mt 17:5), nor when the resounding voice was heard, *I have both glorified it* (my name) *and will glorify it again* (Jn 12:28), but it was the Father's voice alone addressing the Son; [A'] although just as Father and Son and Holy Spirit are inseparable, so do they work inseparably. This is also my faith inasmuch as it is the Catholic faith (*De trinitate* 1.7, 69-70).[43]

First (A), Augustine discusses divine relations from an intratrinitarian standpoint. Father, Son and Holy Spirit exist in an "inseparable equality of one substance." Thus, we must speak of *one* God. At the same time (B), real distinctions exist among the persons that are grounded in relations of origin. Third (B'), Augustine discusses the relations of the divine persons from an economic standpoint. It was not the three who were born of the virgin Mary but only the Son. It was not the three who "descended" as a dove but only the Spirit. It was not the three that "spoke" at Jesus' baptism but only the Father. His summary draws to a close (A') with an affirmation that the divine persons act inseparably. It is important to observe how A/A' and B/B' mirror one other in such a way that A constitutes the basis for A', while B constitutes the basis for B'. This citation offers a compact summary of Augustine's teaching on divine relations. Our discussion of divine relations will follow the order outlined as (A, B, B', A').

---

[43]For a discussion of this summary, see Ayres, *Augustine and the Trinity*, pp. 95-114. Whereas Ayres sees this text as divided into three sections, I follow many other commentators in seeing four.

Unity and equality of the divine persons* ad intra *(A). Following a theological tradition that can be traced to Tertullian, Augustine locates the equality of the divine persons in a unity of substance.[44] Father, Son and Spirit "are of one and the same substance (*substantia*) or essence (*essentia*)" (*De trinitate* 1.4, 67). Although he frequently speaks of one *substantia*, Augustine's vocabulary is somewhat flexible, such that he also speaks of one *essentia,* one *divinitas* or one *deitas.*[45] Augustine explains that *substantia* has the same meaning as *ousia* in Greek: "By 'being' [*essentia*] I mean here what is called *ousia* in Greek, which we more usually call substance [*substantia*]" (*De trinitate* 5.9-10, 195-96). The essence of God is unchanging and eternal (*De trinitate* 1.3, 66).

In order to demonstrate that the divine persons are one substance, Augustine attempts to show that the Son and the Holy Spirit are consubstantial (*consubstantialis*) with the Father. One of the "clearest and most consistent divine testimonies" showing Jesus Christ is God can be found in John 1:1-3 (*De trinitate* 1.9, 71). The "Word of God" in this passage is none other than the "Son of God" who became incarnate (cf. Jn 1:14). John 1:1-3 "clearly shows that he is not only God but also of the same substance as the Father" (*De trinitate* 1.9, 71). Augustine arrives at this conclusion by observing that in John 1:2 the Word of God (which must be recognized as the Son of God) created "all things." If the Son of God created all things and was not himself among the all things that were created, then "he is of one and the same substance as the Father," based on the assumption that whatever is not created must be God (*De trinitate* 1.9, 71). Thus the Son is not only God but also "true God." A few paragraphs later he offers a similar argument by reading 1 Corinthians 8:6 alongside John 1:2. First Corinthians 8:6 affirms that God the Father created all things through the Son while

---

[44]There is for Augustine an important sense in which the equality of the three divine persons can be traced to the Father. As Ayres notes, the Father is the "cause and source of the Trinitarian communion" (ibid., p. 264). The Father's role as *principium* will be discussed later.

[45]For a discussion of the terms *substantia* and *essentia* in Augustine's theology, see ibid., pp. 200-208.

John 1:2 affirms that the Son created all things.

Together these passages preclude the idea that the Father made some things and the Son others; it is clear that the Father made *all* things and the Son made *all* things. If the Father created all things and the Son created all things, then they must have created the same things. This implies that "the Son is equal to the Father" (*De trinitate* 1.12, 72). One of the most important texts affirming the consubstantiality of the Son to the Father is Philippians 2:6. Notice how he emphasizes the word *equal*: "In any case the apostle did not fail to use the very word 'equal,' and said as plainly as could be, *who being in the form of God did not think it robbery to be equal to God* (Phil 2:6), here using 'God' as a proper name for the Father, as he does in another text, *But the head of Christ is God* (1 Cor. 11:3)" (*De trinitate* 1.12, 73.) Another important text for Augustine in affirming the consubstantiality of the Son to the Father is John 10:30.[46]

Augustine's argument for the deity of the Holy Spirit proceeds in a parallel fashion. First, he argues that the Holy Spirit is not a creature but God (both by appealing directly to Scripture as well as to biblical "testimonies" that have been collected by others). For example, if the Holy Spirit is a creature, then how can Paul say (1 Cor 6:19) that Christian bodies are the temple of the Holy Spirit? "Could anything be more insanely sacrilegious than to have the effrontery to call the members of Christ the temple of a creature who is inferior, in these people's opinion, to Christ himself?" (*De trinitate* 1.13, 73). Augustine notes that four verses earlier (1 Cor 6:15) Paul claims that believers' bodies are "members of Christ."

> But if things that are the members of Christ are the temple of the Holy Spirit, then the Holy Spirit is not a creature, since we cannot but owe, to one whom we offer our bodies to as a temple, that service by which

---

[46]Richard Bauckham argues that "one" in John 10:30 functions as a monotheistic claim confirming Augustine's reading (see Richard Bauckham, *Jesus and the God of Israel: God Crucified and Other Studies on the New Testament's Christology of Divine Identity* [Grand Rapids: Eerdmans, 2008], pp. 104-6).

only God is to be served, which in Greek is called *latreia*. So he says in conclusion, *Glorify God therefore in your bodies* (1 Cor 6:20). (*De trinitate* 1.13, 73)

Implicit in his argument is an assumption—rooted in Augustine's reading of Romans 1:25—that genuine *latreia* must only be offered only to God and not to any creature. If the Holy Spirit is God, then he must be "absolutely equal to the Father and the Son, and consubstantial and co-eternal in the oneness of the three" (*De trinitate* 1.13, 73).

***Distinction of divine persons* ad intra (B).** If Father, Son and Holy Spirit are one substance, then no inequality may exist among them. Although this affirmation eliminates all ontological subordination, it leaves an important question unanswered. If the divine persons share one nature, in what sense and on what basis are they distinct? According to Augustine, real distinctions exist among the divine persons, which are grounded in relations of origin. Because the Father has begotten the Son, the Father is not the Son. Because the Son is begotten by the Father, the Son is not the Father. Similarly, because the Spirit proceeds from the Father and the Son, the Spirit is distinct from the Father and the Son. The generation of the Son and procession of the Holy Spirit constitute the basis for the distinction of the divine persons in Augustine's trinitarian theology.[47]

---

[47]Augustine's opponents argued that the terms *unbegotten* and *begotten* describe the essence of the Father (unbegotten) and the essence of the Son (begotten). Because *begotten* and *unbegotten* differ, the essence of the Father must be distinct (and different) from the essence of the Son. Thus Father and Son cannot be equal. The philosophical assumption behind the Homoian argument is that terms like *begotten* and *unbegotten* must name God's essence since, in the case of God, nothing can be "accidentally" predicated of God's nature. (In the background of this debate is the Aristotelian distinction between "accident" and "substance." An accidental quality is something an object may or may not have [e.g., "love in the life of a human person]. Although we use "accident" words like *good* and *great* to speak about God, no accidents can be predicated of God in terms of Aristotle's categories. All accident words, when used of God, are really substance words.) Augustine responded by drawing a distinction between "substance" and "relation." While God can have no accidents, it does not follow from this that every statement about God must be a substance statement: "With God, though, nothing is said modification-wise [in terms of accident], because there is nothing changeable with him. And yet not everything that is said of him is said substance-wise. Some things are said with reference to something else, like Father with reference to Son and Son with reference to Father; and this is

Generation of the Son. Augustine was not the first to articulate a doctrine of eternal generation as a way of explicating the Son-Father relationship. On the contrary, eternal generation is a central feature of pro-Nicene exegesis (both Latin and Greek).[48] Augustine's exposition of John 5:26 in his *Tractates on the Gospel of John* offers a helpful window into his understanding of eternal generation. "For as the Father has life in himself, so he has granted the Son also to have life in himself." What does it mean that the Father has "life in himself"? Among other things it means that the Father's life is completely different from human life. Whereas the life of the soul is mutable and dependent, the life of God is immutable and dependent on nothing outside God (*Tractates* 19.8, 149).[49] Augustine points out that the Son possesses a form of life identical to that of the Father—"life in himself." The only difference is that the Son possesses "life in himself" which was "given" to him while the Father possesses "life in himself" which was given by no one. The fact that the Son possesses "life in himself" rules out the possibility that the Son possesses a mutable form of life akin to human life.[50]

How, Augustine asks, did the Son receive "life in himself"? His answer is both simple and profound: the Father begat the Son. "The Father is life, not by a 'being born'; the Son is life by a 'being born.' The Father [is] from no Father; the Son, from God the Father" (*Tractates*

---

not said modification-wise, because the one is always Father and the other always Son—not 'always' in the sense that he is Son from the moment he is born or that the Father does not cease to be Father from the moment the Son does not cease to be Son, but in the sense that the Son is always born and never began to be Son" (Augustine, *De trinitate* 5.6, 192). Terms like *unbegotten* and *begotten*, when applied to God, do not name God's substance but relations that exist among the divine persons.

[48]Lewis Ayres, *Nicaea and Its Legacy: An Approach to Fourth-Century Trinitarian Theology* (New York: Oxford University Press, 2004), p. 236. "Augustine places Latin Nicene emphasis on the Son's being generated from the substance of the Father at the heart of his theology" (Ayres, *Augustine and the Trinity*, p. 180).

[49]English citations from Augustine's *In Johannis evangelium tractatus* will be taken from Saint Augustine, *Fathers of the Church*, vol. 79, *Tractates on the Gospel of John, 11-27*, trans. John W. Rettig (Washington D.C.: Catholic University of America Press, 1988).

[50]Augustine devotes several paragraphs to a discussion of the difference between the dependent life of the soul and the self-existent life of God.

19.13, 152). Augustine suggests that the phrase "has been given" is roughly equivalent in meaning to "has been begotten" (*Tractates* 19.13, 152).[51] Here we see Augustine invoking the concept of eternal generation to explain the judgment this text renders regarding the relationship of the Son to the Father.[52] Although Father and Son both possess "life in himself," they possess it in differing ways: "Therefore, the Father remains life, the Son also remains life; the Father, life in himself, not from the Son, the Son, life in himself, but from the Father. [He was] begotten by the Father to be life in himself, but the Father [is] life in himself, unbegotten" (*Tractates* 19.13, 153).[53] The Father did not beget a "lesser Son" who would one day become his equal. He timelessly begat a coeternal Son. In a beautiful turn of phrase, Augustine exhorts his readers to "hear the Father through the Son. Rise, receive life that in him who has life in himself you may receive life which you do not have in yourself" (*Tractates* 19.13, 153).[54] That the Son receives

---

[51]Augustine's interpretation of the phrase "has been given" as "has been begotten" in John 5:26 may strike some readers as a huge leap. It is important to remember that Christian theologians frequently employ terms not explicitly found in the biblical text (eg., Trinity, person, essence, nature, etc.) in order to explain what the text affirms. For example, most theologians interpret "life" in v. 26 as referring to God's essence even though the term *essence* is not found in John 5:26.

[52]It is crucial that we distinguish the "judgment" this text renders regarding the relationship of the Son to the Father from the "conceptuality" used to express this judgment (i.e., "generation"). For more on this important distinction, see David S. Yeago, "The New Testament and the Nicene Dogma: A Contribution to the Recovery of Theological Exegesis," *Pro Ecclesia* 3 (1994): 152-64.

[53]It is important to see the way the Creator-creature distinction provides the context for his analysis of John 5:26. "Life in himself" can only be understood on the Creator side of this distinction.

[54]There is much to commend Augustine's reading of John 5:26. Commenting on this text, D. A. Carson explains, "A full discussion of John 5:26 could demonstrate that it most plausibly reads as an *eternal grant* from the Father to the Son, a grant that inherently transcends time and stretches Jesus' Sonship into eternity past. When Jesus says that the Father has 'life in himself,' the most natural meaning is that this refers to God's self-existence. He is not dependent on anyone or anything. Then Jesus states that God, who has 'life in himself,' 'has granted the Son to have life in himself.' This is conceptually far more difficult. If Jesus had said that the Father, who has 'life in himself,' had granted to the Son to have life, there would be no conceptual difficulty, but of course the Son would then be an entirely secondary and derivative being. What was later called the doctrine of the Trinity would be ruled out. Alternatively, if Jesus had said that the Father has 'life in himself' and the Son has 'life in himself,' there would be no conceptual difficulty, but it would be much more difficult to rule out ditheism. In fact what

"life in himself" from the Father is not merely dependent on his exegesis of individual texts like John 5:26. Augustine marshals a wide variety of biblical evidence for eternal generation.[55]

Augustine's account of eternal generation includes several important elements. First, the generation of the Son by the Father is incorporeal and should not be understood in the manner of human generation. Unfortunately, some people make the mistake of "transfer[ing] what they have observed about bodily things to incorporeal and spiritual things" (*De trinitate* 1.1, 65). Second, the generation of the Son is "timeless," through generation "the Father bestows being on the Son *without any beginning in time*" (*De trinitate* 15.47, 432, italics mine). Thus, the Son is coeternal with the Father. Third, the Son is begotten by the Father in an equality of nature. The Father did not beget a "lesser Son" who would eventually become his equal. Commenting on John 5:26, Augustine explains that the Father begot the Son "timelessly in such a way that the *life* which the Father gave the Son by begetting him is coeternal with the *life* of the Father who gave it" (*De trinitate* 15.47, 432, italics mine). Through generation the Son receives the life—that is, the nature or substance—of the Father. Fourth, it is "necessary" in the sense that the Son is begotten *not* by the will of the Father but rather of

---

Jesus says is that the Father has 'life in himself' and He has *granted* to the Son to have 'life in himself.' The expression 'life in himself' must mean the same thing in both parts of the verse. But how can such 'life in himself,' the life of self-existence, be granted by another? The ancient explanation is still the best one: This is an eternal grant. There was therefore never a time when the Son did not have 'life in himself.' This eternal grant establishes the nature of the eternal relationship between the Father and the Son. But if this is correct, since Father and Son have always been in this relationship, the Sonship of Jesus is not restricted to the days of His flesh" (D. A. Carson, "God Is Love," *Bibliotheca Sacra* 156 [1999]: 139. See also Marianne Meye Thompson, *The God of the Gospel of John* [Grand Rapids: Eerdmans, 2001], pp. 77-80).

[55]Although he offers traditional readings of many of texts typically cited in support of eternal generation (e.g., Ps 2:7; Prov 8:22-25), Augustine's argument for eternal generation draws on a wide variety of biblical materials that can be organized in five different groups. See Keith E. Johnson, "What Would Augustine Say to Evangelicals Who Reject the Eternal Generation of the Son?" unpublished paper presented at the Evangelical Theological Society in Atlanta, Georgia, on November 17, 2010. It should be noted, therefore, that Augustine's doctrine of eternal generation is deeply embedded in his reading of the Gospel and is not dependent on the translation of the Greek word *monogenēs*. This point seems be missed by those who claim that little or no biblical warrant exists for a doctrine of eternal generation.

the substance of the Father (*De trinitate* 15.38, 425).[56] Fourth, the Son is begotten by the Father in an equality of nature. Fifth, a likeness to the generation of the Son can be found in the nature of "light." We should not think of the generation of the Son like "water flowing out from a hole in the ground or in the rock, but like light flowing from light" (*De trinitate* 4.27, 172). The Son's light is equal in its radiance to the light of the Father. Finally, the generation of the Son is incomprehensible.[57]

Procession of the Holy Spirit. Although earlier theologians recognized that the procession of the Spirit clearly differed from the generation of the Son (such that it would be inappropriate to speak of the Spirit as a second Son), many were at a loss to offer a theological rationale for this distinction. Augustine made an important contribution by suggesting that the Holy Spirit proceeds jointly from the Father and the Son as from one principle.[58] This discussion will be important for our assessment of Yong's trinitarian pneumatology, as rejection of the procession of the Spirit *from the Son* plays a role in Amos Yong's case for a distinct economy of the Holy Spirit. Augustine succinctly summarizes his position in the following statement:

> And just as for the Holy Spirit his being the gift of God means his proceeding from the Father, so his being sent means his being known to proceed from him. Nor, by the way, can we say that the Holy Spirit does not proceed from the Son as well; it is not without point that the same Spirit is called the Spirit of the Father and of the Son. (*De trinitate* 4.29, 174)

Augustine sees biblical warrant for affirming the Son's role in the procession of the Spirit in the way that Scripture speaks of the Holy

---

[56]To say that the Son is generated by the will of the Father is to say that the Son is a creature.

[57]The incomprehensibility of the triune God is a major theme in Augustine's theology. He repeatedly reminds his readers of this throughout *De trinitate*.

[58]In order to avoid confusion, I will use the term *filioque* ("and the Son") exclusively in reference to the controversial interpolation in the Nicene Symbol, while I will use the phrase "procession from the Father and Son" to refer to Augustine's position. The failure to distinguish these results in confusion.

Spirit as the "Spirit of the Father and the Son" (e.g., Gal 4:6). Further evidence for the Son's role in the procession of the Holy Spirit can be seen in the bestowal of the Spirit upon the disciples by Christ following the resurrection (Jn 20:22).

Two of the most important biblical texts for Augustine regarding the procession of the Spirit are John 14:26 and John 15:26. "By saying then, *Whom I will send you from the Father* (Jn 15:26), the Lord showed that the Spirit is both the Father's and the Son's. Elsewhere too, when he said, *whom the Father will send*, he added, *in my name* (Jn 14:26)" (*De trinitate* 4.29, 174). The logic of this is quite clear: if temporal sending reveals an eternal procession, and if the Son "sent" the Spirit, then the Spirit must proceed not only from the Father but also from the Son. Like the generation of the Son, the procession of the Holy Spirit is immaterial, timeless and results in equality of nature (*De trinitate* 15.47, 432).

Although he affirms that the Spirit proceeds from the Father and the Son, Augustine offers an important qualification. John 15:26 does not say, "whom the Father will send from me" but rather "whom I will send from the Father." By this, "he [Christ] indicated that the source [*principium*] of all godhead [*divinitatis*], or if you prefer it, of all deity [*deitatis*], is the Father. So the Spirit who proceeds from the Father and the Son is traced back, on both counts, to him of whom the Son is born" (*De trinitate* 4.29, 174). Thus, Augustine affirms that the source and origin of deity (*principium deitatis*) is the Father. The Father's status as *principium* is a core element of Augustine's trinitarian theology.[59]

One final issue merits attention in relation to the Holy Spirit. According to Augustine, names like "Son" and "Father" signify relations

---

[59]As Ayres explains, "the Father's *monarchia*, his status as *principium* and *fons*, is central to Augustine's trinitarian theology. . . . For Augustine, the Father's status as *principium* is eternally exercised through his giving the fullness of divinity to the Son and Spirit such that the unity of the God will be eternally found in the mysterious unity of the *homoousion*" (Ayres, *Augustine and the Trinity*, p. 248). Augustine's account of trinitarian communion holds in tension the Father's role as *principium* with full divinity and equality of the Son and Holy Spirit with the Father. Ayres summarizes this reality well when he says "Augustine's mature account of the Trinity" involves "an ordered communion of equals established by the Father" (ibid., p. 197).

that obtain among the divine persons. A problem, however, arises in the case of the Spirit in that the name "Holy Spirit" does not initially appear to suggest a relation. Augustine finds a solution in the language of "gift": "This relationship, to be sure, is not apparent in this particular name [Holy Spirit], but it is apparent when he is called *the gift of God* (Acts 8:20; Jn 4:10)" (*De trinitate* 5.12, 197). *Gift* implies relationship: "So when we say 'the gift of the giver' and the 'the giver of the gift,' we say each with reference to the other. So the Holy Spirit is a kind of inexpressible communion or fellowship of the Father and Son, and perhaps he is given this name just because the same name can be applied to the Father and the Son" (*De trinitate* 5.12, 197). Appealing to gift language also provides a way to distinguish generation and procession: while the Son comes forth "as being born," the Spirit comes forth "as being given" (*De trinitate* 5.15, 199). Thus, we should not speak of the Spirit as a second "son."

***Distinction of divine person* ad extra (B').** Having examined the divine relations *ad intra*, we will now consider the distinction of the persons by examining the central economic concept in *De trinitate*—the divine "missions." This discussion will play a key role in my evaluation of Yong's distinct economy of the Spirit and Dupuis's distinction between the working of the incarnate Logos and non-incarnate Logos. In chapter three we examined the relation between "mission" and "generation/procession," highlighting Augustine's central insight that the temporal missions reveal the eternal generation of the Son and eternal procession of the Spirit. If the missions of the Son and Spirit closely correspond to their eternal generation and procession, this suggests that the intratrinitarian order (*taxis*), Father-Son-Holy Spirit, represents one of the keys to understanding the interrelationships of the divine persons in the economy of salvation.[60] Indeed this is precisely what we discover: the Father—the source and origin of deity (*principium*)—is the one who sends, while the Son (who proceeds from the Father) and the Spirit (who

---

[60]See Ayres, *Augustine and the Trinity*, p. 247.

proceeds from the Father and Son) are the ones sent.

Sending of the Son. Augustine links the "sending" of the Son to the incarnation: "What constituted the sending of the Lord was his being born in the flesh, his issuing, so to speak, from the hidden invisibility of the Father's bosom and appearing to the eyes of men in the form of a servant" (*De trinitate* 3.3, 129). The sending of the Son represents a unique moment in salvation history, such that we cannot properly speak of the Son being "sent" prior to the incarnation. Two key differences exist between Old Testament theophanies and the sending of the Son in the incarnation. First, the latter involved the direct presence of the Son in the world, while the former were mediated by angels (*De trinitate* 3.27, 144). Second, the New Testament sending of the Son differed in purpose from the divine appearances in Old Testament. In book 4, Augustine engages in a protracted discussion of the work of Christ, in which he appears to digress from his argument. Augustine discusses the reality of humans under sin and how Jesus Christ, as Mediator, solved this problem. It is not until the final part of book 4 that the reader discovers the purpose of this apparent digression: "There you have what the Son of God has been sent for; indeed there you have what it is for the Son of God to have been sent" (*De trinitate* 4.25, 171). In other words, Augustine's digression in the first part of book 4 was intended to explicate the purpose for which the Son was sent—namely, to restore fallen humans into a relationship of communion with the triune God.[61]

Sending of the Spirit. Augustine's claim that the Son appeared in a "created bodily form" while, in his "uncreated spiritual form," he remained hidden also enables us to understand the sense in which the Holy Spirit was sent. The Holy Spirit was "visibly displayed in a created guise which was made in time, either when he descended on our Lord himself *in bodily guise as a dove* (Mt 3:16), or when ten days after his ascension *there came suddenly from heaven on the day of Pentecost a sound as of*

---

[61]"Mediation" represents the central concept through which Augustine narrates the work of Christ (see Augustine, *De trinitate* 4.12, 161).

a violent gust bearing down, and there appeared to them divided tongues as of fire, which also settled upon each one of them (Acts 2:2)" (*De trinitate* 2.10, 104). The sending of the Holy Spirit differs from the sending of the Son in that the Holy Spirit did not join a created reality "to himself and his person to be held in an everlasting union" (*De trinitate* 2.11, 104). For this reason, we cannot say that the Spirit is "God and dove" or "God and fire," as we say of the Son "that he is God and man" (*De trinitate* 2.11, 104). This raises an important question: inasmuch as the divine manifestations in the Old Testament also involved the temporary appropriation of a created reality, in what sense does the sending of the Holy Spirit at Pentecost differ from these earlier appearances? Augustine offers two responses. First, he points out that John 7:39 teaches that "there was going to be a kind of giving or sending of the Holy Spirit after Christ's glorification such as there had never been before" (*De trinitate* 4.29, 174). Second, he suggests that uniqueness of the Spirit's sending can be seen in its result. Nowhere prior to Pentecost do we read of people speaking languages they did not previously know. The Holy Spirit's

> coming needed to be demonstrated by perceptible signs, to show that the whole world and all nations with their variety of languages were going to believe in Christ by the gift of the Holy Spirit, in order to fulfill the psalmist's prophetic song, *There are no languages or dialects whose voices are not heard; their sound has gone out to all the earth, and their words to the end of the world* (Ps 19:3). (*De trinitate* 4.29, 175)

Augustine sees a special significance in the perceptible sign through which the bestowal of the Spirit is manifested (i.e., bearing witness to Christ in multiple languages): it not only underscores the unique role of the Holy Spirit in the economy of salvation but also offers a proleptic fulfillment of the ultimate goal of the Holy Spirit's mission—namely, leading people in every nation to confess Jesus Christ as Savior and Lord.

Two sendings—one goal. Having examined the roles of the Son and the Holy Spirit, we must now bring our discussion to close by considering how these two "sendings" relate to one another. This discussion will play an important role in my Augustinian critique of Yong and Dupuis. First and foremost we must remember that these sendings have one ultimate goal—bringing men and women into eternal contemplation of the Father, the Son and the Holy Spirit:

> Contemplation in fact is the reward of faith, a reward for which hearts are cleansed through faith, as it is written, *cleansing their hearts through faith* (Acts 15:9). Proof that it is that contemplation for which hearts are cleansed comes from the key text, *Blessed are the clean of heart, for they shall see God* (Mt 5:8). (*De trinitate* 1.17, 77)

Augustine is careful to point out that it is not merely the Father who is the object of eternal contemplation but also the Son and the Spirit (*De trinitate* 1.17-18, 77). This contemplation is the source of eternal joy: "For the fullness of our happiness, beyond which there is none else, is this: to enjoy God the three in whose image we are made" (Augustine, *De trinitate* 1.18, 77). In the second half of *De trinitate*, Augustine leads his reader into contemplation of the triune God through consideration of the divine image in human soul, which represents a mirror through which we may perceive—albeit it dimly—the triunity of God.

Although it customary to speak about the "missions" (plural) of the Son and the Holy Spirit, Augustine does not actually speak about these two missions in quite the same way *mission* is frequently used in contemporary English. He uses the Latin noun *missio*, which means "sending," along with the Latin verb *mitto*, which means "to send." Although the English term *mission* is derived from *missio*, these terms have slightly different connotations. The emphasis of the Latin term *missio* is on the act of sending, while the emphasis of the English term *mission* is often more on the purpose for being sent. Perhaps it might be more faithful to Augustine (and Scripture) to speak of two sendings (with reference to the *act* of sending) and one mission (with regard to the ultimate *purpose* of the sendings). This distinction seems to be missed by those who want to talk about an economy of the Spirit which is separate or distinct from the economy of the Son.

Unity of operation **ad extra** *(A')*. According to Augustine, Father, Son and Holy Spirit act inseparably (*De trinitate* 1.7, 70). The inseparable action of the divine persons represents a fundamental axiom of Augustine's trinitarian theology.[62] He inherited this axiom from pro-Nicene theologians like Ambrose and Hilary.[63] Anti-Nicenes argued that the distinct activity of the Father, Son and Holy Spirit indicated that the divine persons were separate beings, with the Father being superior. In response, pro-Nicenes argued that Scripture shows the activity of the divine persons to be one (i.e., all three persons are involved in acts of creation, providence and redemption). Thus, Father, Son and Holy Spirit share one nature.

What does it mean, therefore, to affirm that the divine persons act inseparably? First, it means that all three persons are involved in *every* action of creation, providence and redemption.[64] Second, it means that Father, Son and Holy Spirit possess one will and execute one power. Inseparable operation is a direct implication and economic expression of intratrinitarian unity (i.e., monotheism). This can be seen clearly in Augustine's summary of Latin pro-Nicene teaching on the Trinity: intratrinitarian (ontological) unity (A) constitutes the basis for inseparable (economic) operation (A').

A helpful overview of the inseparable action can be found in a sermon Augustine preached on Matthew 3:13-17 around 410. It succinctly summarizes the teaching set forth in *De trinitate*. In the baptism of Jesus, Augustine sees a clear revelation of the divine persons: "So we have the three, somehow or other, clearly distinguished: in the

---

[62]Lewis Ayres, "The Fundamental Grammar of Augustine's Trinitarian Theology," in *Augustine and His Critics: Essays in Honour of Gerald Bonner*, ed. Robert Dodaro and George Lawless (New York: Routledge, 2000), pp. 55-56.

[63]Ibid., p. 56.

[64]We cannot formally assign different external works to the divine persons as distinct agents. The divine persons enact a single agency in creation, providence and redemption. When a biblical text mentions one divine person, this should *not* be seen as excluding the others: "It is to make us aware of the trinity that some things are even said about the persons singly by name; however, they must not be understood in the sense of excluding the other persons, because this same three is also one, and there is one substance and godhead of Father and Son and Holy Spirit" (Augustine, *De trinitate* 1.19, 79).

voice the Father, in the man the Son, in the dove the Holy Spirit. There is no need to do more than just remind you of this; it's easy enough to see" (*Sermon* 52.1, 50).[65] Surprisingly, this separable mani-festation of the persons raises a problem: "Now someone may say to me, 'Demonstrate that the three are inseparable. Remember you're speaking as a Catholic, speaking to Catholics'" (*Sermon* 52.2, 51). The Catholic faith, rooted in Scripture and apostolic truth holds "with the firmest and most orthodox faith, that Father, Son, and Holy Spirit are one inseparable trinity or triad; one God, not three gods; but one God in such a way that the Son is not the Father, that the Father is not the Son, that the Holy Spirit is neither the Father nor the Son, but the Spirit of the Father and of the Son" (*Sermon* 52.2, 51). How, then, can this be reconciled with the Son coming *separately* in human flesh, the Holy Spirit descending *separately* and the voice of the Father sounding *separately* from heaven?

After reminding his readers of the biblical basis for Catholic teaching regarding the inseparable action of the persons, Augustine restates the problem: "If the Father does nothing without the Son and the Son nothing without the Father, won't it follow, presumably, that we have to say the Father too was born of the Virgin Mary, the Father suffered under Pontius Pilate, the Father rose again and as-cended into heaven?" (*Sermon* 52.6, 52-53). To answer this question affirmatively would be to fall into the same error as the Patripas-sians.[66] This raises a dilemma. It appears that either Augustine must abandon his claim that the Son never acts without the Father or he must acknowledge that the Father suffered, the Father died and the Father rose again. After rejecting both these options, Augustine of-fers the following solution: "the Son indeed, and not the Father, was born of the Virgin Mary; but this birth of the Son, not the Father,

---

[65]English citations from Sermon 52 will be taken from Saint Augustine, *The Works of Saint Augustine: A Translation for the 21st Century*, vol. 3.3, *Sermons III (51-94) on the New Testament*, trans. Edmund Hill, ed. John E. Rotelle (Brooklyn: New City Press, 1991).

[66]Patripassianism is the error that the Father suffered on the cross. Theologians like Tertullian (rightly) argue that modalism entails Patripassianism.

from the Virgin Mary was the work of both Father and Son. It was not indeed the Father, but the Son who suffered; yet the suffering of the Son was the work of both Father and Son. It wasn't the Father who rose again, but the Son; yet the resurrection of the Son was the work of both Father and Son" (*Sermon* 52.8, 53-54). Having stated his solution, Augustine turns back to Scripture in order to demonstrate that the birth, death and resurrection of the Son were the work of the Father and the Son, yet that it was only the Son who was born, died and rose.

The inseparable action of the persons reflects the intratrinitarian *taxis*–Father, Son and Holy Spirit.[67] A clear example of this can be seen in Augustine's discussion of John 5:19. "So Jesus said to them, 'Truly, truly, I say to you, the Son can do nothing of his own accord, but only what he sees the Father doing. For whatever the Father does, that the Son does likewise.'" The reason the Son can do nothing on his own is because he is not—so to speak—"of himself." Rather he is *from* the Father. Notice the how the mode of operation directly reflects the mode of being of the divine persons in Augustine's explanation of John 5: "So the reason for these statements [John 5:19, 26] can only be that the life of the Son is unchanging like the Father's, and yet is from the Father [v. 26]; and that the work of Father and Son is indivisible, and yet the Son's working is from the Father [v. 19] just as he himself is from the Father" (*De trinitate* 2.3, 99).

That inseparable action of the divine persons is grounded in the intratrinitarian *taxis* can also be seen in his application of John 5:19 to creation in his *Tractates on the Gospel of John*. Genesis 1 teaches that God created light. What light did the Son create? It certainly cannot be a different light. Rather, it must be the same light: "Therefore, we understand that the light was made by God the Father, but through the Son" (*Tractates* 20.7, 170). Similarly, the Father created the world. The Son did not create another world by watching the Father. On the

---

[67]As Ayres rightly notes, "all operations *ad extra* [for Augustine] are founded in the ordering of the divine life" (Ayres, *Augustine and the Trinity*, p. 247).

contrary, the world was created by the Father *through* the Son. Thus, the reason the Son can do nothing of himself (Jn 5:19) is simply because "the Son is not of himself" (*Tractates* 20.8, 171). Summarizing his discussion of the creative work of the triune God, Augustine explains, "The Father [made] the world, the Son [made] the world, the Holy Spirit [made] the world. If [there are] three gods, [there are] three worlds; if [there is] one God, Father and Son and Holy Spirit, one world was made by the Father through the Son in the Holy Spirit" (*Tractates* 20.9, 172).

Augustine's mature account of trinitarian agency involves two elements. On the one hand, the work of the Father, Son and Holy Spirit is inseparably the work of the three *ad extra*. On the other hand, in this single act, the divine persons work according to their personal properties *ad intra*.[68] The Father acts with the other divine persons according to his mode of being "from no one" (unbegotten). The Son acts with the other divine persons according to his mode of being "from the Father" (generation). The Spirit acts with the other divine persons according to his mode of being "from the Father and the Son" (procession). A reciprocal relationship exists for Augustine between inseparable action of the persons and their inseparable nature. On the one hand, inseparable action implies inseparable nature (*De trinitate* 1.12, 72). On the other hand, inseparable nature implies inseparable action (*De trinitate* 1.19, 79).[69]

YONG'S TRINITARIAN PNEUMATOLOGY: AN AUGUSTINIAN EVALUATION

Inasmuch as Yong's pneumatological theology of religions is rooted in a

---

[68]In other words, *inseparability* for Augustine does not mean interchangeability: "Divine action has to be attributed inseparably to Father, Son and Holy Spirit, but not as if it was carried out through the distribution of tasks to three equal sources of action. *In reality, the unique divine action has its source in the Father and is performed through the Son, in the Holy Spirit*" (Luigi Gioia, *The Theological Epistemology of Augustine's* De trinitate [Oxford: Oxford University Press, 2008], pp. 162-63).

[69]Inseparable action should not be confused with modalism. Modalism denies the distinction of persons—something Augustine clearly affirms.

distinction between the economy of the Son and the economy of the Spirit, his proposal raises important questions about the relations among the trinitarian persons both within the divine life of the triune God (*ad intra*) and within the economy of salvation (*ad extra*). In the discussion that follows, I will argue that Yong's proposal ultimately fails to offer an adequate account of the relation of the Holy Spirit to the Son and Father.

Insufficient trinitarian framework. Although Yong acknowledges that the mission of the Spirit must ultimately be understood in a trinitarian context, he offers no comprehensive trinitarian framework at the outset within which to relate the work the Father, Son and Holy Spirit.[70] Although he frequently refers to the missions of the Son and Spirit, he offers no substantive discussion of the content of these missions from a salvation historical perspective. Echoing several contemporary theologians, he simply asserts that the Spirit operates in an economy distinct from that of the Son, brackets the economy of the Son, and then focuses almost exclusively on the economy of the Holy Spirit.

At the level of the immanent Trinity, Yong offers no account of the relations of the divine persons *ad intra* as ground for his understanding of the divine missions. Inasmuch as his distinction between the economy of the Son and the economy of the Spirit depends on the hypostatic distinction between the Son and Spirit, some discussion of intratrinitarian relations seems to be required. Yong, however, rejects out of hand any attempt to speculate about the immanent Trinity.[71] The closest he comes to a discussion of intratrinitarian relations is a brief discussion of the procession of the Spirit in which he rejects the traditional Western view that the Spirit proceeds jointly from the Father and the Son (in order to maintain a theological basis for an independent economy of the Holy Spirit).[72] However, inasmuch as compelling rea-

---

[70]Yong, *Discerning the Spirit(s)*, p. 58.

[71]Ibid., pp. 68-69.

[72]Ibid., p. 64. Rejection of the *filioque* has become standard fare among many who commend pneumatological approaches. See, e.g., Clark Pinnock, *Flame of Love: A Theology of the Holy Spirit* (Downers Grove, Ill.: InterVarsity Press, 1996), pp. 185-214.

sons exist to affirm the procession of the Spirit from the Father and the Son, Yong's rejection of the procession of the Spirit from the Father and the Son is unwarranted.[73] Furthermore, evidence *against* the twofold procession of the Spirit *ad intra* does not count as positive evidence *for* a separate economy of the Spirit *ad extra*. Yong seems to assume that by problematizing the procession of the Spirit from the Father and Son, he gains positive ground for dual economies. But the latter does not follow from the former. Finally, it is possible to affirm the full equality of the Spirit to the Son (a concern that drives Eastern rejection of the procession of the Spirit from the Father and the Son) without positing dual economies.[74]

Severing the "two hands" of the Father. Throughout *Discerning the Spirit(s)*, Yong repeatedly appeals to Irenaeus's image of the Son and Spirit as the "two hands" of God as a way of conceptualizing the Son-Spirit relationship.[75] His use of this image, however, stands in tension

---

[73]The *filioque* clause was inserted into the Nicene-Constantinopolitan Creed at the Third Council of Toledo in 589—over 170 years after Augustine wrote *De trinitate*. Thus, the question regarding the formal legitimacy of the insertion of the *filioque* clause into the creed must be distinguished from the substantive theological question of whether the Holy Spirit proceeds from the Father *and the Son*. These two issues are frequently (and wrongly!) conflated. In other words, one might acknowledge that the Western church was wrong unilaterally to insert the *filioque* into the creed while, at the same time, affirming that the Spirit proceeds from the Father and the Son. For an explanation and defense of Augustine's position, see Ayres, *Augustine and the Trinity*, pp. 263-68.

[74]See Kilian McDonnell, *The Other Hand of God: The Holy Spirit as the Universal Touch and Goal* (Collegeville, Minn.: Liturgical Press, 2003), pp. 86-97, 196-201, 228-29.

[75]Yong refers to the Son and Spirit as the "two hands" of God on at least sixteen different occasions in *Discerning the Spirit(s)*. This image is read not only as illustrating the equality of the Son and Spirit (in contrast to the alleged subordination of Spirit to the Son in the Western church as evidenced by the *filioque*) but it is also seen as providing epistemic warrant for an economy of the Spirit separate from that of the Son. Yong follows Khodr on this point. Notice how Khodr reads "two hands" in terms of dual economies: "The Spirit is present everywhere and fills everything by virtue of an economy distinct from that of the Son. Irenaeus calls the Word and the Spirit the 'two hands of the Father'. This means we must affirm not only their hypostatic independence but also that the advent of the Holy Spirit in the world is not subordinated to the Son, is not simply a function of the Word" (Khodr, "Christianity and the Pluralistic World," pp. 125-26). Yong appears to follow Khodr on this point: "Khodr's suggestion, echoed by Samartha, Dupuis and Knitter, is that a retrieval of Irenaeus's theological metaphor allows us to recognize the different economies of the Word and the Spirit" (Yong, *Discerning the Spirit(s)*, p. 62).

with his emphasis on a "distinct economy" of the Spirit. From an economic standpoint, the two-hands imagery is not about a left hand doing one activity and the right hand doing another (which seems to be implied by associating a distinct economy with each hand). It is fundamentally about the Father acting through the Son and Holy Spirit to a particular end.[76] Two-hands imagery underscores unity of action, combining hypostatic distinction at the intratrinitarian level (i.e., Father, Son and Spirit) with unity of action at the economic level.[77] As a heuristic device, Yong is free to use the two-hands imagery as he sees fit; however, it must be noted that this image, in the broader context of Irenaeus's trinitarian theology, offers no theological warrant for a separate economy of the Spirit.[78] On the contrary, Yong's use of this image causes me to wonder if his proposal implicitly severs the two hands of the Father.[79]

Like Irenaeus, Augustine emphasizes the unity of the divine persons *ad extra*. Father, Son and Holy Spirit work together in a single economy of salvation. Although the sendings of the Son and Spirit are distinct in such a way that we must speak of *two* sendings (Gal 4:4-6), these two sendings have *one* ultimate goal—bringing human beings into communion with the triune God. Yong's trinitarian pneumatology is deficient not because it attributes different economic roles to the Son and the Spirit (e.g., the fact that the Son alone became incarnate). Rather, it is deficient because it affirms two distinct economies—one associated with the Son and other with the Spirit. From two sendings (*missiones*)

---

[76]In the original context of Irenaeus's trinitarian theology, the two-hands metaphor served to highlight the direct nature of God's involvement in the world over and against Gnostics who posited a chain of intermediaries between God and the world. For a discussion of the two-hands image in Irenaeus, see Eric Osborn, *Irenaeus of Lyons* (Cambridge: Cambridge University Press, 2001), pp. 89-93.

[77]"A striking way of expressing the divine unity and its embrace is through the description of the word and spirit as the hands of God" (ibid., p. 91).

[78]Moreover, as heuristic device, it is not particularly helpful in expressing a distinct economy of the Spirit.

[79]In fairness to Yong it should be noted that in many places where he employs the two-hands metaphor, he explicitly acknowledges that the Son and Spirit work together (e.g., Yong, *Discerning the Spirit(s)*, p. 116).

we should not infer two separate economies.[80] As Kilian McDonnell explains,

> To insist on the equality of the Spirit and of the Spirit's mission, it is neither necessary nor advisable to postulate a "distinct economy of the Spirit," as does Vladimir Lossky. There is one economy from the Father constituted by the missions of the Son and the Spirit, each of the missions being present and active at the interior of the other.[81]

To speak of two economies in such a way that they represent two foci could lead to a form of economic tritheism.[82] The sendings issue from the Father and lead back to the Father.[83] By positing two economies, Yong implicitly severs the two hands of the Father and undermines the unity of the economy of salvation.

Further evidence that Yong's trinitarian pneumatology severs the two hands of the Father can be seen in the way he relates the work of the Spirit to the Son. Although he emphasizes the empowering role of the Spirit in the incarnation and earthly ministry of Christ,[84] Yong

---

[80]Yong makes the mistake of equating *mission* and *economy*. Notice how he uses these terms interchangeably in the following statement: "Preliminarily then, a pneumatological theology of religions that validates the distinction between the *economy* of the Word and Spirit holds the christological problem in abeyance. For now, it is sufficient to grant that there is a relationship-in-autonomy between the two divine *missions*" (Yong, *Discerning the Spirit(s)*, p. 70 [italics added]).

[81]McDonnell, *Other Hand of God*, p. 198.

[82]Ibid., pp. 199-200. Perhaps it would be more accurate to say that positing two economies could lead to economic bitheism.

[83]Yong not only brackets a christological perspective but he also brackets what might be called a patrological perspective. If the Spirit represents divine *presence* in Yong's proposal, we might rightly say with McDonnell that the Father symbolizes divine *purpose:* "The Father is the origin of the downward (outward) movement and the goal of ascending (returning) movement. Creation and the church are the immediate goal of the outward movement, achieved in the Spirit. The Father is the point of departure and ultimate goal of the two movements. The Spirit is both the point of contact with the world and the church on the downward movement and the turning around point on the journey back from the world and church to the Father. The primary earthly locus of this movement is baptism and the church, in which believers are touched and transformed by the Spirit, and made bearers of the prophetic Spirit who leads to the Son, bringing them to the Father" (ibid., pp. 94-95). By bracketing the Father, Yong effectively obscures the goal of the economy of salvation.

[84]At several points Yong highlights the biblical basis for and benefits of "Spirit-Christology" for a pneumatological theology of religions (see Yong, *Discerning the Spirit(s)*, pp. 118-20).

fails to take seriously biblical teaching regarding the Spirit's unique role in bearing witness to and glorifying the risen Christ (e.g., Jn 15:26-27; 16:7-15; Acts 1:6-9; 4:24-31).[85] In his discussion of Pentecost (Acts 2), Augustine discerns a special significance in the sign through which the bestowal of the Spirit was manifested (i.e., bearing witness to Christ in multiple languages): it offers a proleptic fulfillment of the goal of the Holy Spirit's work—namely, leading people in every nation to believe in Jesus Christ (*De trinitate* 4.29, 175). It is precisely in this sense that the Spirit universalizes the work of Jesus Christ. This universal work of the Spirit constitutes the basis for the evangelistic mission of the church. Commenting on John 16:14, Augustine explains that the Spirit "glorifies" Christ by pouring out love in the hearts of Christ's followers so that they will proclaim him and spread his fame throughout the world (*Tractates* 100.1, 229). Thus, from a salvation-historical perspective, the redemptive work of the Spirit (along with the Father and Son) among adherents of other religions should be understood in terms of *praeparatio evangelica*.[86] No grounds exist for positing a distinct salvation-historical economy of the Spirit leading to some other end. Inasmuch as Yong's proposal attempts to move beyond a *praeparatio evangelica* approach to the Spirit's work in the lives of non-Christians (including adherents of other religions), it severs the two hands of the Father.

A final way Yong's trinitarian pneumatology severs the two hands

---

[85]In the Pauline Epistles we see further evidence that Holy Spirit bears witness to and glorifies the Son. The Spirit glorifies Christ by witnessing to the sonship of the redeemed (Rom 8:1-17), empowering the preaching of the gospel (Rom 15:14-21; 1 Cor 2:2-5), enabling believers to confess Jesus as Lord (1 Cor 12:2-3), removing the veil so that men and women can see the glory of Christ who is the image of God (2 Cor 3:7–4:6), enabling believers to become conformed to the image of the Son (Rom 8:26-30), producing the fruit of Christ in the lives of believers (Gal 5:15-24), and enabling believers to know and experience the love of Christ (Eph 3:14-21).

[86]Adopting this view does not require us to deny the presence of truth and goodness in the lives of adherents of other religions. These can be accounted for in terms of a Christian anthropology informed by the doctrines of creation and Fall. For a helpful discussion of the implications of Christian anthropology for a Christian theology of religions, see Harold A. Netland, *Encountering Religious Pluralism: The Challenge to Christian Faith and Mission* (Downers Grove, Ill.: InterVarsity Press, 2001), pp. 308-48.

of the Father is by bracketing christological criteria for discerning God's work:

> The value of a pneumatological theology of religions can now be seen in clearer light. I have argued that insofar as Word and Spirit are related but yet distinct as the two hands of the Father, we should be able to identify dimensions of the Spirit's presence and activity that are not constrained by that of the Word.[87]

According to Yong, earlier pneumatological approaches failed precisely because they were unable to move beyond christological criteria. For example, because of Karl Rahner's commitment to the *filioque,* Yong suggests that Rahner was ultimately unable to distinguish the economy of the Son and the Spirit. This left Rahner unable to articulate non-christological criteria for discerning God's presence. According to Yong, even Clark Pinnock, who rejects the *filioque,* yields too quickly "to the theological pressure exerted by Christology."[88] If, however, as Augustine rightly insists, the Father, Son and Spirit are working together in a *single* economy that exists to draw men and women into the life of the triune God, then any criteria for discerning the Spirit's redemptive work must include a christological element. Thus, it should not be surprising that Rahner, Pinnock and others who affirm the universal work of the Spirit nevertheless want to preserve some type of christological criterion for discerning the Spirit's presence.

Before I draw this evaluation to a close, we must briefly consider Yong's discussion of his proposal in his more recent book *Beyond the Impasse: Toward a Pneumatological Theology of Religions.*[89] In this work Yong tempers his proposal in two ways. First, he acknowledges, to a greater degree, the inherent economic relatedness of the two hands of the Father.[90]

---

[87]Yong, *Discerning the Spirit(s)*, p. 136.

[88]Ibid., p. 201.

[89]Amos Yong, *Beyond the Impasse: Toward a Pneumatological Theology of Religions* (Grand Rapids: Baker Academic, 2003).

[90]This shift can be seen in his reading of Khodr. In *Discerning the Spirit(s)* Yong reads Khodr almost solely as emphasizing an independent economy of the Holy Spirit, effectively bracket-

Although a pneumatological theology of religions initially seems to be promising in emphasizing a distinct economy of the Spirit, he explains that its distinctiveness must be qualified: "Because of the relationality between Spirit and Son, any Christian theology of religions that begins pneumatologically must ultimately include and confront the christological moment."[91] Second, Yong seems more aware of the problems associated with a search for non-christological criteria for discerning the Spirit's presence. Nevertheless, none of these acknowledgements leads to any explicit revision of his earlier proposal. On the contrary, he continues to affirm a distinct economy of the Spirit and still wants to maintain the legitimacy of non-christological criteria for discerning the Spirit's presence and activity.[92] Thus, in the final analysis, a significant tension remains. Inasmuch as Yong emphasizes a distinct economy of the Spirit in order to legitimize a non-christological approach to other religions, he implicitly severs the two hands of the Father. However, inasmuch as he acknowledges the intrinsic relatedness of the two hands under pressure of classical Christian concerns regarding the doctrine of the Trinity, he undermines his quest for non-christological criteria.

DUPUIS'S TRINITARIAN CHRISTOLOGY: AN AUGUSTINIAN EVALUATION

Although at first glance Dupuis appears to be faithful to the Catholic trinitarian tradition, I will argue that his proposal introduces subordinationism into the Father-Son relationship, undermines the unity of

---

ing Khodr's discussion of how this distinct economy of the Spirit inherently points to Christ (see Yong, *Discerning the Spirit(s)*, pp. 60-64). In *Beyond the Impasse* he acknowledges the christological dimension of Khodr's proposal (which he nevertheless seems to view as problematic): "Khodr's presentation is nevertheless not free from tension. Theologizing as he does from within the framework of Orthodox trinitarianism, he sees the missions of the Son and Spirit as much more connected than not. While the religions may be the working of the economy of the Spirit, yet they are at the same time in a very real sense connected to the economy of the Son" (Yong, *Beyond the Impasse*, p. 89).

[91]Yong, *Beyond the Impasse*, p. 103.

[92]In a far more restrained form, similar claims can also be found in chap. 6 of Amos Yong, *The Spirit Poured Out on All Flesh: Pentecostalism and the Possibility of Global Theology* (Grand Rapids: Baker Academic, 2005).

the economy of salvation, and severs the economic and the immanent Trinity.[93]

Subordinationism in the Father-Son relationship. In order to make space for other saviors and mediators, Dupuis appeals to a trinitarian Christology in which Christ is recognized not as "absolute" Savior but merely as "constitutive" Savior. Only God (i.e., the Father) is the absolute Savior in the sense of being the primary and ultimate source of salvation. Jesus Christ is Savior only in a secondary and derivative sense:

> In the Hebrew Bible, the title "Savior" has to do primarily with God; in the New Testament it is applied to God, and only secondarily to Jesus Christ—without gainsaying that God remains the ultimate cause and original source of salvation. The object of faith, according to New Testament theology, remains primordially God the Father; likely, according to that theology, it is primarily God who saves, and not primarily but conjointly, Jesus Christ: God saves through his Son (cf. Jn 3:16-17).[94]

Prima face it may sound as if Dupuis merely wants to affirm the traditional notion that the Father is the source (*principium*) of divinity. In the latter context it is quite appropriate to speak of the Father as the primary source of salvation; however, when Dupuis speaks of Jesus Christ as constitutive Savior, he appears to have more in mind. That Jesus Christ is constitutive Savior means, among other things, that he is not the *goal* of salvation but merely the constitutive *means* of salvation.[95] What is troubling about the latter claim is the obvious attempt to distinguish the salvific role of incarnate Son (constitutive Savior) from that of the Father (absolute Savior) by limiting the Son to an *in-*

---

[93]In addition to *Toward a Christian Theology of Religious Pluralism*, I will also draw upon a more recent work: *Christianity and the Religions: From Confrontation to Dialogue*, trans. Phillip Berryman (Maryknoll, N.Y.: Orbis, 2002).

[94]Dupuis, *Christianity and the Religions*, p. 167.

[95]"[Christocentrism] never places Jesus Christ in the place of God; it merely affirms that God has placed him at the center of his saving plan for humankind, not as the end but as the way, not as the goal of every human quest for God but as the universal 'mediator' (cf. I Tim 2:5) of God's saving action toward people" (ibid., p. 88).

strumental role in salvation.[96] Within his "inclusive pluralism," the Father is absolute Savior as the one who *wills* salvation, while the Son is constitutive Savior as the one who *effects* salvation.

The latter assumption seems to be implicit in his claim that God's saving *will* is not limited to the Christ event: "While the Christ event is the 'universal sacrament' of God's will to save humankind and of his saving action, it need not be thereby and exclusively the only possible expression of that will. God's saving power is not exclusively bound by the universal sign God has designed for his saving action."[97] To suggest that the salvific role of Jesus Christ is *merely* instrumental sounds suspiciously subordinationist. Earlier in this chapter I noted that one of the fundamental axioms of Augustine's theology is that the Father, Son and Holy Spirit act with *one will* in the economy of salvation. Of particular relevance is Augustine's discussion of the Passion. In contrast to Dupuis, Augustine argues that the decision leading to the Passion involved not only the Father but also the Son.[98] Inasmuch as Jesus Christ is Savior precisely as God-incarnate (*homoousios* with the Father), we must affirm on the basis of inseparable operation that the Son also willed salvation along with the Father. If we instead insist that Jesus Christ is merely a constitutive means of salvation and did not also will it (along with the Father and the Spirit), then it would seem that some form of subordinationism is unavoidable.

Subordinationism can also be seen in Dupuis's claim that Jesus Christ, as the incarnate Son, is not the *goal* of salvation. Contra Dupuis, Augustine insists that the object of contemplation in the eschaton will not only be the Father but all three divine persons: "For we shall contem-

---

[96]Ibid., p. 92. A similar claim can be found in Dupuis, *Christian Theology of Religious Pluralism*, p. 306.

[97]Dupuis, *Christianity and the Religions*, p. 176. Commenting on 1 Tim 2:5, Dupuis notes, "The universal 'saving will' toward all humankind is attributed not to the risen Christ but to God. That universal divine will is the 'absolute' element that constitutes the salvation of the world; it is the focal point for a correct understanding of the affirmation of faith in human salvation" (ibid., p. 41).

[98]Augustine notes that while Rom 8:32 attributes the giving of the Son to the Father, Gal 2:20 attributes the Son's death to his own decision (see Augustine, *Sermon* 52.12, 55).

plate God the Father and Son and Holy Spirit" when the work of the Mediator is complete (*De trinitate* 1.20, 80). Similarly, when Jesus Christ "brings the believers to the contemplation of God and the Father, he will assuredly bring them to the contemplation of himself, having said, *I will show myself to him* (Jn 14:21)" (*De trinitate* 1.18, 79). Thus,

> Whether we hear then "Show us the Son," or whether we hear "Show us the Father," it comes to the same thing, because neither can be shown without the other. They are indeed one, as he tells us, *I and the Father are one* (Jn 10:30). In a word, because of this inseparability, it makes no difference whether sometimes the Father alone or sometimes the Son alone is mentioned as the one who is to fill us with delight at his countenance. (*De trinitate* 1.17, 77)

To deny that the Son is also the goal of salvation necessarily leads to subordinationism in the Father-Son relationship.

As a Catholic theologian, Dupuis is aware of this problem. In order to avoid positing subordinationism in the immanent life of the triune God, he appeals to the distinction between the human and divine natures of Jesus Christ as the basis for his claim that Jesus Christ is merely constitutive Savior:

> The unique closeness that exists between God and Jesus by virtue of the mystery of the incarnation may never be forgotten, but neither can the *unbridgeable distance* that remains between the Father and Jesus in his human existence. . . . While it is true that Jesus the man is uniquely the Son of God, it is equally true that God (the Father) stands beyond Jesus.[99]

In other words, when pressed with the subordinationism inherent in his notion of Jesus Christ as constitutive Savior, Dupuis can respond by insisting that he is only speaking about Jesus Christ in his human nature. Although this move may solve the problem of subordinationism, it does so only by undermining the unity of the two natures in *one* per-

---

[99]Dupuis, *Christianity and the Religions*, p. 92 (italics added).

son. It was not a *nature* that the Father sent to save the world but a *person*. It was not a *nature* that died on the cross but a *person*. That person was the Son of God, who became incarnate by taking on human nature. To speak of Jesus Christ as "constitutive Savior" is to speak of the *person* of the Son as "constitutive Savior," and it is precisely at this point that subordination arises. The only way Dupuis can avoid subordinationism is by sharply distinguishing the two natures of Jesus Christ in a way that undermines their unity.

Initially it might appear that the distinction Dupuis makes between the two natures is virtually identical to the distinction Augustine makes between the Son in the "form of God" and the Son in the "form of servant." A subtle but important difference exists between Augustine and Dupuis. It will be helpful to quote Augustine at length:

> However, if it were not one and the same person who is Son of God in virtue of the form in which he is, and Son of man in virtue of the form of a servant which he took, the apostle Paul would not have said, *If they had known, they would never have crucified the Lord of glory* (1 Cor 2:8). It was in the form of a servant that he was crucified, and yet it was the Lord of glory who was crucified. For that "take-over" was such as to make God a man and a man God. Yet the careful and serious and devout reader will understand what is said of him for the sake of which, and what in virtue of which. For example, we said above that it is in virtue of his being God that he glorifies his followers—in virtue, obviously, of his being the Lord of glory; and yet the Lord of glory was crucified, because it is quite correct to talk even of God being crucified—owing to the weakness of flesh, though, not to the strength of godhead. (*De trinitate* 1.28, 86)

Although he speaks of two "forms," Augustine makes it quite clear that these two forms exist in one person—the Son of God. Although we can say that that the Son was crucified in the form of a servant, we must never forget that it was "the Lord of glory" (i.e., the eternal Son) who was crucified. Thus, when Augustine speaks of the *subject* of the incarnation, he always speaks of the Son. In contrast, when Dupuis speaks of his constitutive Savior, he consistently refers to the *human* person, Jesus Christ. By doing this, Dupuis subtly obscures the fact that the subject of the incarnation is the eternal Son. In the previous citation, Augustine describes the unity of two natures in a way that anticipates later creedal developments at Chalcedon. The unity of the two natures can be seen most clearly in his claim that it is appropriate to speak of "God being crucified."[100] It is precisely the latter kind of speech that is undermined by Dupuis's absolute-constitutive distinction. Although Dupuis acknowledges the hypostatic unity of the natures, in reality he consistently emphasizes their distinction in a way that cannot be reconciled with a full Chalcedonian Christology.

At the end of the day Dupuis faces a serious dilemma. He cannot continue to affirm that Jesus Christ is merely constitutive Savior and uphold an orthodox trinitarian Christology. If, on the one hand, he suggests that Jesus Christ is merely the constitutive *means* of salvation and did not will it along with the Father, he necessarily introduces subordinationism into the Father-Son relationship. If, on the other hand, he attempts to overcome this problem by emphasizing the "unbridgeable distance" between God the Father and Jesus Christ in his human nature, he undermines the union of the two natures.

Undermining the unity of the economy of salvation. We might assume that Dupuis would appeal to the independent action of the Holy Spirit as the basis for the salvific work of the triune God among non-Christian religions. Although he affirms the universal presence and work of the Spirit, Dupuis's proposal is fundamentally *christological* in its orientation. Central to Dupuis's proposal is a distinction between the work of the Logos *ensarkos* (the incarnate Logos) and the work of the Logos *asarkos* (the nonincarnate Logos).[101] On the basis of this distinction

---

[100]Because of the influence of Jürgen Moltmann and others, it has become fashionable to speak of God suffering in his immanent life. This is not what Augustine is affirming here. He is simply saying that the one who suffered on the cross was the eternal Son. The Son, however, suffered in his human nature.

[101]Dupuis, *Christian Theology of Religious Pluralism*, p. 299. It should be noted that official teaching from the Roman Congregation for the Doctrine of the Faith explicitly denies any

Dupuis claims that an enduring work of the Logos *asarkos* continues following the incarnation: "There is a salvific working of the Word as such, distinct from that of the Word operating through his human being in Jesus Christ, risen and glorified, though in 'union' with it."[102] The activity of the Logos *ensarkos* therefore does not exhaust God's saving action following the incarnation.

The distinction Dupuis draws between the economic activity of Logos *ensarkos* and economic activity of the Logos *asarkos* prompts a crucial question from an Augustinian standpoint: Does the work of the Logos *asarkos* constitute a second economy of salvation existing in parallel with the first? Although Dupuis would insist it does not,[103] the way he employs the Logos *ensarkos*–Logos *asarkos* distinction seems to require two parallel economies of salvation.[104] This problem becomes clear when we compare the economic activity of the Logos *asarkos* with that of the Logos *ensarkos*. Through the work of the Logos *ensarkos* (and the Spirit), the Christian Scriptures contain the Word of God.[105] Through the work of the Logos *asarkos* (and the Spirit),[106] the Qur'an and other non-Christian scriptures contain the Word of God.[107] Through the work of the Logos *ensarkos*, there is one mediator between

---

distinction between the salvific action of the Logos *asarkos* and Logos *ensarkos* following the incarnation (see "Declaration *Dominus Iesus:* On the Unicity and Salvific Universality of Jesus Christ and the Church," Congregation for the Doctrine of the Faith, August 6, 2000).

[102]Dupuis, *Christianity and the Religions*, p. 139.

[103]Dupuis repeatedly affirms there is only one economy of salvation. Moreover, he criticizes those who, through an appeal to the work of the Logos *asarkos* or to the universal action of the Holy Spirit, posit a second economy of salvation distinct from the economy of the incarnate Word (Logos *ensarkos*) (see Dupuis, *Christianity and the Religions*, pp. 82-83).

[104]I am not suggesting that any kind of distinction between the Logos *ensarkos* and Logos *asarkos* necessarily implies two economies of salvation. I am simply arguing that the specific way Dupuis employs this distinction requires two economies.

[105]Although I am focusing on the work of the "Logos," Dupuis is careful not to sever the action of the Logos from the action of the Spirit. It will become clear that Dupuis does not sever the unity of the economy of salvation by severing the Word from the Spirit as Yong does, but rather by severing the work of the Logos *ensarkos* from the work of the Logos *asarkos*.

[106]See previous footnote. In the rest of this paragraph, it should be understood that the Spirit is included when I speak of the work of the Logos *ensarkos* or the Logos *asarkos*.

[107]See ibid., pp. 115-37. Dupuis suggests that while Jesus Christ represents the "qualitative fullness" of revelation, he does not represent the "quantitative fullness" of revelation.

humans and God. Through the work of the Logos *asarkos*, other mediators exist between humans and God (although these mediators somehow participate in the mediation of Christ). Through the work of the Logos *ensarkos*, the church mediates salvific grace. Through the work of the Logos *asarkos*, the worship of Hindu images mediates salvific grace.[108] Through the work of the Logos *ensarkos*, men and women are reconciled to God and incorporated into Christ's church. Through the work of the Logos *asarkos*, men and women are not incorporated into the church but become members of "the kingdom of God."[109]

The latter contrast is particularly revealing. Moving beyond Karl Rahner, Dupuis no longer wants to talk about "anonymous Christians."[110] Following Christ's resurrection, how can one be savingly related to the Father without concomitantly being included in Christ's church? The way Dupuis distinguishes kingdom and church seems to require a second parallel economy. The result is two parallel economies that converge only eschatologically. In the present stage in salvation history, they exist more or less in parallel. From an Augustinian perspective no epistemic warrant exists for positing a second economy of salvation in parallel with that of the incarnate Word. Augustine is quite clear that the sending of the Son and the sending of the Spirit have one goal: bringing men and women into fellowship with the triune God *by* leading people in every nation to confess Jesus as Savior and Lord.[111] Inasmuch as Dupuis implicitly posits two economies, he undermines the unity of the economy of salvation.

Moreover, if it is true that Dupuis distinguishes the work of the Logos *asarkos* and Logos *ensarkos* in a way that undermines the unity of

---

[108]Ibid., p. 303.

[109]See Dupuis, *Christianity and the Religions*, pp. 195-217.

[110]Karl Rahner coined the term *anonymous Christian* to describe individuals who experienced Christian salvation without knowing it.

[111]According to Augustine, the Spirit glorifies (and universalizes) the Son by pouring out love in hearts of men and women so that, filled with the confidence of love, they may spread Christ's fame in every nation. The evangelistic mission of the church therefore represents an extension of the temporal missions of the Son and the Spirit.

the economy of salvation, this suggests a further deficiency in his Christology (inasmuch as the distinction between the work of the Logos *asarkos* and Logos *ensarkos* is grounded in the distinction of the divine and human natures). In rejecting a distinction between the salvific working of the Logos *asarkos* and Logos *ensarkos* following the incarnation, the Congregation for the Doctrine of Faith (in *Dominus Iesus*) rightly links this move to the union of Christ's two natures:

> It is likewise contrary to the Catholic faith to introduce a separation between the salvific action of the Word as such and that of the Word made man. With the incarnation, all the salvific actions of the Word of God are always done in unity with the human nature that he has assumed for the salvation of all people. The one subject which operates in the two natures, human and divine, is the single person of the Word. Therefore, the theory which would attribute, after the incarnation as well, a salvific activity to the Logos as such in his divinity, exercised "in addition to" or "beyond" the humanity of Christ, is not compatible with the Catholic faith.

When we combine Dupuis's emphasis on the "unbridgeable gap" between God and Jesus Christ in his human nature as the basis for his constitutive Christology along with his insistence on the distinction between the divine and human natures as the basis for a distinct and continuing action of the Logos *asarkos,* it appears that his "trinitarian Christology" may implicitly undermine the unity of the divine and human natures of Jesus Christ in a Nestorian fashion.[112]

Severing the unity of the economic and immanent Trinity. One final trinitarian problem should be noted. On the one hand, Dupuis claims that "the mystery of the Triune God—Father, Son, Spirit—corresponds objectively to the inner reality of God, even though only analogically."[113] On the other hand, he insists that *authentic* economic manifestations of the triune God can be found in other religious com-

---

[112]Nestorius talked about the two natures of Christ in a way that undermined their unity in one person.

[113]Dupuis, *Toward a Christian Theology of Religious Pluralism*, p. 259.

munities.[114] Obviously a number of these economic manifestations of the triune God are conflicting, and in some cases, even contradictory. Buddhists, for example, envision the triune God as "emptiness" while Muslims conceive of the triune God as a personal absolute. This leads to a problem. Inasmuch as these conflicting economic manifestations of the triune God are to be viewed as *authentic,* we seem to encounter a situation in which a kind of "God-above-God" must be posited with the result that the unity of the economic Trinity with the immanent Trinity is implicitly undermined.[115] One reason Christian theologians have insisted that the economic Trinity is the immanent Trinity (the first half of Rahner's axiom) is precisely to avoid any possibility of a God-above-God. Dupuis's answer to this dilemma is found in his analysis of religious experience. Although adherents of other religions have authentic experiences of the triune God,[116] they do not possess adequate conceptualizations.[117] The economic faces they posit are, objectively speaking, false. Although this may solve the problem of conflicting economic manifestations, it seems to undercut their *authenticity.* To the extent Dupuis emphasizes that these economic faces are *false* (ostensibly to protect his trinitarian grammar), he undercuts their authenticity. To the extent Dupuis emphasizes the *authenticity* of these alternative economic manifestations, he implicitly severs the unity of the economic and the immanent Trinity. His proposal rests on a deficient trinitarianism. This reality casts a dark shadow over his claim that the triune God constitutes a key to a Christian theology of religious pluralism.

---

[114]Ibid., p. 279.

[115]Or, at the very least, we would encounter a situation in which the epistemic priority of the Christian economic manifestation of the triune God is effectively marginalized.

[116]"Wherever there is genuine religious experience, it is surely the God revealed in Jesus Christ who enters into the lives of men and women" (Dupuis, *Christianity and the Religions*, p. 122).

[117]Dupuis makes a critical distinction between religious experience and one's formulation or interpretation of religious experience. Any authentic religious experience represents an experience of "the God revealed in Jesus Christ" (ibid., p. 122). Christians interpret their religious experiences as experiences of the Father of Jesus Christ. Non-Christians experience the Father of Jesus Christ but interpret this God using other categories.

IMPLICATIONS FOR THE CHRISTIAN
THEOLOGY OF RELIGIONS

One pressing question raised by current appeal to divine relations in the Christian theology of religions concerns the relationship of the Holy Spirit to the Son. Assumptions about the Son-Spirit relationship constitute the trinitarian key to Yong's proposal. He rejects all subordination of the Spirit to the Son at the ontological level in order to clear space on the economic level for an economy of the Spirit distinct (i.e., separate) from that the Son. On the basis of this distinction, Yong justifies the use of non-christological criteria for discerning the Spirit's presence in order to affirm the work of the Spirit among adherents of other religions. Yong is not alone in appealing to a separate economy of the Spirit as the basis for a Christian theology of religions. We encounter this claim with increasing frequency.[118] For example, in a monograph exploring the implications of Paul Tillich's trinitarian theology for a Christian theology of religions, Pan-Chiu Lai argues that an exclusivist theology of religions is rooted in a wrongful subordination of the Spirit to the Son (as expressed in the *filioque*) and that one can move beyond exclusivism, (as well as Christocentrism and theocentrism) by recognizing that the Spirit operates in an economy distinct from that of the Son.[119] According to Lai, a trinitarian theology of religions is able "to integrate the centrality of Christ and the freedom of the Holy Spirit within the framework of the doctrine of the Trinity." By stressing "the economy and sovereignty of the Holy Spirit," a trinitarian theology of

---

[118]See Fredrick E. Crowe, "Son of God, Holy Spirit and World Religions," in *Appropriating the Lonergan Idea*, ed. Michael Vertin (Washington, D.C.: Catholic University of America Press, 1989), pp. 324-43; Paul F. Knitter, "A New Pentecost? A Pneumatological Theology of Religions," *Current Dialogue* 19 (1991): 32-41; Stanley J. Samartha, "The Holy Spirit and People of Other Faiths," *Ecumenical Review* 42 (1990): 250-63; Michael E. Lodahl, *Shekhinah/Spirit: Divine Presence in Jewish and Christian Religion* (New York: Paulist Press, 1992); Peter C. Hodgson, "The Spirit and Religious Pluralism," in *The Myth of Religious Superiority: Multifaith Explorations of Religious Pluralism*, ed. Paul F. Knitter (Maryknoll, N.Y.: Orbis, 2005), pp. 135-50; and Roger Haight, "Trinity and Religious Pluralism," *Journal of Ecumenical Studies* 44 (2009): 525-40.

[119]See Pan-Chiu Lai, *Towards a Trinitarian Theology of Religions: A Study in Paul Thought*, Studies in Philosophical Theology, 8 (Kampen, Netherlands: Kok Pharos, 1994), pp. 37-44.

religions is able to affirm both the universality of salvation and the value of openness toward other religions.[120]

By way of contrast, an Augustinian understanding of divine relations holds three implications for the Son-Spirit relationship in the Christian theology of religions. First, because the Son-Spirit relationship can only be understood within a trinitarian context, greater attention must be paid to the trinitarian framework in which claims about the role of the Holy Spirit are being articulated. One of the striking features about *De trinitate* is the rigorous trinitarian framework that Augustine develops for understanding the relations of the divine persons. This framework is precisely what is lacking in many trinitarian proposals in the Christian theology of religions.

Second, a proper account of the Son-Spirit relationship combines hypostatic distinction at an intratrinitarian level (*ad intra*) with inseparable operation at the economic level (*ad extra*). Because the divine persons act inseparably, we must think about the operation or agency of the Son and Spirit in the context of inseparable operation. That the divine persons act inseparably *ad extra* in a way that reflects their relative properties *ad intra* is an assumption Augustine shares not only with the entire Latin pro-Nicene tradition but also the Greek-speaking theologians of the East (e.g. the Cappadocians).[121] For example, in his "Answer to Ablabius," Gregory of Nyssa offers the following explanation of the inseparable action of the Father, Son and Holy Spirit:

> We do not learn that the Father does something on his own, in which the Son does not co-operate. Or again, that the Son acts on his own

---

[120]Ibid., p. 43.

[121]"Although this doctrine is fundamental to late fourth-century, orthodox, Latin theology, it is important that we do not think of 'inseparable operation' as a peculiarly Latin phenomena. The inseparable operation of the three irreducible persons is a fundamental axiom of those theologies which provide the context for the Council of Constantinople in AD 381 and for the reinterpretation of Nicaea, which came to be the foundation of orthodox or catholic theology at the end of the fourth century. It is a principle found in all the major orthodox Greek theologians of the later fourth and fifth centuries, and enters later Orthodox tradition through such figures as John of Damascus in the eighth century" (Ayres, "The Fundamental Grammar of Augustine's Trinitarian Theology," p. 56).

without the Spirit. Rather does every operation which extends from God to creation and is designated according to our differing conceptions of it have its origin in the Father, proceed through the Son, and reach its completion by the Holy Spirit. It is for this reason that the word for the operation is not divided among the persons involved. For the action of each in any matter is not separate and individualized. But whatever occurs, whether in reference to God's providence for us or the government and constitution of the universe, occurs through the three Persons, and it not three separate things.[122]

Thus, if one chooses to dismiss Augustine's explanation, one must also dismiss the entire pro-Nicene tradition. Moreover, medieval theologians like Thomas Aquinas deploy Augustine's grammar of inseparable action, albeit in a more sophisticated form.[123] Furthermore, the inseparable action of the divine persons is affirmed by many post-Reformation theologians.[124] For example, commenting on the work of the Trinity in redemption, John Owen explains, "The agent in, and chief author of, this great work of our redemption is the whole blessed Trinity; for all the works which outwardly are of the Deity are undivided and belong equally to each person, their distinct manner of subsistence and order being observed."[125] In light of inseparable action, no epistemic warrant exists for inferring a distinct economy of the Spirit on the basis of the hypostatic distinction that exists between the Son and the Spirit in the immanent Trinity.

---

[122]Gregory of Nyssa, "An Answer to Ablabius: That We Should Not Think of Saying There Are Three Gods," in *Christology of the Later Fathers*, Library of Christian Classics, ed. Edward R. Hardy (Louisville: Westminster John Knox, 1954), pp. 261-62.

[123]For an incisive analysis of trinitarian agency in Thomas Aquinas, see Giles Emery, *Trinity, Church and the Human Person: Thomistic Essays* (Naples: Sapientia Press, 2007), pp. 115-53.

[124]See Heinrich Schmid, *The Doctrinal Theology of the Evangelical Lutheran Church*, trans. Charles A. Hay and Henry E. Jacobs, 3rd ed. (1899; reprint, Minneapolis: Augsburg, 1961), pp. 129-59; Richard A. Muller, *Post-Reformation Reformed Dogmatics: The Rise and Development of Reformed Orthodoxy, ca. 1520 to ca. 1725*, vol. 4, *The Triunity of God* (Grand Rapids: Baker Academic, 2003), pp. 255-74; and Heinrich Heppe, *Reformed Dogmatics: Set Out and Illustrated from the Sources*, trans. G. T. Thomson (Grand Rapids: Baker, 1950), pp. 105-32.

[125]John Owen, *The Death of Death in the Death of Christ* (Grand Rapids: Christian Classics Ethereal Library, 1967), p. 26.

Finally, the Son and the Spirit work together in a single economy of salvation, which has as its goal drawing men and women into the life of the triune God. Thus, our exploration of Augustine's trinitarian theology serves to remind us that the missionary nature of the church is rooted not in an outdated form of cultural imperialism but in the very life of triune God.[126] The sending of the church is rooted in the dual sendings of the Son and the Spirit (Gal 4:4-6). Just as the Father sent the Son into the world, so the Son sends his followers into the world (Jn 20:21). The Spirit, who is sent into the world by the Father and the Son, bears witness to the Son by preparing the way for and empowering the witness of Christ's disciples (Jn 15:26-27; Acts 1:8). As Lesslie Newbigin explains,

> The Spirit is the Spirit of Christ. The decisive mark of his presence is the confession that Jesus Christ is Lord (1 Cor. 12:1-3; 1 Jn. 4:1-3). His coming in power is the fruit of hearing and believing the Gospel of Jesus Christ crucified and risen. He takes the things of Christ and shows them to us. He leads men to Christ, in whom we are baptized into one body, the body of Christ. He is no will-o'-the-wisp, leading men to all sorts of individual vagaries, but the one who binds men to Jesus Christ in the fellowship of his one body. It is true that he is free and sovereign; he goes ahead of the Church, as every missionary knows—but it is (if one may put it so) the Church that he goes ahead of.[127]

It is ironic that at the very time advocates of Spirit Christology argue that one should not think about Christ apart from the Spirit, some of these very same theologians seem to suggest it is appropriate to think about the Spirit apart from Christ in a way that ultimately severs the two hands of the Father. Surely Yves Congar is much closer to the mark when he insists, "If I were to draw but one conclusion from the whole

---

[126]For more on this theme, see Stephen R. Holmes, "Trinitarian Missiology: Towards a Theology of God as Missionary," *International Journal of Systematic Theology* 8 (2006): 72-90.

[127]Lesslie Newbigin, *Trinitarian Doctrine for Today's Mission* (Carlisle, U.K.: Paternoster, 1998), pp. 79-80.

of my work on the Holy Spirit, I would express it in these words: no Christology without pneumatology and no pneumatology without Christology."[128] Congar, therefore, rightly recognizes that it is "not possible to develop a pneumatology separately from the Word."[129]

---

[128]Yves M. J. Congar, *Word and Spirit*, trans. David Smith (San Francisco: Harper & Row, 1983), p. 1. Congar repeatedly emphasizes the joint work of the Word and Spirit work in the economy of salvation: "The glorified Lord and the Spirit do the same work. The unity of the glorified Christ and the Spirit is functional, that is to say, it is an operative unity. The work to be done in believers is common to both of them and the two 'hands' proceeding from the Father do conjointly whatever the Father, who is Love, wishes to do" (ibid., p. 25).

[129]Ibid., p. 131.

5

VESTIGES OF THE TRINITY IN
THE THEOLOGY OF RELIGIONS

◆

Several Christian theologians have suggested that reflections of the
Trinity can be discerned in non-Christian religious experience and that
this reality bears witness to the validity of non-Christian religions.
Chapter five will offer a critical assessment of this claim. Notice how
Jacques Dupuis explicitly appeals to traces (*vestigia*) of the Trinity in his
Christian theology of religious pluralism:

> As the tradition has persistently sought and found "traces" of the Trinity
> (*vestigia Trinitatis*) in creation and, more especially, in the spiritual ac-
> tivity of the human being, so must we search for and discover similar
> traces, outside the Biblical tradition, in the religious life of individual
> persons and the religious traditions to which they belong. They too in
> some way echo in history the Father's eternal uttering of the Word and
> issuing of the Spirit.[1]

Reasoning from an assumption that all human religious experience
possesses a "trinitarian structure,"[2] Dupuis claims that extrabiblical

---

[1]Jacques Dupuis, *Toward a Christian Theology of Religious Pluralism* (Maryknoll, N.Y.: Orbis,
  1997), pp. 227-28.
[2]Ibid., pp. 276-77.

traditions "bear an imprint of the economic Trinity."[3] Similarly, William Cenkner argues that triadic structures can be discerned in Taoism and Buddhism, which bear witness, albeit it dimly, to the Trinity.[4] Along similar lines, Bede Griffiths suggests that a triadic pattern can be discerned in the major religious traditions: (1) the "supreme Principle" beyond any name or form, (2) "the manifestation of the hidden reality," and (3) the "Spirit."[5] Finally, Mark Heim's argument for the validity of other religions explicitly appeals to the trinitarian structure of reality: "There is an irreducible variety in what is ultimately true or of greatest significance. Christians find validity in other religions because of the conviction that the Trinity represents a universal truth about the way the world and God actually are."[6]

One of the most substantive appeals to the trinitarian structure of non-Christian religious experience can be found in Raimundo Panikkar's *The Trinity and the Religious Experience of Man*.[7] Panikkar suggests that recognition of the trinitarian structure of religious experience could lead to greater human unity: "The deepening into the trinitarian structure of religious experience and of human beliefs may here again offer a possibility of fecundation, agreement and collaboration not only among religions themselves, but also with modern man at large, so often torn apart by religious subtleties which he does not understand."[8]

---

[3]Ibid., p. 227. See also Jacques Dupuis, *Christianity and the Religions: From Confrontation to Dialogue*, trans. Phillip Berryman (Maryknoll, N.Y.: Orbis, 2002), p. 2.

[4]See William Cenkner, "Interreligious Exploration of Triadic Reality: The Panikkar Project," *Dialogue & Alliance* 4 (1990): 80-81.

[5]Bede Griffiths, *Universal Wisdom: A Journey Through the Sacred Wisdom of the World* (San Francisco: HarperCollins, 1994), pp. 41-42.

[6]S. Mark Heim, *The Depth of the Riches: A Trinitarian Theology of Religious Ends*, Sacra Doctrina (Grand Rapids: Eerdmans, 2001), p. 127.

[7]Raimundo Panikkar, *The Trinity and the Religious Experience of Man: Person-Icon-Mystery* (Maryknoll, N.Y.: Orbis, 1973). Other important works by Panikkar include *The Unknown Christ of Hinduism*, rev. ed. (London: Darton, Longman & Todd, 1984); *The Intra-Religious Dialogue* (New York: Paulist, 1978); *Blessed Simplicity: The Monk as Universal Archetype* (New York: Seabury, 1982); *The Silence of God: The Answer of the Buddha* (Maryknoll, N.Y.: Orbis, 1989); and *The Cosmotheandric Experience: Emerging Religious Consciousness* (Maryknoll, N.Y.: Orbis, 1993).

[8]Panikkar, *Trinity and the Religious Experience of Man*, p. xiv.

The purpose of this chapter is to offer an Augustinian critique of the trinitarian theology in Panikkar's proposal. After outlining his proposal, we will consider how Ewert Cousins, an interpreter of Panikkar, attempts to relate Panikkar's proposal to the vestige tradition. Next, I will explore Augustine's search for reflections of the Trinity in the functioning of the human soul in books 8-15 of *De trinitate*. Finally, in conversation with Augustine, I will offer a critical assessment of Panikkar's theology of religious experience. Readers will want to pay careful attention to the relationship between Panikkar's three types of religious experience and the doctrine of the Trinity. Although Panikkar appeals to the logic of the vestige tradition, there are significant problems in the way he employs this tradition.

RAIMUNDO PANIKKAR'S THEANDRIC SPIRITUALITY

Three forms of spirituality. In the first section of *The Trinity and the Religious Experience of Man,* Panikkar identifies three irreducible forms of spirituality,[9] which he identifies as "iconolatry," "personalism" and "mysticism."[10] These three spiritualities parallel the Hindu ways of action (*karmamārga*), devotion (*bhaktimārga*), and knowledge (*jnana-marga*).[11] Iconolatry involves the "the projection of God under some *form,* his objectivation, his personification *in* an *object* which may be mental or material, visible or invisible, but always reducible to our human 'representation.'"[12] We might think of iconolatry as a legitimate form of idolatry. False idolatry denotes worship that fails to rise to God because it terminates in a created object.[13] By way of contrast, iconola-

---

[9]Underlying Panikkar's proposal is a distinction between "spirituality" and "religion." *Spirituality* denotes the "mass of rites, structures, etc., that are indispensable to all religions," whereas *religion* represents "an attitude of mind" independent of any particular tradition (Panikkar, *The Trinity and the Religious Experience of Man,* p. 9). Several spiritualities may be found in one religious tradition.

[10]Ibid., p. 10. Elsewhere he describes them as "apophatism, personalism and divine immanence" (ibid., p. 55).

[11]Ibid., p. 10.

[12]Ibid., p. 15.

[13]According to Panikkar, false idolatry involves the "transference to a creature of the adoration due to God alone, i.e. an adoration which stops short at the object without going beyond it in

try involves worship that ascends *from* an object on which divine glory rests *to God*. As such, it represents a legitimate form of human religious consciousness that can be found not only in the Judeo-Christian tradition (with its emphasis on the human person as the image of God and the world as vestige of the divine) but also in the way of sacred action in Hinduism:

> The fundamental attitude, however, of an iconolatric spirituality is the cultic *act* of adoration of an "image" of God, believed to represent each time the true God. It is this action which allows us to call this spirituality *karmamārga* or the way of action in order to reach "salvation," i.e., the end and fulfillment of man in whatever way it is interpreted.[14]

While *iconolatry* for Panikkar is rooted in "cosmo-anthropomorphism," *personalism* denotes a form of religious consciousness founded "on the concept of *person*." "We call God a personal being *because* we ourselves are persons. We consider God a Being because we ourselves are beings." In a personalist context, love is no longer "unconscious ecstasy but a mutual giving."[15] Similarly, worship does not involve negation of the self but represents a voluntary response to the divine person. Panikkar points out that personalism should not be viewed as the essence of religion. It simply represents one form of spirituality among several possible forms. In itself, it is unable to exhaust the richness of the Absolute. Personalism is found not only in Christian faith but also in Hindu way of devotion and love (*bhaktimārga*).

A third and final form of spirituality is *advaita* or "mysticism." Panikkar explains that a personalist concept of the Absolute faces a number of conceptual problems. For example, if God is a person, then God appears to be indifferent to evil and suffering. Furthermore, in what seems like sheer cruelty, God requires the blood of his Son. Moreover, God seems powerless to create a better world. Although various Christian

---

an ongoing movement toward the Creator, the Transcendent, is without doubt the gravest of sins" (ibid., p. 16).

[14]Ibid., p. 18.

[15]Ibid., pp. 21-22.

theologies have sought to address these problems, these limitations suggest that "an exclusively personal" conception of the Absolute cannot do adequate justice to it.[16] Hinduism rightly teaches that the mystery of God cannot be "exhausted in his unveiling as *Person*."[17] At the center of this third form of spirituality is an experience of divine immanence: "An immanent God cannot be a God-person, 'someone' with whom I could have 'personal' relationship, a God-other. I cannot *speak* to an immanent God."[18] Hindus refer to this immanent ground as *Brahman*. The relationship that one forms with *Brahman* "consists in the rupture and negation of every alleged relation."[19] Thus, "The sole way of discovering *brahman* is by revelation in the sense of an unveiling of all the veils of *existence*, including that of the *ego*, i.e. of the one who undertakes the ascent, or rather the descent, in search of *brahman*."[20] It is the latter experience to which the Upanishads bear witness. Whereas praise, prayer and dialogue are central to personalism, mysticism involves silence, abandonment and nonattachment.[21] The Hindu way of "knowledge" (*jnanamarga*) exemplifies this spirituality.

   Panikkar's doctrine of the Trinity. After identifying these three spiritualities, Panikkar presents his understanding of the Trinity. He notes that his primary objective is not to "expound the doctrine of the Trinity" but rather "to show how in the light of the Trinity the three forms of spirituality described above can be reconciled."[22] According to Panikkar, only a "trinitarian understanding of Reality" allows for "a synthesis between these three apparently irreducible concepts of the Absolute."[23] On the one hand, Panikkar insists that "a very real continuity [exists] between the theory of the Trinity" he presents and Chris-

---

[16]Ibid., p. 28.
[17]Ibid., p. 29.
[18]Ibid., p. 31.
[19]Ibid., p. 34.
[20]Ibid., p. 35.
[21]Ibid., p. 39.
[22]Ibid., p. 41.
[23]Ibid.

tian teaching.[24] In this context, he avers that his proposal is "authentically orthodox."[25] On the other hand, he acknowledges that his formulation of the Trinity moves beyond the traditional Christian explanation.[26] Moreover, he also asserts that a trinitarian understanding of the Absolute is not merely a Christian insight: "It is simply an unwarranted overstatement to affirm that the trinitarian conception of the Ultimate, and with it of the whole reality, is an exclusive Christian insight or revelation."[27] Adherents of other religions experience the same trinitarian mystery but simply describe it in different terms.

Father. All religious traditions recognize that the Absolute is ineffable and has no name. One may call the Absolute *Brahman* or *Tao*, but these merely represent human designations. According to Christian teaching, the Absolute has a distinctive title: "the Father of our Lord Jesus Christ."[28] Although Christians refer to the Absolute as "the Father of Jesus Christ," neither "Father" nor "God" represent proper names. These are merely human designations.

"The Father is the Absolute, the only God, *ó theós*."[29] This is why early Christian formulas "do not speak of the Father, the Son and the Spirit, but of God, Christ and the Spirit. Neither the Son nor the Spirit is *God*, but, precisely, the Son of God and the Spirit of God, 'equal' to the One God (*ó theós*) as God (*theós*)."[30] One should not think of the divinity as a fourth thing alongside the Father, Son and Holy Spirit. Rather, the Father must be recognized as the "substratum" of the divinity.[31]

---

[24]Ibid., p. 43.

[25]"I emphasize once and for all that I *believe* this interpretation to be authentically *orthodox*— i.e., which gives to God a truly right (*orthos*) honour and glory (*doxa*)—and to be thus fully ecclesial" (ibid., p. 6).

[26]Panikkar justifies this move on the ground that dogmatic formulations are simply unable "to encompass the totality of the divine reality which overflows their limits on all sides to an infinite degree" (ibid., p. 41).

[27]Ibid., p. viii.

[28]Ibid., p. 44.

[29]Ibid.

[30]Ibid., p. 45.

[31]Panikkar explains that his approach to the Trinity builds on the "more dynamic thrust of the

According to Panikkar, the generation of the Son by the Father is complete inasmuch as the Father gives himself away fully: "Everything that the Father *is* he transmits to the Son," with the result that "the Son is the *is* of the Father."[32] Thus, we cannot speak of the Father *qua* Father because the Father "is not."[33] If we ask what the Father is, the answer must be "the Son." As the Absolute, "the Father, *is not*."[34] Hence, the Father "has no *ex-sistence*, not even that of Being. In the generation of the Son he has, so to speak, given everything. In the Father, an apophatism (the *kenosis* or emptying) of Being is real and total."[35] The Buddhist experience of emptiness is grounded therefore in the Father. In Buddhist thought, "One is led onwards toward the 'absolute goal' and at the end one finds nothing, because there is nothing, not even Being."[36] Formally speaking, "the spirituality of the Father is not even a spirituality. It is like the invisible bedrock, the gentle inspirer, the unnoticed force which sustains, draws and pushes us. God is truly transcendent, infinite."[37] This ultimate ground can be grasped only through an image or icon—the Son. This is the meaning of the biblical statement that one comes to the Father only through the Son. Thus, the only proper response to the Father is silence.[38] Iconolatry is the religion of the Father.

Son. Whereas we might describe the Father as "God-from" or "Source of-God," the Son is best designated as "of-God." It is the Son who *is*. It is the Son who *acts*. It is the Son who *creates*. Everything exists *in the Son*. According to Panikkar, *person* is not a term that can be applied univocally to Father, Son and Holy Spirit: "Thus, strictly speaking, it is not true that God is *three* persons. 'Person' here is an equivocal term

---

greek patristic tradition" as well as the "latin bonaventurian scholastic" tradition (ibid., p. 45).

[32]Ibid., p. 46.

[33]Ibid.

[34]Ibid.

[35]Ibid.

[36]Ibid., p. 47. To speak about the Father is impossible. Every statement about the Father can only refer to the Son.

[37]Ibid., p. 50.

[38]Ibid., p. 47.

which has a different meaning in each case."[39] To speak of person in a univocal sense would be to imply a fourth element that the Father, Son and Spirit share in common; however, God is *not* a quaternity consisting of Father, Son, Holy Spirit plus a "God-divine nature."[40] The Father *is* his Son through his Spirit. Thus, "Only the Son is Person, if we use the word in its eminent sense and analogically to human persons: neither the Father nor the Spirit is a Person."[41] We can speak of the Father and Spirit as persons in a weaker sense if we bear in mind that we are speaking about "real relative oppositions at the heart of the divine mystery."[42] As a result, "it is only with the Son than man can have a personal relationship. The God of theism, thus, is the Son."[43]

The Son is the "Mystery" to which the Scriptures point and which was revealed in Christ. "Christ," in Panikkar's terminology, refers to the Principle or Being that is given various names in other traditions.[44] "It is Christ, then, known or unknown—who makes religion possible."[45] This Christ is the "mediator," that is to say, the link between the finite and the infinite. In speaking of Christ as mediator, Panikkar explains that he is not "presupposing its identification with Jesus of Nazareth."[46] Christians have never affirmed such an unqualified identification. They have simply claimed that Jesus of Nazareth has a special relationship to what John calls the "Logos."[47] In this context, Jesus of Nazareth

---

[39]Ibid., pp. 51-52.

[40]Ibid., p. 52.

[41]Ibid.

[42]We must be careful, however, not to attempt to speak about the persons *in se*. "A person is never in himself, but by the very fact that he is a person is always a constitutive relation—a *pros ti*" (ibid., p. 52).

[43]Ibid.

[44]"The nomenclature that I personally would like to suggest in this connection is as follows: I would propose using the Lord for that Principle, Being, Logos or Christ that other religious traditions call by a variety of names and to which they attach a wide variety of ideas. . . . Each time that I speak of Christ I am referring (unless it is explicitly stated otherwise) to the Lord of whom christians lay no monopoly" (ibid., p. 53).

[45]Ibid.

[46]Ibid.

[47]Ibid.

represents one manifestation of a broader Christ principle.[48] Panikkar explains that he continues to use the term *Christ* simply because it best embodies the key characteristics of the mediator between divine and human.[49] Personalism is the spirituality of the Son.

Holy Spirit. Whereas the revelation of the Father is an unveiling of divine *transcendence,* the revelation of the Spirit is an unveiling of divine *immanence:* "Essentially it signifies the ultimate inner-ness of every being, the final foundation, the *Ground* of being as well as of beings."[50] Formally speaking, the idea of revelation can be applied only to the Son. Neither divine transcendence nor divine immanence can be revealed. In the case of divine transcendence, what is revealed is "the revelation *of it,* i.e., God, the Son, the Logos, the Icon."[51] Similarly, divine immanence is also "incapable of revealing itself, for that would be a pure contradiction of terms."[52]

Our experience of the trinitarian mystery teaches us "that in reality God is immanent to himself."[53] At the deepest level of divinity, there is the Spirit. Speaking metaphorically, we might say

> that in spite of every *effort* of the Father to "empty himself" in the generation of the Son, to pass entirely into his Son, to give him everything that he *has,* everything that he *is,* even then there remains in this first procession, like an irreducible factor, the Spirit, the non-exhaustion of the source in the generation of the Logos.[54]

The Spirit is immanent both to the Father and the Son, passing, so to

---

[48]The church, therefore, is not the religion for all humanity but simply "the place where Christ is fully revealed" (ibid., p. 55).

[49]"It is not my task here to discuss the other names and titles that have been accorded to this manifestation of the Mystery in other religious traditions. The reason I persist in calling it Christ is that it seems to me that phenomenologically Christ presents the fundamental characteristics of the mediator between divine and cosmic, eternal and temporal, etc., which other religions call *Isvara, Tathāgata* or even Jahweh, Allah and so on—at least when they are not seeking to distinguish between a *saguna* and *nirguna* brahman" (ibid., p. 54).

[50]Ibid., pp. 58-59.

[51]Ibid.

[52]Ibid., p. 59.

[53]Ibid., p. 59.

[54]Ibid., p. 60.

speak, from Father to Son and from Son to Father. Because true unity is trinitarian, there is no Self in the divine life. The Son is the Self of the Father. The Father's "in himself" is the Spirit. The Son is the Thou of the Father. In this context, we cannot speak of the Spirit *in se:* "There is only the Spirit *of* God, of the Father and Son."[55] The Spirit is neither an I nor Thou, but a we between Father and Son. *Advaita* can help us in expressing this inner-trinitarian dynamic: the Father and Son are neither two nor one. The Spirit distinguishes and unites them.

It is not possible to have a personal relationship with the Spirit. "One can only have a non-relational union with him."[56] For this reason, we should not pray to the Spirit but rather "in" the Spirit. The spirituality of the Spirit, therefore, does not consist in discovering and dialoging with someone but in attaining a consciousness that one is not outside reality but already included in it.[57] This form of spirituality is marked by complete passivity: "there is no longer any *me* to save, for one has grasped that there is an I who calls one by a new and completely hidden name."[58] Mysticism is the spirituality of the Spirit.

Panikkar offers the following summary of his understanding of the Trinity. The Father is Source, the Son is Being (Thou) and the Spirit is the "Return of Being" (we).[59] A parallel can be seen in the trinitarian structure of Ephesians 4:6. The Father is "over all" (i.e., Source of Being), the Son is "through all" (Being as that which all beings participate in), and the Spirit is "in all" (divine immanence, the end or return of Being).[60]

Theandric spirituality. On the one hand, Panikkar claims that each of the spiritualities previously outlined represent legitimate responses to the triune God. On the other hand, he argues that no single spiritu-

---

[55]Ibid., p. 61.
[56]Ibid., p. 63.
[57]Ibid., p. 64.
[58]Ibid.
[59]Ibid., p. 68. Elsewhere Panikkar offers a similar analogy in terms of water. The Father is the source of the river. The Son is the river that flows from the source. The Spirit is the ocean into which the river flows (ibid., p. 63).
[60]Ibid., p. 68.

ality is sufficient in and of itself. As an *exclusive* spiritual attitude each possesses inherent limitations. Iconolatry (the spirituality of the Father), if pursued exclusively, can degenerate into nihilism. Nihilists are "present-day witnesses to a spirituality which was directed to the Father but to a Father 'severed' from the living Trinity."[61] Personalism (the spirituality of the Son), if pursued exclusively, can degenerate into "humanism." Finally, *advaita* (the spirituality of the Spirit), if pursued exclusively, can degenerate into "pantheism."[62] Only a trinitarian understanding of religious experience can provide "the synthesis and mutual fecundation of the different spiritual attitudes which comprise religions, without forcing or doing violence to the fundamental intuitions of the different spiritual paths."[63]

Rather than calling the resulting triad of spiritualities "trinitarian," Panikkar prefers to use the term *theandric.*[64] The latter term was originally used to describe the union of the divine and human natures of Christ. This term is helpful in expressing two constitutive elements of spirituality: the human element and the "transhuman factor which gives it inner life and its transcendent result."[65] The central insight of theandrism involves the recognition that humans possess "an infinite capacity which links up to the asymptotic limit called God."[66] Theandrism has been intuitively grasped by thinkers through the ages. Central to Panikkar's theandric spirituality is an assumption that reality itself is theandric: "There are not two realities: God *and* man (or the world); but neither is there one: God *or* man (or the world), as outright atheists are dialectically driven to maintain. Reality is itself theandric."[67]

Panikkar and the vestige tradition. In a book titled *Christ of the 21st*

---

[61]Ibid., p. 78.
[62]Ibid., p. 82.
[63]Ibid., p. 43.
[64]Ibid., p. 71.
[65]Ibid., p. 72.
[66]Ibid., p. 74.
[67]Ibid., p. 75.

Century, Ewert Cousins, a Catholic theologian, commends Panikkar's proposal and attempts to build upon it by explicitly linking it to the vestige tradition.[68] Reasoning from the assumption that creation reflects its Creator, Christian theologians have, throughout the history of the church, searched for traces of the triune God (*vestigia Trinitatis*) within structures of creation. A vibrant expression of the vestige tradition can be found in Bonaventure's *Itinerarium Mentis in Deum*, written in the middle of the thirteenth century. Bonaventure outlines a six-step process through which the soul ascends to union with God by contemplating the Trinity through the vestiges in creation, through the divine image and through God's essential and personal attributes. Although they may search for reflections of the Trinity in differing facets of creation, theologians including Augustine, Bernard of Clairvaux, Richard of St. Victor, Bonaventure and others share a conviction that certain created realities possess a discernible trinitarian structure.

According to Cousins, the meeting of religions constitutes one of the most important challenges facing contemporary theology in a globalized world. This challenge calls for a new kind of systematic theology "that will encompass within its horizons the religious experience of humankind."[69] Cousins laments the fact that theologians have focused almost exclusively on the question of "divine providence in salvation history" and generally have not attempted to enter into the unique religious experiences of other traditions and relate these to the Christian faith.[70] To remedy this situation the primary doctrines of the Christian

---

[68]Ewert H. Cousins, *Christ of the 21st Century* (Rockport, Mass.: Element, 1992). Cousins's discussion of Panikkar builds on an earlier essay: "The Trinity and World Religions," *Journal of Ecumenical Studies* 7 (1970): 476-98. Similar discussions can also be found in Ewert H. Cousins, *Bonaventure and the Coincidence of Opposites* (Chicago: Franciscan Herald Press, 1978), pp. 281-84; "Panikkar's Advaitic Trinitarianism," in *The Intercultural Challenge of Raimon Panikkar*, ed. Joseph Prabhu (Maryknoll, N.Y.: Orbis Books, 1996), pp. 119-30; and "Raimundo Panikkar and the Christian Systematic Theology of the Future," *Cross Currents* 29 (1979): 141-55. Others have followed Cousins in affirming the way he relates Panikkar's proposal to the vestige tradition (see William Cenkner, "Interreligious Exploration of Triadic Reality: the Panikkar Project," *Dialogue & Alliance* 4 [1990]: 71-85).

[69]Cousins, *Christ of the 21st Century*, p. 77.

[70]Ibid.

theology (e.g., Trinity, Christ, redemption) "must be explored in such a way that they will be open to, in relation with, and enriched by the religious experience of humankind."[71] This cannot be done in an objectivist mode. Christian theologians must enter into the subjectivity of other religions. This process will lead to a new kind of theology—a theology that possesses a "global consciousness."

In the past when Christian theologians attempted to encompass a broader religious horizon, they frequently turned to Christology. Justin Martyr related Christianity to Greek philosophy by appealing to Christ as the "eternal Logos." Similarly, Clement of Alexandria claimed that Plato was influenced by the eternal Logos. Although a Logos Christology may provide a useful point of contact with Western culture, it is not particularly helpful in building bridges to the East. On the contrary, two of the most important doctrines of the East (the Buddhist doctrine of *nirvana* and Hindu doctrine of nonduality of the self and the Absolute) are incompatible with logos doctrine. How then are Christians to enter into dialogue with the East? It is here that Panikkar's proposal represents a "major breakthrough in both the theology of the Trinity and interreligious dialogue,"[72] arising both from rich engagement with the Christian theological tradition as well as Buddhism and Hinduism. Unlike christological approaches that tend to be imperialistic (reducing every religious expression to a single form), Panikkar's trinitarian approach embraces diversity:

> The Trinitarian model of pluralism is not a class model, in which all individuals have to be fitted together under a least common denominator; nor is it an atomistic model, in which all individuals remain eternally aloof; nor is it a unitary model, in which all individuals are absorbed into a single one. Rather it is a model of unity in diversity, of profound interpenetration and yet individual identity.[73]

Although the Trinity represents a Christian concept, it possesses a "two-

---

[71]Ibid., p. 78.
[72]Ibid., p. 82.
[73]Ibid., p. 83.

fold universality."[74] First, it reflects core elements of religious experience in such a way that a kind of trinitarian pattern can be found in other religions. Second, it provides an overarching pattern for the unity of individual spiritual attitudes. "With the Trinity as a model, Christians can see the great spiritual traditions as dimensions of each other."[75]

While Panikkar's approach offers a "pluralistic model for dialogue," Cousins acknowledges that it raises some important questions. "Is it," he asks, "a radically new approach to the Trinity, or does his application of the doctrine to the world religions have at least some antecedents in the Christian tradition?"[76] We can discern two trajectories in the history of trinitarian thought: (1) a restrictive trajectory that limits the work of the Trinity to the salvific action of the Son and Spirit, and (2) a universalizing trajectory that connects the Trinity to the entire universe in creation and all history.[77] If Panikkar's proposal is situated against the backdrop of "three universalizing currents in the history of Trinitarian theology" (i.e., the medieval vestige doctrine, the trinitarian doctrine of creation in the early Greek fathers, and the scholastic doctrine of appropriations), "it can be seen to harmonize with each of them and at the same time to draw each into a new level."[78]

Although vestige doctrine has roots in the East, Cousins explains that it flourished primarily in Western medieval thought: "Basing their position on the metaphysics of exemplarism, inherited from Platonism, theologians reasoned that if, as Christian revelation teaches, the first cause of all things is Trinitarian, then its Trinitarian stamp must have been left on the physical universe and human beings."[79] Thus, by contemplating the universe, Christians can come to know more deeply the triune God, even in the smallest particle of matter. Robert Grosseteste,

---

[74]Ibid.
[75]Ibid.
[76]Ibid., p. 85.
[77]Ibid.
[78]Ibid., p. 84.
[79]Ibid., p. 86.

for example, contemplated the Trinity in a speck of dust. A speck of dust comes into being by a great power. Therefore, it reflects the Father.[80] Second, because this speck has form, it reflects the Son who is the wisdom and image of the Father.[81] Finally, because the speck is useful for contemplation, it reflects the Spirit.[82] Hence power, wisdom and goodness are reflected in a speck of dust, which represents a vestige of the Father, Son and Holy Spirit. Contemplation of the vestiges plays a central key role in Bonaventure's *Itinerarium Mentis in Deum*. In the first stage of the journey, Bonaventure views the material universe as a "vast mirror" that reflects the Father, Son and Holy Spirit.[83] Bonaventure invites his readers to contemplate the whole of creation from seven perspectives: origin, fullness, multitude, beauty, fullness, activity and order. "From each angle of vision, [Bonaventure] sees the universe manifesting the power, wisdom and goodness of the Triune God."[84] This reflects Bonaventure's conviction that the world is like a book in which the Trinity shines forth. In the third stage of the soul's journey, Bonaventure contemplates the divine image in the human person, viewing the soul as "a mirror in which the Trinity is reflected."[85] God shines in the soul as the light of truth. Through the mirror of the soul (specifically in the mental activities of memory, understanding and love) one can glimpse three coeternal, coequal and consubstantial persons.[86] One final example of the medieval vestige tradition can be seen in the writings of Richard of St. Victor. Building upon Augustine, Richard discerns a reflection of the Trinity in "human interpersonal community."[87]

---

[80]Power became associated with the Father in medieval thought because the Father is the source and origin of divinity.

[81]The form of the speck reflects the wisdom by which it was made. Thus, it reflects the Son who is both the wisdom of the Father and the image of the Father.

[82]"Again, in an ancient theological tradition, goodness is associated with the Spirit since he is the fullness and completion of the Trinity and the Gift in whom all gifts are given" (ibid.).

[83]Ibid., p. 87.

[84]Ibid.

[85]Ibid., p. 88.

[86]Ibid.

[87]Ibid.

Cousins suggests that a logical progression can be seen in the vestige tradition: movement from contemplation of a speck of dust in Grosseteste to contemplation of the entire universe in Bonaventure, as well as movement from the human soul as image of the Trinity (Bonaventure) to interpersonal community as a reflection of the Trinity (Richard of St. Victor). In such a context,

> It is not a major step, then, to rise to the larger human community and take into account its historical development to the point of its highest spiritual achievement. At this level it would not be surprising, then, to discover, as Panikkar does, a reflection of the Father, Son and Spirit. To extend the vestige tradition into the sphere of religion and philosophy is not without precedent in Christian theology. From the early centuries, Christian theologians explored what they considered to be the foreshadowing of the Trinity in the Old Testament and the reflection of the Trinity in Greek philosophy. . . . At the present time, if Christians are to expand their horizons beyond the Mediterranean world and relate Christianity to a larger spectrum of human experience than is found in Judaism and Greek philosophy, it would not be inappropriate to encompass within this vestige doctrine humankind's religious experience as this has developed in its highest forms.[88]

Against this backdrop Cousins suggests that Panikkar's three forms of spirituality (iconolatry, personalism, mysticism) represent a vestige of the Trinity (*vestigium trinitatis*). By explicitly linking Panikkar's proposal to the vestige tradition, Cousins provides an important clue to understanding Panikkar's proposal. Following Cousins's lead, we will examine Augustine's search for reflections of the Trinity in creation and then use the results of our investigation to evaluate Panikkar's proposal. We will see that whereas Augustine interprets created reality in light of the Trinity, Panikkar violates the basic grammar of the vestige tradition by reinterpreting the doctrine of the Trinity on the basis of non-Christian religious experience.

---

[88]Ibid.

AUGUSTINE ON THE *VESTIGIA TRINITATIS*

In books 8-15 of *De trinitate*, Augustine searches for reflections of the Trinity in the highest functions of the human soul. Because these books are frequently misunderstood, I want to provide some context before examining Augustine's search for traces of the Trinity. Three elements provide a crucial backdrop for Augustine's search: his quest to know God, scriptural teaching about the Trinity, and the redemptive work of Christ.[89] The second half of *De trinitate* should not be read as an abstract treatise on theological anthropology. It represents a vital search to know and understand the God in whom Augustine believes. Psalm 105:3-4 (104:3-4 LXX) provides the impetus for Augustine's search with its invitation continually to seek the face of God. Augustine explicitly cites this text at the beginning of book 1 (*De trinitate* 1.5, 68); the beginning of book 9, when he initiates his quest for the image of God in the human soul (*De trinitate* 9.1, 270); and at the end of his investigation (*De trinitate* 15.2, 395). He also alludes to this text at numerous other points (*De trinitate* 1.31; 2.1; 8.14; 15.3, 13, 51). Augustine invites his readers to join him in a quest to seek the face of God. Reflecting on his objective at the beginning of book 15, he explains that his plan has been "to train the reader *in the things that have been made* (Rom 1:20), for getting to know him by whom they were made" (*De trinitate* 15.1, 395).[90] Augustine specifically invites his readers to contemplate the triune God through the divine image in the mind (*mens*), which he believes has been created in the image of the Trinity.[91]

Scriptural teaching about the Trinity also provides an important backdrop for his search. In books 8-15 Augustine is not attempting to offer a rational proof for the Trinity unaided by revelation. On the con-

---

[89]These books also serve a polemical purpose inasmuch as Augustine has not forgotten about the Latin Homoian theologians he wrestles with in bks. 1-7.

[90]If Ps 105:3-4 explains the *motive* of Augustine's search, Rom 1:20 informs the *method* for his search. In addition to bk. 15, Augustine cites Rom 1:20 at several key points: *De trinitate* 2.25, 4.21, 6.12, 13.24.

[91]The Latin terms *mens*, which Augustine uses throughout the second half of *De trinitate*, is difficult to render adequately in English. I will use the English words *soul* and *mind* to translate it.

trary, he believes that God is triune on the basis of Scripture and wants to understand this belief, inasmuch as this is humanly possible. As A. N. Williams rightly notes, "The *vestigia*, then, are a tool for penetrating belief and grasping it yet more fully, not a means for establishing the content of faith independently of, or prior to, Scripture."[92] The centrality of Scripture in his search can be seen in three ways. First, his reading of Scripture prompts Augustine to see the image of God in the human soul as trinitarian. Second, scriptural teaching about the Trinity, as narrated in the first half of *De trinitate,* provides the blueprint for the trinitarian image in the *mens.*[93] Finally, scriptural teaching about the Trinity provides the criterion for evaluating the viability of the various trinities Augustine discovers. For example, in describing why he rejects the idea that the trinitarian image of God can be found in three persons (specifically, the union of a man and a woman and their offspring), Augustine explains,

> The reason then why we dislike this opinion is not that we are afraid of thinking about inviolate and unchanging charity as the wife of God the Father, who comes into being from him, though not as offspring, in order to bring to birth the Word *through whom all things were made* (Jn 1:3), but that the divine scripture shows quite clearly that it is false. (*De trinitate* 12.6, 325)

The redemptive work of Christ constitutes a third backdrop for Augustine's search. He offers a dramatic account of the trinitarian image in the human soul. This becomes especially clear in books 12-14, where he describes the effacement of the divine image by sin (bk.

---

[92] A. N. Williams, "Contemplation: Knowledge of God in Augustine's *De trinitate,*" in *Knowing the Triune God: The Work of the Spirit in the Practices of the Church,* ed. James J. Buckley and David S. Yeago (Grand Rapids: Eerdmans, 2001), p. 123.

[93] As Edmund Hill rightly notes, "In the dogmatic sense, Augustine's doctrine about the divine processions has already been given; it is the *datum* of orthodoxy which he is investigating through the image in order to be able to understand or see it" (Augustine, *The Trinity,* trans. Edmund Hill [Brooklyn: New City Press, 1991], p. 65). In light of this, Hill suggests that it might be best to speak of Augustine "constructing" the trinitarian image in the human person (as opposed to merely discovering it), inasmuch he chooses psychological activities to fit "the linguistic standards" he has outlined in the first half of *De trinitate* (ibid., p. 54).

12), the restoration of the image through the work of Christ (bk. 13) and the future perfection of the divine image (bk. 14).[94] This restoration can only be brought about by grace (*De trinitate* 14, 21, 387). As Augustine explains in book 4, "And in the sixth age of the human race the Son of God came and was made the Son of man in order to refashion us to the image of God" (*De trinitate* 4.7, 158). Conversion represents the first step in the lifelong process of renewal (*De trinitate*, 14.23, 389). When the soul "comes to the perfect vision of God," it will "bear God's perfect likeness" (*De trinitate* 14.23, 390).[95] The image of God is increasingly actualized as the soul remembers, understands and loves God. With this background in mind, we will explore Augustine's search in greater detail.

Fundamentally, it is Augustine's doctrine of creation that prompts him to search for traces of the Trinity (*vestigia trinitatis*) in the functioning of the soul. He claims that everything in creation bears a certain likeness to its Creator:

> Is there anything, after all, that does not bear a likeness to God [*similitudinem Dei*] after its own kind and fashion, seeing that God made all things very good for no other reason than that he himself is supremely good? Insofar then as anything as is good, to that extent, it bears some likeness, even though a very remote one, to the highest good, and if this is a natural likeness it is of course a right and well-ordered likeness; if it is faulty, then of course it is a sordid and perverted one. . . . It is true that not everything in creation which is like [*simile*] God in some way or another is also to be called his image [*imago*], but only that which he alone is higher than. That alone receives his direct imprint [*exprimitur*] which has no other nature interposed between him and itself. (*De trinitate* 11.8, 310)

There are several things we should observe in this extended state-

---

[94]For a helpful discussion of the role of Christology in bk. 13, see Lewis Ayres, "The Christological Context of Augustine's *De trinitate* XIII: Toward Relocating Books VIII-XV," *Augustinian Studies* 29 (1998): 111-39.

[95]The two biblical texts that shape Augustine's understanding of this process are 2 Cor 3:18 and 1 Jn 3:2.

ment. First, the scope of this likeness (*similitudo*) is universal, reaching to all of creation. Second, goodness constitutes the point of connection between God and creation. Insofar as something is good, it bears some likeness to God. Third, this likeness obtains even under the condition of sin. Finally, Augustine identifies varying degrees of likeness within creation. This can be seen clearly in his distinction between likeness (*similitudo*) and image (*imago*). Although everything that is good in creation bears some similitude to God, not everything that is good bears God's image. The divine image, which "alone receives his direct imprint," bears a unique likeness to the Trinity.

As the second half of *De trinitate* unfolds, it becomes clear that Augustine is not interested in the *vestigia* in general (i.e., the sense in which various facets of creation bear a likeness to the triune God) but rather the divine image in the human mind (*mens*) as it reflects—albeit dimly—the divine processions.[96] That Augustine's interest is directed toward the divine image becomes quite clear when we compare the relative frequency of *vestigium* and *imago*. *Vestigium* occurs only ten times in *De trinitate*, while *imago* occurs almost 250 times.[97] Furthermore, of the ten occurrences of *vestigium*, only two occurrences are used in reference to the triune God. The clearest example of the latter use is the following statement in book 6: "So then, as we direct our gaze at the creator by *understanding the things that were made* (Rom 1:20), we should understand him as triad, whose traces [*vestigium*][98] appear in creation in a way that is fitting" (*De trinitate* 6.12, 213).[99] Although

---

[96]Helpful discussion of the divine image in Augustine's theology can be found in John E. Sullivan, *The Image of God: The Doctrine of St. Augustine and Its Influence* (Dubuque: Priory Press, 1963); Luigi Gioia, *The Theological Epistemology of Augustine's* De trinitate (Oxford: Oxford University Press, 2008), esp. chap. 11; and Lewis Ayres, *Augustine and the Trinity* (Cambridge: Cambridge University Press, 2010), chaps. 11 and 12.

[97]These numbers were generated using the search engine in the *Library of Latin Texts* (CLCLT) (Turnhout: Brepols, 2005), www.brepolis.net; accessed March 14, 2006.

[98]Although the Latin text uses the singular *vestigium*, Hill translates *vestigium* as a plural noun in his English translation.

[99]The other instance can be found in bk. 11: "No one will doubt that just as the inner man is endowed with understanding, so is the outer man with sensation. Let us try then if we can to pick out some trace of trinity [*vestigium Trinitatis*] in this outer man too" (*De trinitate* 11.1,

Augustine believes that all creation in some way reflects the Trinity, he restricts his search for reflections of the Trinity to the highest point in creation—the image of God in the human mind (*mens*).[100]

Augustine's belief that a reflection of the triunity of God can be found in the divine image in the mind (*mens*) is rooted in his reading of Genesis 1:26-27. It will be helpful to begin with a "misreading" of Genesis 1:26-27 (at least a misreading from Augustine's perspective). It was common Patristic practice to read the phrase "God created man in his image" (Gen 1:27) as the Father created human beings in the image of the Son.[101] Augustine rejects this reading. Notice how he reads the pronoun *our* in Genesis 1:27 in a trinitarian fashion:

> God said *Let us make man to our image and likeness* (Gn 1:26), and a little later on it adds, *And God made man to the image of God* (Gn 1:27). "Our," being plural in number, could not be right in this place if man were made to the image of one person, whether of the Father or the Son or the Holy Spirit; but because in fact he was made in the image of the trinity, it said *to our image.* (*De trinitate* 12.6, 325)

For Augustine, the pronoun *our* implies that human beings have been created in the image of the three persons of the Trinity and not merely in the image of the Son as a number of earlier interpreters had proposed.

Reading Genesis 1:26-27 alongside several New Testament texts (especially Eph 4:23 and Col 3:9-10), Augustine concludes that the divine image must exist in the mind: "After all, the authority of the apostle as well as plain reason assures us that man was not made to the image of God as regards the shape of his body, but as regards his rational mind [*rationalis mens*]" (*De trinitate* 12.12, 328-29). Why is the mind the locus of the image? Augustine believes that soul, or more

---

303). Augustine's assumption that creation in general possesses a kind of trinitarian stamp is rooted in a trinitarian reading of Rom 11:36 and Wisdom 11:20 (see Sullivan, *Image of God*, pp. 87-89).

[100]In other words Augustine is not really interested in finding a *vestigium trinitatis* but rather *imago trinitatis* (see *De trinitate* 12.5, 324).

[101]See Sullivan, *Image of God*, pp. 165-203.

specifically mind (*mens*), represents the highest aspect of human nature.[102] Among created things, it is the most like God.[103] Second, Augustine explains that something that is made in God's image must not be perishable: "So whatever it is that must be called the image of God, it must be found in something that will always be, and not in the retention, contemplation, and love of faith, which will not always be" (*De trinitate* 14.4, 372). Finally, the image of God involves the ability to know God—a central capacity of the mind (*mens*). It is important, however, to remember that being made in God's image does not imply any kind of equality with God.[104]

Armed with the conviction that the divine image exists in the mind and must reflect the three persons, Augustine commences his search for created reflections of the Trinity. Although he explores a number of "trinities" in the inner man and the outer man,[105] the most important trinity he identifies is the mental triad of memory (*memoria*), understanding (*intelligentia*) and will (*voluntas*).[106] He introduces this triad in book 10 and returns to it in book 14. What does this triad reveal if understood as a reflection of the triune God? It is helpful to remember that Augustine is looking for trinities in the functions of the mind that will shed light on the processions he has outlined in part one. Notice how his summary of the functions of memory, understanding and will parallels his earlier discussion of the processions:

---

[102]*Mens* is commonly translated "mind"; however, it has a much broader semantic range in Latin.

[103]"For although the human mind [*mens humana*] is not of the same nature as God, still the image [*imago*] of that nature than which no nature is better is to be sought and found in that part of us than which our nature also has nothing better" (*De trinitate* 14.11, 379).

[104]According to Augustine, the phrase "to the image of God" (*ad imaginem Dei*) in Genesis 1:27 implies both similarity and dissimilarity in relation to God (see *De trinitate* 7.12, 231).

[105]In bk. 8 Augustine introduces the triad of lover, beloved and love. In bk. 9 he suggests the possibility of mind, self-knowledge and self-love. In bk. 10 he outlines his most important triad: memory, understanding and will. In bk. 11 he explores a triad in the outer man, namely, memory, internal sight and will. Clearly not every trinity Augustine discovers is an image of triune God. For example, all the trinities he discovers within the "lower" functions of the human psyche are excluded from being the image of God.

[106]For a helpful discussion of this triad along with its background in Latin thought, see Ayres, *Augustine and the Trinity*, pp. 297-318.

These three then, memory [*memoria*], understanding [*intellegentia*], and will [*voluntas*], are not three lives but one life, nor three minds but one mind [*una mens*]. So it follows of course that they are not three substances but one substance [*una substantia*]. When memory is called life, and mind, and substance, it is called so with reference to itself; but when it is called memory it is called so with reference to another. I can say the same about understanding and will; both understanding and will are so called with reference to another. But each of them is life and mind and being with reference to itself. For this reason these three are one in that they are one life, one mind, one being; and whatever else they are called together with reference to self, they are called it in the singular, not in the plural. But they are three in that they have reference to each other. And if they were not equal, not only each to the other but also each to them all together, they would not of course contain each other (*De trinitate* 10.18, 298).

In this lengthy passage we see the payoff of Augustine's investigation. His investigation of the divine image in the soul (*mens*) potentially sheds light on the way that the three persons of the Trinity are distinct yet also one. Memory, understanding and will (respectively representing Father, Son and Holy Spirit) are each distinct, yet they are also one mind (corresponding to the one nature of the triune God). Just as the Father is called "God" with respect to the divine nature, so memory is called "mind" with respect to the whole. Just as the Father is called "Father" with respect to the Son, so memory is called "memory" with respect to understanding. This triad also sheds light on the processions. We might understand memory as the mind's "self-presence."[107] We remember ourself via this self-presence. Once the mind is activated, this self-presence generates an act of understanding through a mental "word."[108] As Edmund Hill explains, "from these two conjoint, co-extensive, conmental acts of minding me, and me saying me to myself, there issues the third co-extensive, conmental act, as it were joining

---

[107]Here I am following Edmund Hill's summary (see Hill, *The Trinity*, p. 53).
[108]Ibid.

together quasi-parent, and quasi-offspring, of me liking me, me willing me, self-willing."[109]

At this point it may sound as if Augustine is rather optimistic regarding the extent to which the divine image in the soul (*mens*) reflects the Trinity that God is. We must conclude our discussion by considering two crucial qualifications to the preceding discussion. First, in book 14 Augustine explains that the divine image is actualized only in the context of redemption: "This trinity of the mind is not really the image of God because the mind remembers and understands and loves itself, but because it is also able to remember and understand and love him by whom it was made" (*De trinitate* 14.15, 383). The ability to "see" God is directly linked to the renewing of the image.[110] Second, despite the numerous similarities he identifies in earlier books, Augustine insists that an enormous difference exists between the triad in the human soul and the Trinity which God is (*De trinitate* 15.12, 403). Thus, aligning memory, understanding and will with Father, Son and Holy Spirit is ultimately problematic. Humans remember nothing apart from their memory, understand nothing apart from their understanding, and love nothing apart from their will. But who would want to say that the Father only understands through the Son or only loves through the Holy Spirit? Moreover, who would want to say that the Son only remembers himself through the Father? Furthermore, who would want to say that the Holy Spirit remembers the Father through the Father or understands the Father only through the Son? If the Son alone is the source of understanding then "we are back at the absurdity of the Father not being wise with himself but with the Son"—a problem Augustine already dealt with in books 5-7 (*De trinitate* 15.12, 403).

At the root of the vast dissimilarity between the divine image in the *mens* and God the Trinity is the Creator-creature distinction, which

---

[109]Ibid., pp. 53-54.

[110]"So then, when this image is renewed to perfection by this transformation, we will be like God *because we shall see him*, not through a mirror but *as he is* (1 Jn 3:2); what the apostle Paul calls *face to face* (1 Cor 13:12)" (*De trinitate* 15.21, 411).

Augustine articulates through a grammar of divine simplicity (or divine immateriality).[111] While humans *have* memory, understanding and will, these faculties exist *in* the human being without *being* the human being. "But can we possibly say that a trinity is in God in such a way that it is something of God's, and is not itself just God?" (*De trinitate* 15.12, 403). The logic of divine simplicity requires a negative answer to this question. While a human being has the image of God, "that trinity he is the image of is nothing but wholly and simply God, nothing but wholly and simply trinity. Nor is there anything belonging to God's nature which does not belong to that trinity; and there are three persons of one being, not, like any single man, just one person" (*De trinitate* 15.12, 403).

What does this mean for the epistemic adequacy of the triad of memory, understanding and will in revealing the *triunity* of God? On the one hand, it means that "the trinity which is God cannot just be read off from those three things which we have pointed out in the trinity of our minds" (*De trinitate* 15.28, 419). Furthermore, because any of the divine perfections one can infer through creation are identical with the divine essence, it is impossible to descry directly the triunity of God through creation in terms of Romans 1:20 (*De trinitate* 15.6-13, 399-405). On the other hand, Augustine believes that we can dimly perceive the triunity of God through the divine image in the *mens* (*De trinitate* 15.39, 426). First Corinthians 13:12 provides language that Augustine uses to express this indirect apprehension of the triune God through the image: "*We see now through a mirror* [speculum] *in an enigma* [aenigmate], *but then it will be face to face* (1 Cor 13:12)" (*De trinitate* 15.14, 405). Augustine focuses on two key terms in this text: *speculum* and *aenigma*. Reading 2 Corinthians 3:18 alongside 1 Corinthians 13:12, Augustine suggests that the "mirror" in 1 Corinthians 13:12 may best be understand as a reference to the image of God: "If we ask what kind of mirror [*speculum*] this might be, the thought occurs to us

---

[111]See Lewis Ayres, *Nicaea and Its Legacy: An Approach to Fourth-Century Trinitarian Theology* (New York: Oxford University Press, 2004), pp. 364-83.

that the only thing ever seen in a mirror [*in speculo*] is an image [*imago*]. So what we have been trying to do is somehow see him by whom we were made by means of his image which we ourselves are, as through a mirror" (*De trinitate* 15.14, 405). The term enigma (*aenigma*) expresses the opaque character of this image.[112] Thus, the best we can hope for in this life is a kind of "limited inference" from this enigmatic likeness (*De trinitate* 15.40, 427).[113] Full sight will come only when the restoration of the image is complete and Christians see God "face to face" (*De trinitate* 15.44, 429).

PANIKKAR'S TRINITARIAN SPIRITUALITY: AN AUGUSTINIAN EVALUATION

My Augustinian evaluation of Panikkar will proceed from two angles. First, following Cousins's suggestion that Panikkar's proposal be situated against the backdrop of vestige tradition, I will evaluate Panikkar's proposal through the lens of the vestige tradition. Then, bracketing Cousins's reading, I will evaluate Panikkar's trinitarian doctrine focusing on the relationship between the immanent Trinity and the economic Trinity.

Flawed appeal to the vestige tradition. By situating Panikkar's proposal in the context of the vestige tradition, Cousins provides an important clue for understanding Panikkar's project; however, rather than strengthening it, this move simply brings the problems with his proposal more sharply into focus.[114]

---

[112]"As far as I can see then, by the word 'mirror' [*speculi*] he wanted us to understand an image [*imaginem*], and by the word 'enigma' [*aenigmatis*] he was indicating that although it is a likeness [*similitudinem*], it is an obscure one and difficult to penetrate" (*De trinitate* 15.16, 407).

[113]Augustine seems to suggest that evidence for the triunity of God, however limited, is available both to those who believe and to those who do not. Some, who do not believe, see the "mirror" (the divine image in the *mens*) but fail to "see by a mirror the one who now can only be seen by a mirror, [so] that they do not even know the mirror they see *is* a mirror, that is to say an image" (*De trinitate* 15.44, 429).

[114]At least two points of continuity exist between Panikkar and the vestige tradition: (1) an assumption that the world possesses a discernible trinitarian structure, and (2) a belief that a specific human reality discernibly reflects the trinitarian persons. At the same time, several important points of discontinuity exist which merit careful scrutiny.

A methodological problem. Although Augustine and Panikkar both believe that reflections of the Trinity can be found in the world, their methodologies differ significantly. Augustine interprets created reality (specifically the divine image in the soul) in light of the doctrine of the Trinity he has gleaned from Scripture. Moreover, Augustine believes he possesses scriptural warrant for seeing a particular created reality (the divine image in the *mens*) as an image of the triune God. In contrast, Panikkar *reinterprets* the doctrine of Trinity in light of non-Christian religious experience. We can see this quite clearly in the structure of Panikkar's argument. First, he identifies three spiritualities that are said to arise purely from an "empirical assessment" of religious experience (independent of any particular religious tradition).[115] Then he offers a novel interpretation of the doctrine of the Trinity, on the basis of these spiritualities, as constitutive ground for them. By reinterpreting the doctrine of the Trinity on the basis of non-Christian religious experience, Panikkar violates the basic theological grammar of the vestige tradition that involves reading the "book of the world" in light of the "book of Scripture."[116]

Karl Barth's discussion of the *vestigia* in *Church Dogmatics* 1/1 helps sheds light on the problem with Panikkar's trinitarian grammar. Barth insists that the root of the doctrine of the Trinity is "the threefold yet single lordship of God as Father, Son and Spirit" (i.e., the biblical concept of revelation).[117] "When we say that the doctrine

---

[115]Panikkar claims that his description of these spiritualities "does not proceed from an *a priori* construction but emerges from an empirical assessment of the situation" (Panikkar, *Trinity and the Religious Experience of Man*, p. 9).

[116]In his introduction to Bonaventure's *Itinerarium Mentis in Deum*, Stephen Brown explains that the first two chapters of the *Itinerarium* are designed to help the wayfarer rightly understand sensible things (that is, the vestiges) from the horizon of Scripture: "Before the fall into sin man had a knowledge of sensible things and through them he was carried up to God to praise, worship and love him. After he fell man lost this kind of knowledge. He no longer could read the book of the world. The book of the sacred Scriptures tells us again the divine meaning of the sensible things and is able to restore the symbolic character of the world, so that it once again leads us to the knowledge, praise and love of God" (Stephen F. Brown, *Bonaventure: The Journey of the Mind to God*, trans. Philotheus Boehner [Indianapolis: Hackett, 1993], p. 50).

[117]Karl Barth, *Church Dogmatics* 1/1, *The Doctrine of the Word of God*, 2nd ed., trans. G. W. Bro-

of the Trinity grows from this root we are saying critically and polemically that it does not stem from any other root."[118] Barth claims that the vestige tradition challenges this single root. His critique of the vestige tradition is driven by the assumption that once we posit a second root for the doctrine of the Trinity, this second root will inevitably swallow up the first. In the language of Barth, Panikkar implicitly posits a second root of the doctrine of the Trinity (non-Christian religious experience), which ultimately swallows the real root (God's self-revelation in Scripture).

At this point one might register the following objection. Inasmuch as Augustine is the progenitor of the vestige tradition, would not Barth's criticisms apply equally to him? Barth's criticisms would apply to Augustine were he to posit a second root for the doctrine of the Trinity; however, it is clear from our previous discussion that Augustine posits a single root for the doctrine of the Trinity—God's self-revelation in Scripture. As Earl Muller rightly notes, "What Augustine believes about the Trinity will guide his quest. He does not argue from the structure of the mind to the structure of the Trinity; rather; the light derived from faith guides his exploration of the mind. It is this, for instance, that determines his description of intellectual activity as a sort of begetting."[119] Although important differences exist between Barth and Augustine, the proper root of trinitarian doctrine is not one of them.[120] Augustine makes it clear that the search for trinitarian reflections in the created world must be guided by the "rule of faith" (*De trinitate* 15.49, 434; 15.51, 436).

Disregarding the Creator-creature distinction. Not only does Panikkar's

---

miley (Edinburgh: T & T Clark, 1975), p. 334.

[118]Ibid.

[119]Earl C. Muller, *Trinity and Marriage in Paul: The Establishment of a Communitarian Analogy of the Trinity Grounded in the Theological Shape of Pauline Thought*, American University Studies 7, Theology and Religion 60 (New York: Peter Lang, 1990), p. 219.

[120]For a helpful discussion of why Barth's critique of the vestige tradition does not apply to Augustine, see David S. Cunningham, "Interpretation: Toward a Rehabilitation of the *Vestigia* Tradition," in *Knowing the Triune God: The Work of the Spirit in the Practices of the Church*, ed. James J. Buckley and David S. Yeago (Grand Rapids: Eerdmans, 2001), pp. 179-202.

reinterpretation of the Trinity on the basis of non-Christian religious experience violate the grammar of the vestige tradition, but it also fails to take into account the epistemic implications of Creator-creature distinction. In book 15 Augustine insists that the Trinity that God is cannot simply be "read off" the divine image in the creature because of the vast dissimilarity that exists between the triune God and the image of God in the soul (*mens*). This fundamental difference (which Augustine explicates through a grammar of divine simplicity) means that no vestige (*vestigium*) could ever adequately reflect the Trinity.

Commenting on his search for an image of the Trinity in the human person, Augustine explains that every time he attempted "to bring out some comparative illustration of this point in that created reality which we are," he discovered that "no adequate expression followed whatever understanding I came to; and I was only too well aware that my attempt even to understand involved more effort than result" (*De trinitate* 15.45, 430). Although he believes he discovered an "image of that supreme trinity," he acknowledges, nonetheless, that the "three things of one person were quite unable to match those three persons in the way our human plan requires, as we have been demonstrating in this fifteenth book" (*De trinitate* 15.45, 430). One of the central themes in book 15 is the inadequacy of the divine image in revealing the Trinity that God is.[121] We must bear in mind that Augustine's comments about the inadequacy of this image are not directed at the "lower" trinities he explores in the "outer man." To the contrary, they are directed at the most adequate trinity Augustine has discovered.

If the aspect of human nature which is most like God (the divine image in the soul) is so inadequate for revealing the Trinity, then no

---

[121]Edmund Hill's title for bk. 15, "The Absolute Inadequacy of the Perfected Image," appropriately expresses this reality. Regarding the inadequacy of the created image to mirror the Trinity, Augustine offers the following warning: "To the memory, sight, and love of this supreme trinity, in order to recollect it, see it, and enjoy it, he should refer every ounce and particle of his life. But I have sufficiently warned him, so it seems to me, that this image, made by the trinity and altered for the worse by its own fault, is not so to be compared to that trinity that it is reckoned similar to it in every respect. Rather, he should note how great the dissimilarity is in whatever similarity there may be" (*De trinitate* 15.39, 426).

epistemic warrant exists for reinterpreting the doctrine of the Trinity on the basis of any potential *vestigium*. Such a move fails to take into account Augustine's warning in book 9: "What we have to avoid is the sacrilegious mistake of saying anything about the trinity which does not belong to the creator but to the creature, or which is fabricated by vain imaginings" (*De trinitate* 9.1, 271). Thus, even if, for the sake of argument, we were to grant Cousins's claim that non-Christian religious experience represents a *vestigium trinitatis* (a claim we will shortly evaluate), no epistemic warrant exists for reinterpreting the doctrine of the Trinity on the basis of non-Christian religious experience in light of the dissimilarity that exists between Creator and creature.

Iconolatry, personalism and mysticism as a vestige of the Trinity? Cousins's argument for viewing Panikkar's three spiritualities as a vestige of the Trinity might be summarized as follows:

P1. The vestige tradition has recognized traces of the Trinity throughout creation.

P2. The vestige tradition should be extended to encompass non-Christian religious experience.

P3. When thus extended, an important trinitarian vestige can be found, namely "iconolatry," "personalism" and "mysticism."

P4. The presence of the latter vestige constitutes evidence that non-Christian religions represent valid means of relating to the triune God.

In order to evaluate Cousins's argument it will be helpful to consider the criteria that implicitly guide Augustine's search for reflections of the Trinity in the functioning of the human soul. Broadly speaking, five criteria guide Augustine's search.[122] First, created reality is the locus of trinitarian reflections. Second, the clearest reflection of the

---

[122]Earl Muller identifies twenty different criteria that guide Augustine's search for an image of the Trinity (see Muller, *Trinity and Marriage in Paul*, pp. 209-43). I have reduced Muller's list by grouping a number of similar elements.

Trinity is to be found in that which bears the greatest likeness to God.[123] Third, Scripture should play a key role in the discernment and evaluation of trinitarian reflections. Augustine believes that biblical warrant exists for viewing the divine image in the soul as a reflection of the Trinity. Fourth, trinitarian reflections should mirror key elements of Christian teaching on the Trinity, including the oneness of the divine substance, the consubstantiality and equality of the divine persons, the commensurability of the persons, inseparability of the persons, perichoresis, relative difference, and mutual relation (generation and procession).[124] The presence of threeness alone does not constitute a sufficient condition for an authentic reflection of the Trinity. Finally, trinitarian reflections should aid our knowledge of the triune God.[125]

How does Cousins's proposal fare in light of these criteria? The first criterion (created reality as locus of trinitarian reflection) raises serious questions about extending the vestige tradition to encompass non-Christian religious experience (P2). All the examples Cousins cites from the vestige tradition (e.g., speck of dust, created universe, human soul, community of persons, etc.) clearly name created realities.[126] "Experience," however, names a relation; experience is always "experience of." Although it makes sense to speak of experience *of* a vestige, it does not seem to make sense to speak of experience *as* a vestige.[127]

The third criterion prompts an important question: What biblical evidence exists for viewing iconolatry, personalism and mysticism as a vestige of the Trinity? Even if one were to grant P2, Cousins provides no biblical warrant for Panikkar's three spiritualities as a vestige of the Trinity. This is simply asserted. Moreover, his theological argument for recognizing iconolatry, personalism and mysticism as a vestige is inher-

---

[123]Because God is incorporeal, bodily analogies for the Trinity (e.g., father, mother and child) are inadequate.

[124]Muller, *Trinity and Marriage in Paul*, pp. 233-37.

[125]It is not an accident that Augustine's search for a reflection of the Trinity centers on the psychological apparatus by which we know the triune God. Augustine is not ultimately searching for reflections of the Trinity in the soul. He is searching for the triune God.

[126]Moreover, the faculties of memory, understanding and will represent created realities.

[127]For Bonaventure the *vestigia* always refer to something in the sensible world.

ently circular. On the one hand, the reading of these spiritualities as *vestigia* arises from the assumption that they are legitimate experiences of the triune God. On the other hand, it is the reading of these three spiritualities as *vestigia* that grounds the claim that they constitute experiences of the triune God.

The fourth criterion prompts the following question: If iconolatry, personalism and mysticism are read as a mirror reflecting the divine persons, what does this *vestigium* reveal about the triune God, and how does the resulting picture comport with Christian teaching regarding the generation of the Son and procession of the Holy Spirit? At first glance, the answer to the first half of this question may appear quite obvious. Panikkar outlines the doctrine of the Trinity that mirrors his triad of spiritualities in the second chapter of *The Trinity and the Religious Experience of Man*. The Buddhist experience of emptiness reflects the Father, who is the "emptying of Being." The Jewish experience of a personal relationship with God reflects the Son who, strictly speaking, is the only Person in the Trinity. The Hindu experience of identity (nonrelational union) with *Brahman* reflects the Holy Spirit, who is "divine immanence." Upon closer inspection, however, the answer to this question is a bit more complicated. If we were to bracket Panikkar's exposition of the Trinity in the second chapter of *The Trinity and the Religious Experience of Man* and then simply to ask what the first chapter (Panikkar's explanation of three spiritualities) reveals about the triune God, it seems unlikely the results would necessarily match the explanation of the Trinity outlined the second chapter.

This brings us to the second part of my question: How does the resulting picture that these *vestigia* provide comport with Christian teaching regarding the generation of the Son and procession of the Holy Spirit? Aside from the number three (a limitation that seems somewhat arbitrary), they bear no witness to the distinction of divine persons, consubstantiality and equality of the divine persons, the commensurability of the persons, exhausting the divine substance in three persons, the inseparability of the persons, the perichoresis of the persons, relative difference, or mutual relation. In short, we cannot infer the Christian Trinity from these three spiritual experiences. Thus, Cousins's reading of iconolatry, personalism and mysticism as a *vestigium* fails to satisfy the fourth criterion.[128]

The fifth criterion reminds us what is at stake—authentic knowledge of the triune God. In light of this criterion, we must consider Cousins's claim that the presence of *vestigia* in the religious experience of non-Christians constitutes the basis for affirming that non-Christian religions represent valid means of experiencing and relating to the triune God (P4). Here we must ask, To what do the vestiges bear witness? From Augustine to Bonaventure the answer is the same: read by the faithful through the lens of Scripture, they bear witness (albeit dimly and indirectly) to the triunity of God. It is difficult to see how this reality might, in any way, constitute the basis for the kind of pluralist view of relationship of Christianity to other religions that Cousins and Panikkar want to affirm. Even if, for the sake of argument, we were to grant P2, no warrant exists for moving from the discernible presence of a *vestigium* in some aspect of human religious experience to the soteriological efficacy of non-Christian religions.[129] Cousins effectively severs the *vestigia* from the economy of salvation; however, the *vestigia* cannot be separated from the economy of salvation.[130]

---

[128]In the following section of this chapter I will offer a detailed examination of Panikkar's doctrine of the Trinity. In response, I might point out that if we were to start with Augustine's description of memory, understanding and will, and then ask what it reveals about the Trinity (apart from his description in bks. 1-7), the result would be similar. The reason this problem exists for Panikkar and not for Augustine is that Panikkar wants to *reinterpret* the Trinity on the basis of religious experience whereas Augustine wants to interpret the image of the Trinity strictly in light of Christian teaching on the Trinity. This brings us back to the methodological problem I outlined earlier.

[129]Augustine, of course, would not deny that all people—Christians and non-Christians alike—have been made in the image of the Trinity. In the functioning of the human soul qua soul, the divine image—albeit defaced—is present: "For we have said that even when it has lost its participation in him it still remains the image of God, even though worn out and distorted. It is his image insofar as it is capable of him and can participate in him; indeed it cannot achieve so great a good except by being his image" (*De trinitate* 14.11, 379). Nevertheless, from the presence of this trinitarian image in a Buddhist, we cannot infer the salvific efficacy of Buddhism.

[130]"Image," for Augustine, is inextricably tied to the redemptive work of the triune God (as is

In sum, Cousins's appeal to the vestige tradition brings to light three problems with Panikkar's trinitarian grammar. First, Panikkar's proposal violates the basic grammar of the vestige tradition by reinterpreting the doctrine of the Trinity on the basis of religious experience. Second, in light of the vast dissimilarity that exists between Creator and creature, no epistemic warrant exists for reinterpreting the doctrine of the Trinity on the basis of non-Christian religious experience. Panikkar's proposal fails to take into account the epistemic implications of this dissimilarity. Third, there are good reasons to question Cousins's claim that iconolatry, personalism and mysticism should be viewed as a vestige of the Trinity (*vestigium trinitatis*).

In response, one might counter that all I have really demonstrated is that Cousins's reading of Panikkar is inadequate and that Panikkar is not doing anything that should be subsumed under the vestige tradition. Although Panikkar does not explicitly appeal to the vestige tradition in the same way Cousins does, he implicitly appeals to the basic grammar of vestige tradition in speaking of the "threefold structure of reality,"[131] "trinitarian structure of religious experience"[132] and world as a "divine 'vestige'" of the triune God.[133] Hence, my criticisms seem to be warranted. Perhaps it would be best to acknowledge that while Panikkar's proposal implicitly draws on elements of the vestige tradition, important discontinuities exist between the latter and the former, and that some of these discontinuities reflect deficiencies in Panikkar's trinitarian grammar. Although the vestige tradition does expose several problems with Panikkar's proposal, it is important that our assessment not be limited to this lens. The ultimate confirmation of these problems can only come through a critical analysis of Panikkar's doctrine of the Trinity. Thus, in the remaining section of this chapter, I

---

abundantly clear in bks. 12-14). It is only as the soul remembers, understands and loves God that image of God can be progressively restored.

[131]Panikkar, *Trinity and the Religious Experience of Man*, p. xi. Elsewhere Panikkar explains that "Every bit of reality has this trinitarian imprint" (Panikkar, *Blessed Simplicity*, p. 128).

[132]Panikkar, *Trinity and the Religious Experience of Man*, p. xiv.

[133]Ibid., p. 18.

will evaluate Panikkar's doctrine of the Trinity with special attention to his understanding of the immanent Trinity and the economic Trinity.

The immanent Trinity and the economic Trinity. According to Panikkar,

> The doctrine of the Trinity, in point of fact, is not there for the sake of satisfying our curiosity about the "immanent" Trinity as an internal affair of the Divinity (*ad intra*), alone. It connects the immanent mystery with the "economic" God (*ad extra*), in which the destiny of the world is at stake. It is not mere speculation about the depths of God; it is equally an analysis of the heights of man.[134]

This statement provides an important clue regarding Panikkar's understanding of his project. He believes that contemporary Christian theology has mistakenly focused upon the immanent Trinity to the neglect of the economic Trinity.[135] One of his central goals in *The Trinity and the Religious Experience of Man* is to reconnect the trinitarian reality ("immanent mystery") with the world. Following this clue, we will evaluate his proposal by considering how he relates the economic and the immanent Trinity. We will see that in his attempt to connect Trinity with the world, Panikkar ultimately undermines the very thing he wishes to accomplish.

The immanent Trinity. At the heart of Panikkar's proposal is a specific understanding of the immanent Trinity which constitutes the ground for the three spiritualities he outlines. The divine "emptying of Being" that marks the life of the Father constitutes the basis for a Buddhist experience of divine emptiness (*Nirvana*). The divine "personality" that marks the life of the Son constitutes the basis for a Christian experience of a personal relationship with God. The "divine immanence" that marks the Spirit constitutes the basis for the Hindu experi-

---

[134]Ibid., p. xii.
[135]According to Panikkar, Christian theology "has too often relegated the trinitarian mystery to the exclusive sphere of the Divinity, 'theology' in the greek use of the word, i.e., the study of God-in-himself totally or almost independent of the 'economy' or study of God in his 'temporal manifestation', i.e., creation and incarnation" (ibid., p. 71).

ence of nonrelational union with *Brahman*. In terms of his trinitarian grammar, Panikkar emphasizes the immanent Trinity as ground for the economic. Although it is true the immanent Trinity constitutes the *ontological* basis for the economic Trinity, it must also be recognized that the economy of salvation revealed in Scripture constitutes the sole *epistemic* foundation for our knowledge of the Trinity. It is in relation to the latter point that the problems begin to emerge in Panikkar's trinitarian grammar. When Panikkar claims that "the trinitarian conception of the Ultimate" is not "an exclusive Christian insight or revelation," he implicitly abandons the epistemic foundation provided by Scripture.[136] Panikkar simply offers a speculative account of the immanent Trinity that is inadequately rooted in Scripture.

From an Augustinian standpoint there are numerous problems with Panikkar's account of the immanent Trinity.[137] For example, in his explanation of the Father, Panikkar implies the Father of Jesus Christ (and by extension the Christian Trinity) is *not* the ultimate reality but merely a penultimate manifestation of a transcendent Absolute, which is beyond name or description. Furthermore, Panikkar seems to suggest that what uniquely constitutes the Father as Father is not a distinct property such as "unbegottenness" but rather "emptiness of being." The Father, he insists, has no existence from the standpoint of Being, because his Being has been emptied, wholly and without remainder, in the generation of the Son. Hence, one cannot even speak about the Father. It is difficult to see how this description of the Father as "emptiness of Being" can be reconciled with the creedal affirmation that the Son is *homoousios* with the Father.[138] Finally, although Panikkar ap-

---

[136]Ibid., p. viii. In another context Panikkar explains, "The Trinity, we have to clarify at the outset, is neither a monopoly of Christianity nor, for our purposes of the Divinity" (Panikkar, *Blessed Simplicity*, p. 128).

[137]Although he appeals to many elements of the Augustinian tradition, he infuses these elements with new meaning.

[138]Panikkar attempts to fend off this objection by pointing out that the divine nature is not a fourth thing alongside the persons: "A certain popular theological language which speaks of the equality among the 'three' persons can certainly be accepted provided we stop short of accepting an objectified divine nature, 'trinitarianly' disincarnated, as it were (the famous

peals to a number of elements in the classic trinitarian tradition (particularly the notion of the Father as the substratum of divinity), his account of the Father as "emptiness of Being" seems uniquely tailored to ground a Buddhist experience of emptiness.[139] By reinterpreting the Father in light of the Buddhist teaching, Panikkar abandons the epistemic foundation for human knowledge of the Trinity.

Although the problems with his understanding of the Son come most sharply into focus at the level of the economic Trinity, at least one issue merits attention in relation to the immanent Trinity.[140] Panikkar offers a very complex explanation of why, among the Father, Son and Spirit, the Son alone should be called a Person. There are at least three problems with Panikkar's explanation. First, it seems to be driven not by reflection on the economy of salvation revealed in Scripture but rather by the need to ground a relational experience of God *exclusively* in the Son. Second, this claim seems to imply that what uniquely constitutes the Son qua Son (distinguishing him from the Father and Spirit) is not eternal generation but personhood (which for Panikkar is roughly synonymous with Being). By distinguishing Father and Son on this basis, Panikkar opens the door to the Homoian argument Augustine works so hard to dismantle in books 5-7. Panikkar therefore faces a dilemma. To the extent he grounds differences between the Father and Son in what implicitly amount to differences of substance between the Father and Son in order to muster support for his theology of reli-

---

rejected *quaternitas*)" (Panikkar, *Trinity and Religious Experience of Man*, p. 45). Since neither Augustine nor any ecumenical council affirms that the divine nature is a "fourth thing," it is difficult to see how this response answers my objection. Panikkar seems to be saying that what distinguishes Father and Son is a respective absence and presence of Being. This undermines their equality of nature.

[139]Notice the influence of Buddhism on Panikkar's description of the Father as silence: "Any attempt to speak about the Father involves almost a contradiction in terms, for every word about the Father can only refer to the one of whom the Father is Father, that is, to the Word, to the Son. It is necessary to be silent. The most diverse religious traditions teach us that God is Silence. This affirmation must be accepted in its unfathomable profundity. God is Silence total and absolute—the silence of Being—and not only the being of silence" (ibid., pp. 47-48).

[140]Panikkar's account of the economic Trinity will be discussed in the following section.

gious experience, he falls into the Homoian error of making Father and Son separate substances. If, on the other hand, he follows the Augustinian tradition in recognizing that everything the Father is, the Son is, except that the Son is not the Father, Panikkar loses the basis for grounding a relational experience of God *exclusively* in the Son. Finally, Panikkar's claim that the Son alone is Person seems to be parasitic upon a view of Jesus Christ that he rejects. It only makes sense to speak of the Son uniquely as Person (in contrast to the Father and Spirit) in the context of a Chalcedonian Christology. Panikkar, however, rejects a strict identification between Jesus of Nazareth and the eternal Son.[141] In so doing he undermines the theological basis for calling the Son a Person in distinction from the Father and Spirit.

As with his discussion of the Father and Son, Panikkar's account of the Holy Spirit seems to be tailored to suit the needs of his theology of religious experience. The central link between Panikkar's third form of spirituality and his discussion of the Spirit is the Hindu concept of *advaita*.[142] According to Panikkar, the concept of *advaita* has been misunderstood in the West. The message of the Upanishads is not monism, dualism or theism but "*advaita*, i.e. the non-dual character of the Real, the impossibility of adding God to the world or *vice versa*, the impossibility of putting in *dvanva*, in a pair, God and the world."[143] God and the world are neither one thing nor two. Consciousness of *advaita* (which Panikkar describes as an experience of divine immanence) is at the center of the third spirituality. *Advaita* also plays a central role in his understanding of the Spirit. Whereas the Father is the revelation of the "divine transcendence," the Spirit "is the revelation of the God immanent."[144] Panikkar explains that the Spirit is the com-

---

[141]See ibid., pp. 53-54.
[142]For a discussion of the role of *advaita* on Panikkar's trinitarian thought, see Ewert H. Cousins, "Panikkar's Advaitic Trinitarianism," in *The Intercultural Challenge of Raimon Panikkar*, ed. Joseph Prabhu (Maryknoll, N.Y.: Orbis, 1996), pp. 119-30.
[143]Panikkar, *The Trinity and the Religious Experience of Man*, p. 36.
[144]Ibid., p. 58.

munion between the Father and the Son.[145] Thus, the Spirit is "immanent to Father and Son jointly."[146] At this point it may sound as if all
Panikkar is doing is offering an Augustinian account of the Spirit as
the mutual bond of love between the Father and Son. Panikkar, however, gives this Augustinian concept a Hindu twist:

> The *advaita* which helps us express suitably the "relation" God-World is
> again a precious aid in elucidating the intra-trinitarian problem. If the
> Father and the Son are not *two*, they are not one either: the Spirit both
> unites and distinguishes them. He is the bond of unity; the *we* in be-
> tween, or rather within.[147]

Thus, we cannot have personal relations with the Spirit. Rather we
can only have "non-relational union with him."[148] In sum, intratrinitarian *advaita* (which is the Spirit) constitutes the ground for an experience of *advaita* (i.e., nonrelational union with the Absolute).
Again we must ask, "What epistemic warrant exists in Scripture for
this understanding of the Spirit?" The primary foundation for this
claim ultimately seems to be a particular reading of the Upanishads:
"Indeed what is the Spirit but the *ātman* of the Upanishads, which is
said to be identical with *brahman*, although this identity can only be
existentially recognized and affirmed once 'realisation' has been
attained?"[149] Turning to a second problem, Panikkar seems to imply
that what uniquely constitutes the Spirit as Spirit is not procession
but immanence or the "foundation of Being." Whereas the Father is
the "emptying of Being" and the Son is "Being," the Spirit is the
"foundation of Being."[150] As I explained earlier, this way of distinguishing Father, Son and Holy Spirit potentially leads Panikkar into
the Homoian trap Augustine criticizes in books 5-7. Like Heim,
Panikkar simply offers a highly speculative account of the immanent

---

[145]Ibid., p. 60.
[146]Ibid.
[147]Ibid., p. 62.
[148]Ibid., p. 63.
[149]Ibid., pp. 64-65.
[150]Ibid., p. 63.

Trinity that is inadequately rooted in Scripture.

The economic Trinity. A second problem centers on Panikkar's doctrine of the economic Trinity. According to Panikkar, the triune God is present and active among the religions of the world.[151] The locus of this divine activity is not the outer structures of "religion" but inner spiritual "experience." Jesus Christ does not represent the definitive revelation of the triune God; rather he represents one manifestation of a broader Christ principle. The Holy Spirit is "pushing the christian forward beyond what we call 'christianity', beyond, I am tempted to add, even the institutional and visible Church."[152] The Spirit is leading Christians to abandon a particularistic perspective and to recognize the true experience of "Christ" in others.[153] "And the Son, the Lord under whatever name, is the symbol for this process."[154] The goal of this process is the greater unity of humankind. Connecting Panikkar's doctrine of the economic Trinity to his three spiritualities, we might say that Panikkar posits three economies: an economy of the Father (iconolatry), an economy of the Son (personalism) and an economy of the Spirit (mysticism). These are summarized in table 5.1.

There are numerous problems with Panikkar's account of the economic Trinity. First, Panikkar severs the identification between Jesus of Nazareth and the eternal Son.[155] This move is incompatible with a

---

[151]Ibid., p. 42.

[152]Ibid., p. 57. This claim depends on an important distinction Panikkar makes between Christian experience and the institutional form of the church: "Let us go further: christian 'stripping' should be complete. The faith of the enlightened christian must strip itself of the 'christian religion' as it actually exists and free itself for a fecundation that will affect all religions both ancient and modern. From the sociological and external point of view christianity is only one religion among others. . . . Christian faith, however, lives within time and in the hearts of men. It requires, therefore to be 'incarnated' in a historical form; but what we call christianity is only one form among other possible ones living and realizing the christian faith" (ibid., pp. 3-4).

[153]According to Panikkar, "If we remain attached exclusively to the 'Saviour', to his humanity and historicity, we block, in a manner of speaking, the coming of the Spirit and thus revert to a stage of exclusive iconolatry" (ibid., p. 58).

[154]Ibid.

[155]Gavin D'Costa offers a similar criticism: "Others like Raimundo Panikkar have sought to

Chalcedonian Christology and undermines the very foundation of orthodox teaching on the Trinity. In addition, by positing multiple economies that bypass the redemptive work of Christ, Panikkar divorces the

Table 5.1 Three Economies in Panikkar

Spirituality	Economy	Description
Iconolatry	Economy of the Father	Experience of divine emptiness or transcendence
Personalism	Economy of the Son	Experience of divine relation
Mysticism	Economy of the Spirit	Experience of divine immanence

work of the Trinity in the world from the redemptive missions of the Son and Spirit revealed in Scripture. Ultimately, Panikkar's three economies represent a form of economic tritheism. Furthermore, Panikkar offers a deficient account of the work of the Spirit. He seems to imply that the Spirit is leading people away from Jesus Christ. This is fundamentally incompatible with scriptural teaching regarding the Spirit's unique role in bearing witness to and glorifying the risen Christ (e.g., Jn 15:26-27; 16:7-15; Acts 1:6-9; 4:24-31).[156] Finally, the three economic manifestations of the Trinity Panikkar identifies (i.e., experience of the Father as emptiness, experience of the Son as personal, and experience of the Spirit as immanence) do not fit with the Christian experience of the triune God described in Scripture. According to Panikkar, experiences of the Father and Spirit are funda-

---

rehabilitate a Logos Christology. However, Panikkar makes the Logos a universal revelation, of which Jesus Christ is one instantiation, and then reads other revelations in a like manner. The prioritizing of the economy of salvation in the particularity of Adam and Eve and Jesus and Mary's history is bypassed, and the series of revelations specified in the Conciliar documents is made subordinate to a higher controlling idea of 'Logos'" (Gavin D'Costa, *The Meeting of Religions and the Trinity* [Maryknoll, N.Y.: Orbis, 2000], p. 110; see also Dupuis, *Toward a Christian Theology of Religious Pluralism*, pp. 151-52).

[156]As I noted in chap. 4, Augustine discerns a special significance in the sign through which the bestowal of the Spirit was manifested at Pentecost (i.e., bearing witness to Christ in multiple languages). It offers a proleptic fulfillment of the goal of the Holy Spirit's work—namely, leading people in every nation to believe in Jesus Christ (see *De trinitate* 4.29, 175).

mentally impersonal, while only an experience of the Son is personal. In contrast, Christian experience of Father, Son and Holy Spirit is fundamentally *personal*. For example, each of the divine persons receives worship. On the basis of a speculative understanding of the immanent Trinity, Panikkar outlines a deficient account of the economic Trinity that ultimately undermines the divine economy revealed in Scripture.

An "alien God." Our discussion of the relationship between the economic and the immanent Trinity simply reinforces the impression gleaned from our examination of Panikkar's proposal through the lens of the vestige tradition. Although Barth's wholesale rejection of the vestige tradition may not be warranted, his concerns regarding the danger of positing a "second root" for the doctrine of the Trinity prove to be well founded. According to Barth,

> The moment it is taken seriously it leads plainly and ineluctably into an ambivalent sphere in which in a trice, even with the best will of the world, we are no longer speaking of the God of whom we want to speak and whose traces we meant to find but of some principle of the world or humanity, of some alien God. The original intention was to speak of God's revelation. But what happened was that talk about the world and man, and this talk, understood as talk about God's revelation, necessarily wound up being talk against God's revelation.[157]

Barth offers a fitting description of Panikkar's project. Panikkar posits a second root for the doctrine of the Trinity (non-Christian religious experience) that ultimately swallows up the first (God's self-revelation in Scripture), with the result that he ends up speaking about an "alien God." In order to garner support for his theology of religious experience, Panikkar subtly replaces a Trinity of divine persons (Father, Son and Holy Spirit) with a trinity of transcendence (or emptiness), relationality and immanence.[158]

---

[157]Barth, *Church Dogmatics* 1/1, p. 344.
[158]Striking similarities can be seen to Mark Heim's theology of religious ends on this point.

IMPLICATIONS FOR THE CHRISTIAN THEOLOGY OF RELIGIONS

Assuming that we follow Augustine in accepting, at least in principle, the possibility of reflections of the triune God in the world, at least two implications follow for the Christian theology of religions. First, no epistemic warrant exists for revising our understanding of the Trinity on the basis of discernible triadic structures—whether in religious experience or elsewhere. Such a move not only fails to take into account the epistemic implications of the Creator-creature distinction but it also requires us to abandon Scripture as the foundation for human knowledge of the Trinity (Barth's legitimate concern). Second, no epistemic warrant exists for inferring the salvific validity of non-Christian religions from the discernible presence of various triadic structures. Mark Heim seems to draw this unwarranted inference when he claims that Christians must affirm the validity of religions because "the Trinity represents a universal truth about the way the world and God actually are."[159] Even if we were to acknowledge, for the sake of argument, that vestiges of the Trinity can be discerned in Buddhist religious experience, no warrant exists for inferring the salvific efficacy of Buddhism from this reality. Augustine would acknowledge that reflections of the triune God (albeit in a defaced form) exist every human being qua human being; however, from the presence of a triadic structure (i.e., the divine image), one cannot infer the salvific activity of the triune God. To the extent that trinitarian structures can be discerned in the world through the eyes of faith, they bear witness, dimly and indirectly, to the triune God.

---

[159]Heim, *The Depth of the Riches*, p. 127.

6

RETHINKING THE RELEVANCE
OF THE TRINITY

◆

In his *Church Dogmatics*, Karl Barth insists that the doctrine of the
Trinity should be "decisive and controlling for the whole of dogmatics."[1]
Following Barth's cue, contemporary theologians are attempting to relate the doctrine of Trinity to a wide variety of issues. There are trinitarian accounts of personhood, gender, marriage, political structures,
models of church government, leadership models, therapeutic methods, environmental ethics, human rights and (in the case of this investigation) religious diversity. While this vision is commendable, some of
the specific strategies for implementing it are not. In the preceding
chapters we have examined several substantive attempts to employ trinitarian doctrine as the foundation for a new interpretation of religious
diversity. The purpose of this chapter is to explore the implications of
this study for both terms in my investigation: the theology of religions
and the doctrine of Trinity. First, I will explore the implications of this
study for trinitarian approaches to religious diversity. Then I will consider the implications of this investigation for contemporary attempts
to relate the doctrine of the Trinity to other issues. I will argue that

---

[1]Karl Barth, *Church Dogmatics* 1/1, *The Doctrine of the Word of God*, 2nd ed., trans. G. W. Bromiley (Edinburgh: T & T Clark, 1975), p. 303.

some of the methodological problems documented in chapters three to five are not limited to theological reflection on religious diversity but reflect larger methodological problems in contemporary theology. In the final section I will consider how Augustine might lead us to reconsider the purpose(s) of trinitarian doctrine.

IMPLICATIONS FOR THE CHRISTIAN THEOLOGY OF RELIGIONS

The purpose of this investigation was to examine critically the claim that a proper understanding of the Trinity provides the basis for a new interpretation of religious diversity. To this end I have offered an Augustinian assessment of the trinitarian doctrine in four recent proposals. In chapter three I explored the relationship between the economic Trinity and the immanent Trinity in Mark Heim's trinitarian theology of religious ends. At the root of Heim's proposal is an assumption that the immanent life of the triune God is constituted by three dimensions: "impersonal," "personal" and "communion." These immanent dimensions constitute the ontological foundation for multiple religious ends. I argued that Heim's proposal gains traction only by radically severing the economic Trinity from the immanent Trinity. First, Heim offers a speculative account of the immanent Trinity as constituted by three dimensions that possesses little basis in the economy of salvation revealed in Scripture. Then, on the basis of a speculative understanding of the immanent Trinity, he develops a deficient account of the Trinity in the economy of salvation that undermines the teaching of Scripture. Ultimately, Heim replaces the Trinity of divine persons with a trinity of dimensions that bears little resemblance to the Trinity confessed in the classic creeds.

In chapter four I explored the relations of the divine persons in two proposals: Amos Yong's pneumatological theology of religions and Jacques Dupuis's Christian theology of religious pluralism. Yong's "foundational pneumatology" is predicated on a distinction between an economy of the Son and an economy of the Spirit. Yong rejects all subordination of the Spirit to the Son at the ontological level in order to create space on the economic level for an economy of the Spirit distinct from that of the Son. On the basis of a distinct (read: second) economy of the Spirit, Yong affirms that the Holy Spirit is present and active among non-Christian religions and justifies the use of non-christological criteria for discerning the Spirit's presence. I argued that Yong's distinct economy of the Spirit ultimately severs the two hands of the Father. On trinitarian grounds, Jacques Dupuis argues that non-Christian religions mediate God's saving grace in such a way that they may legitimately be called "channels of salvation." In order to create theological space for other saviors and mediators, Dupuis develops a trinitarian Christology in which Jesus Christ is recognized not as "absolute" Savior but merely as "constitutive" Savior. In this context he insists that God's saving action is not limited to the Christ event; on the contrary, an enduring work of the Logos *asarkos* (distinct from the Logos *ensarkos*) continues following the incarnation. I showed that Dupuis's proposal introduces subordinationism into the Father-Son relationship, undermines the unity of the economy of salvation, and severs the economic and the immanent Trinity.

In chapter five I explored the appeal to vestiges of the Trinity in Raimundo Panikkar's trinitarian account of religious experience. Panikkar claims that the doctrine of the Trinity—an insight not limited to Christians—provides the key to reconciling three irreducible forms of religious experience: "iconolatry," "personalism" and "mysticism." These three forms of spirituality correspond to the divine persons: iconolatry corresponds to the Father; personalism corresponds to the Son; and mysticism corresponds to the Spirit. Ewert Cousins builds on Panikkar's proposal by explicitly linking it to the vestige tradition. He suggests that Panikkar's three forms of spirituality represent a vestige of the Trinity. I argued that Panikkar's approach violates the basic theological grammar of vestige tradition: rather than interpreting created realities in light of the Trinity, Panikkar reinterprets the doctrine of the Trinity on the basis of an empirical analysis of religious experience. I argued that no epistemic warrant exists for reinterpreting the doctrine of the Trinity on the basis of non-Christian religious experience. Moreover, I demonstrated that good reason exists to reject Cousins's claim that iconolatry, personalism and mysticism should be viewed as a vestige of the Trinity. Finally, I argued that Panikkar severs the economic Trinity and the immanent Trinity by severing the identification between Jesus of Nazareth and the eternal Son, affirming multiple economies that bypass the redemptive work of Christ and positing economic manifestations of the triune God, which are incompatible with Christian experience of the Trinity as narrated in Scripture. In order to muster support for his theology of religious experience, Panikkar subtly replaces a Trinity of divine persons (Father, Son and Holy Spirit) with a trinity of divine transcendence (or emptiness), divine relationality and divine immanence.

Current use of trinitarian doctrine in the Christian theology of religions appears to be having a deleterious effect on the doctrine. Under pressure to accommodate religious pluralism, Heim, Dupuis, Yong and Panikkar reinterpret trinitarian doctrine in order to support their constructive accounts of religious diversity. To argue for the validity of other religious ends, Heim substitutes a trinity of dimensions for the Trinity of persons. To argue that non-Christian religions are channels of salvation, Dupuis posits subordination in the immanent life of the triune God. To argue for a distinct economy of the Spirit, Yong severs the two hands of God. To argue for the validity of three irreducible forms of religious experience, Panikkar replaces the Trinity of divine persons with a trinity of emptiness, relationality and immanence.

A more blatant form of the problem of reinterpreting trinitarian doctrine to support a problematic interpretation of religious diversity can be seen in the work of John Hick. In an essay titled "Rethinking Christian Doctrine in Light of Religious Pluralism," Hick suggests that in order for Christians to address the challenge of religious diversity, they do not have to abandon any of the great teachings of the Christian faith.[2] Rather, these "themes" simply need to be "reinterpreted" in ways that are consistent with the affirmation that other religions represent independent ways of experiencing "salvation/liberation." Christians, for example, need not reject "Son of God" language; they simply must understand this language as describing a special servant of God rather than denoting an ontological incarnation. Similarly, "We do not need to reject the idea of the Trinity, but to understand it in its modalistic rather than ontological sense."[3] When we think of Trinity as describing "three ways in which the one God is humanly thought and experienced," no problem exists with affirming "the idea of the Trinity" alongside the validity of non-Christian religions.[4] I am at all not suggesting that the theologians examined in the preceding chapters hold a view of the Trinity similar to that of Hick. Rather, I am pointing out that a similar methodological process seems to be at work—namely, revising trinitarian doctrine in order to affirm (in varying ways) the validity of non-Christian religions.

Inasmuch as the proposals of Heim, Yong, Dupuis and Panikkar are representative of current appeal to trinitarian doctrine in the Christian theology of religions, there seems to be good reason to reject the claim that the doctrine of the Trinity offers a privileged path to a new understanding of religious diversity. On the contrary, an inverse relationship exists between the orthodoxy of the trinitarian doctrine employed and the extent to which trinitarian doctrine can be used to marshal theological support for the validity of non-Christian religions. It appears that some theologians who commend "trinitarian" approaches to the theology of religions appeal to the Trinity precisely to avoid inflecting the discussion of non-Christian religions through other theological loci

---

[2]"In order to continue to be Christians in a religiously plural world, we do not have to reject any of the great traditional themes of Christian thought; but we do need to use them in ways that are appropriate to our own situation in a world which has become consciously one" (John Hick, "Rethinking Christian Doctrine in the Light of Religious Pluralism," in *Christianity and the Wider Ecumenism.*, ed. Peter C. Phan [New York: Paragon House, 1990], p. 101).

[3]Ibid., p. 101.

[4]Ibid., p. 98.

like the doctrines of sin and salvation. The proposals of Heim and Panikkar reflect this problematic tendency.[5]

Christian reflection on religious diversity—a legitimate and important endeavor—should be inflected through the doctrines of creation, Fall and redemption, and not merely through a speculative account of the immanent Trinity.[6] For example, elements of truth and goodness in the lives of adherents of non-Christian religions (which need not be denied) can be accounted for on the basis of a Christian anthropology informed by the doctrines of creation, common grace and general revelation.[7] Although Scripture criticizes non-Christian religion, Dutch Reformed theologian Herman Bavinck points out, "it is precisely the general revelation it teaches that enables and authorizes us to recognize all elements of truth that are present also in pagan religions."[8] Moreover, while Reformed theologians did not generally connect common grace to non-Christian religions, "an operation of God's Spirit and of his common grace is discernible not only in science and art, morality and law, but also in the religions."[9] Thus, one might—with John Calvin—affirm that there is an "awareness of divinity" (*divinitatis sensum*) or "seed of religion" (*divinitus religionis*) within every human being and that human religious life arises in response to this reality.[10] In the latter

---

[5]Heim does discuss the doctrine of salvation, but all the heavy lifting in his theology of religions is done by the doctrine of the Trinity. Heim uses a speculative account of the immanent Trinity (Trinity as three dimensions) to ground soteriological claims regarding multiple religious ends. Similarly, Panikkar uses a speculative account of the immanent Trinity to ground soteriological claims regarding the legitimacy of three forms of religious experience.

[6]For helpful reflections on the implications of these doctrines for Christian reflection on religious diversity, see Herman Bavinck, *Reformed Dogmatics*, vol. 1, *Prolegomena*, ed. John Bolt, trans. John Vriend (Grand Rapids: Baker Academic, 2003), pp. 314-20. One of the interesting features of Bavinck's systematic theology is the way in which the reality of religious diversity provides a backdrop for his exposition of Christian doctrine. See also Harold A. Netland, *Encountering Religious Pluralism: The Challenge to Christian Faith and Mission* (Downers Grove, Ill.: InterVarsity Press, 2001), pp. 308-48. Netland develops the framework for an evangelical theology of religions drawing upon these doctrines.

[7]"There is no reason to maintain that everything taught by non-Christian religions is false or that there is nothing of value in them" (Netland, *Encountering Religious Pluralism*, p. 333).

[8]Bavinck, *Reformed Dogmatics*, 1:318.

[9]Ibid., p. 319.

[10]John Calvin, *Institutes of the Christian Religion* 1.3.1, ed. John T. McNeill, trans. Ford L. Bat-

context we might view non-Christians religions "as expressions of a genuine, although misguided, search and longing for God" by those who have been created in the image of God.[11] This has important implications for how to relate to followers of other religions. Followers of Christ can relate to adherents of non-Christian religions first and foremost as human beings created in the image of God, and only secondarily in terms of their specific religious identity.[12]

On the other hand, as Harold Netland rightly notes, non-Christian religions should not to be viewed merely as "benign expressions of humanity reaching out to God."[13] The doctrine of sin reminds us that every aspect of human life, including religious life, has been tainted by the Fall.[14] Thus, human religious life is marked by a deep paradox. On the one hand, it can reflect and express a longing for God.[15] On the other hand, it can also reflect and express human rebellion against God. It is striking that some of Jesus' most stinging critiques were directed toward deeply religious people (e.g., the Pharisees).[16] A third biblical theme that must ground a proper understanding of human religious life is the demonic—a theme that Amos Yong legitimately attempts to account for in his theology of religions. While it is certainly wrong to attribute all non-Christian religion to demonic influence, Scripture teaches that "the god of this world has blinded the minds of the unbelievers, to keep them from seeing the light of the gospel of the glory of Christ, who is the image of God" (2 Cor 4:4). Moreover, in the

---

tles (Philadelphia: Westminster Press, 1960), and ibid., 1.4.1. For Calvin this awareness of God grounds human accountability before God: "Yet there is, as the eminent pagan [Cicero] says, no nation so barbarous, no people so savage, that they have not a deep-seated conviction there is a God" (ibid., 1.3.1). Scripture does not teach that this awareness of God is identical for every person and culture. Degrees of understanding vary from person to person and culture to culture (Netland, *Encountering Religious Pluralism*, p. 332).

[11]Netland, *Encountering Religious Pluralism*, p. 334.

[12]Ibid., pp. 333-34.

[13]Ibid., p. 334.

[14]After reminding his readers that God has planted a "seed of religion" (*divinitus religionis*) within every human being, Calvin explains that all people "degenerate from true knowledge of [God]" (Calvin, *Institutes of the Christian Religion* 1.4.1).

[15]Netland, *Encountering Religious Pluralism*, p. 335.

[16]Ibid.

context of exhorting believers not to eat food offered to idols, Paul reminds his readers "that what pagans sacrifice they offer to demons and not to God. I do not want you to be participants with demons" (1 Cor 10:20).[17]

Because they have rebelled against God, all human beings—including adherents of non-Christian religions—stand in need of the redemption that is initiated by the Father, accomplished by the incarnate Son and applied by the Holy Spirit. The church plays a central role in God's redemptive plan as it graciously and courageously presents Jesus Christ, in word and deed, to all people in every nation as the way, the truth and the life (Mt 28:18-20).[18] Theological reflection on non-Christian religions should support this mandate rather than subverting it.

Do the foregoing criticisms mean that the doctrine of the Trinity has no relevance to a Christian theology of religions? Not at all. The doctrine of the Trinity offers a definitive answer to the question of the identity of God.[19] Furthermore, inasmuch as inseparable links exist between Trinity and gospel, Trinity and Scripture, as well as Trinity and church, this doctrine has great relevance to an evangelical theology of religions. Barth was right: the doctrine of the Trinity

---

[17]Netland points out that one common form of deception involves "the common tendency to blur the distinction between the Creator and the creature. Eve was tempted by the suggestion that she, a mere creature, could become like God (Gen 3:4-5). The tendency to blur the distinction between God and humankind—either to bring God down to our level or to deify human beings—is a common feature of religion and can be found in the polytheistic religions of the ancient world as well as in many modern-day traditions" (ibid., p. 336). Augustine would agree that distortions in our understanding of God often involve blurring the Creator-creature distinction (De trinitate 1.1, 65).

[18]One of the recurring objections to the Christian faith is that Christianity is exclusive and intolerant. Underlying this objection is an assumption that Jesus Christ cannot possibly represent the focal point for human unity and that some form of religious pluralism (a la John Hick) offers the only hope for the unity of humankind. For a helpful critique of this assumption, see Gavin D'Costa, The Meeting of Religions and the Trinity (Maryknoll, N.Y.: Orbis, 2000); Ajith Fernando, The Supremacy of Christ (Wheaton, Ill.: Crossway, 1995); Lesslie Newbigin, The Gospel in a Pluralist Society (Grand Rapids: Eerdmans, 1989); and Netland, Encountering Religious Pluralism, pp. 181-307.

[19]See Kevin J. Vanhoozer, "Does the Trinity Belong in a Theology of Religions? On Angling in the Rubicon and the 'Identity' of God," in The Trinity in a Pluralistic Age, ed. Kevin J. Vanhoozer (Grand Rapids: Eerdmans, 1997), p. 70.

should be "decisive and controlling" for Christian theologian reflection. Every Christian theology of religions contains implicit trinitarian assumptions regardless of whether the doctrine of the Trinity is mentioned. Moreover, every Christian theology of religions should be *explicitly* trinitarian. Despite their many weaknesses Heim, Yong, Dupuis and Panikkar are to be commended for explicitly attempting to relate trinitarian doctrine to the theology of religions. A (proper) trinitarian approach to the Christian theology of religions has several benefits. First, it keeps the issue of religious truth central in a cultural context in which truth is often seen as relative to the individual. The triune God as confessed in Scripture and creeds and worshiped in the Christian church is not merely one manifestation of an unknown divine reality (as pluralists like frequently John Hick assert). Second, a trinitarian approach keeps Jesus Christ central. Not only does orthodox trinitarianism depend on a high Christology that affirms Christ as fully God and fully human, forever joined in one person, but the incarnate Son is also at the center of the trinitarian economy. It is ironic that some Christian theologians have attempted to use trinitarian approaches to undermine christological approaches to religious diversity. Third, a trinitarian approach holds together the work of the Son and the Spirit within a single economy of salvation—an economy of salvation that has as its goal drawing men and women into the life of the triune God. Pneumatological approaches like that of Amos Yong sever the work of the Spirit from the work of the Son (and Father) resulting in a kind of economic bitheism. What God has joined together let no one draw asunder! Finally, a trinitarian approach reinforces the mission of the church by reminding us that the missionary character of the church (which it cannot surrender without ceasing to be the church) is rooted in the immanent life of triune God.[20] The

---

[20]"The sending of the church to the world is a continuation of the Father's sending of the Son and the Spirit. It is the aim of these sending operations to awaken faith, to baptize, and to start new communities of discipleship. The Holy Spirit leads the church to open new fields of mission, continuing the apostolic history that began at Pentecost in Jerusalem. . . . Should the church today continue to evangelize the nations in the name of the triune God? That is basi-

sending of the church is rooted in the dual sendings of the Son and the Spirit. Just as the Father sent the Son into the world, so the Son sends his followers into the world. The Spirit, who is sent into the world by the Father and the Son, bears witness to the Son by preparing the way for and empowering the witness of the church regarding the person and work of Christ. The work of the triune God among adherents of other religions must be understood in the context of the *missio Dei*.[21] In these ways the doctrine of the Trinity provides a foundational framework for Christian reflection on religious diversity.

Perhaps one the most pressing questions raised by this study for the future of the Christian theology of religions concerns the question, Whose Trinity? Stephen Williams (rightly) notes that, missing from many trinitarian proposals in the theology of religions is any susbtantive discussion of criteria for what constitutes the basis for a legitimate (i.e., orthodox) understanding of the Trinity. Commenting on several recent trinitarian proposals, Williams observes, "One striking feature of both of these contributions [Panikkar and Smart-Konstantine] is the absence of any discussion of the question of criteria. The criteriological question that must be answered is this: what enables something to

---

cally the same question as: Should the church continue to be the church? The church is constituted by the structure of the trinitarian mission of God in the history of salvation. The church is the eschatological creation of God's Word serving to unite all humankind" (Carl E. Braaten, "The Triune God: the Source and Model of Christian Unity and Mission," *Missiology* 18 [1990]: 425).

[21]The term *missio Dei* emerged out of a missionary conference in Willingen, Germany, in 1952. It emphasizes, first and foremost, that mission is rooted in and reflects God's nature and will (based on the assumption that the economic Trinity corresponds to and closely reflects the immanent Trinity). "The *ultimate basis* of mission is the triune God—the Father who created the world and sent his Son by the Holy Spirit to be our salvation. The *proximate basis* of mission is the redemption of the Son by his life, death and resurrection, and the *immediate power* of mission is the Holy Spirit. It is, in trinitarian terms, a *missio Dei*. Thus mission is based on the will, movement, and action of the grace and love of God—Father, Son and Holy Spirit" (John Thompson, *Modern Trinitarian Perspectives* [New York: Oxford University Press, 1994], p. 72). Although Barth's trinitarian theology may have influenced the historical development of the *missio Dei* at Willingen, the roots of a *missio Dei* can be found in Augustine (see Edward W. Poitras, "St. Augustine and the *Missio Dei*: A Reflection on Mission at the Close of the Twentieth Century," *Mission Studies* 32 [1999]: 28-46).

count as a formulation of the doctrine of the Trinity?"[22] Although theologians like Heim, Dupuis, Yong and Panikkar may agree that the Trinity offers the key to understanding religious diversity, no consensus currently exists among them as to *whose* doctrine of the Trinity holds the key. Each offers a different account of this doctrine as constitutive ground for a particular understanding of religious diversity. By appealing to the trinitarian theology of Augustine (whose theology does not stand in sharp contrast to that of the Cappadocians), this study offers a potential answer.

Finally, many of the proposals examined in this study sever intrinsic links that exist between Trinity and Scripture, Trinity and church, as well as Trinity and the redemption accomplished by the incarnate Son and applied by the Spirit. This process is abetted by focusing exclusively on the doctrine of the immanent Trinity and bracketing (or worse, reinterpreting) the doctrine of economic Trinity. Appropriate trinitarian approaches should reinforce rather than sever these links.

SIMILAR TRINITARIAN PROBLEMS IN CONTEMPORARY THEOLOGY

We might be tempted to assume that the trinitarian problems outlined in chapters three to five are limited to a select group of theologians reflecting on religious diversity. Unfortunately, such an assumption would be mistaken. To the contrary, some of the trinitarian problems documented here reflect broader patterns in contemporary theology. In the discussion that follows, I will focus on one specific methodological problem related to use of immanent Trinity. Namely, in their quest to relate trinitarian doctrine to a wide variety of contemporary issues, many theologians employ a doctrine of the immanent Trinity as a blue-

---

[22]Stephen Williams, "The Trinity and 'Other Religions,'" in *The Trinity in a Pluralistic Age*, ed. Kevin J. Vanhoozer (Grand Rapids: Eerdmans, 1997), p. 28. Putting the question a slightly different way, Williams asks, "How do we justify a claim that we have offered a reformulation of the doctrine of the Trinity as opposed to offering something different? Panikkar and Smart use trinitarian vocabulary and triadic patterns, but never once address, let alone answer, this question" (ibid., p. 29).

print for everything from political structures to the proper functioning of the environment.[23] First, I will briefly survey several recent attempts to relate trinitarian doctrine to society, politics, ecology, marriage and mission. Then, I will identify six methodological problems that arise from this type of direct appeal to the immanent Trinity. I will not be able to develop these examples at length or provide in-depth critique. I simply want to draw attention to problems related to use of the immanent Trinity.

Immanent Trinity as blueprint: Contemporary examples. Trinity and society. In *Holy Trinity, Perfect Community*, Leonardo Boff presents the "perfect community" of the Father, Son and Holy Spirit as the blueprint for societal relations.[24] Boff wants to see an earthly society developed that will reflect the perichoretic unity of the divine persons: "We seek a society that will be more an image and likeness of the Trinity, that will better reflect on the earth the trinitarian communion of heaven, and that will make it easier for us to know the mystery of communion of the divine three."[25] Boff suggests that the longing for egalitarian forms of society finds its basis in the communion of the divine persons.[26]

Reflecting on the relationships of men and women in society, Margaret Farley argues that "the very life of the Trinitarian God" should be the "ultimate normative model" for male-female relationships.[27] In the latter context "equality, mutuality and reciprocity" serve as "a norm against which every pattern of relationship may be measured," as well

---

[23]As Kathryn Tanner explains, "When contemporary theologians want to form judgments about social and political matters they often turn immediately to the trinity for guidance. Rather than Christology, a theology of the trinity is enlisted to support particular kinds of human community.... What the Trinity is like is thought to establish how human societies should be organized" (Kathryn Tanner, *Christ the Key*, Current Issues in Theology [Cambridge: Cambridge University Press, 2009], p. 207).

[24]Leonardo Boff, *Holy Trinity, Perfect Community* (Maryknoll, N.Y.: Orbis, 2000), p. 66.

[25]Ibid., p. xiv.

[26]Ibid., p. xiii.

[27]Margaret A. Farley, "New Patterns of Relationship: Beginnings of a Moral Revolution," *Theological Studies* 36 (1975): 645.

as a goal toward which every relationship moves.[28] Similar themes regarding the Trinity as model for societal relations are echoed in the writings of many contemporary theologians.

Trinity and politics. In *Trinity and the Kingdom,* Jürgen Moltmann argues that the doctrine of the Trinity provides a blueprint for proper political structures.[29] Moltmann claims that Christians won over educated members of the Roman Empire by proclaiming a deficient doctrine of God.[30] Their philosophical *monotheism* proved to be a "seductive religious-political ideology" when it was used to support the hegemony of the Roman Empire: "The universal ruler in Rome had only to be the image and correspondence of the universal ruler in heaven."[31] A more adequate doctrine of Trinity begins by recognizing that the unity of the Father, Son and Holy Spirit is not found in "the homogeneity of the one divine substance" but "in the *perichoresis* of the divine Persons."[32] Properly understood, *perichoresis* rules out all subordination within the divine life.[33] A political theology that is explicitly Christian will support structures that reflect the perichoretic unity (and equality) of the Father, Son and Holy Spirit.[34] The doctrine of the Trinity is a "doctrine of freedom" inasmuch as it counters political monotheism: "It is only when the doctrine of the Trinity vanquishes the monotheistic notion of the great universal monarch in heaven, and his divine patriarchs in the world, that earthly rulers, dictators and tyrants cease to find any justifying religious archetypes any more."[35] Similarly, a clerical theology that reflects the perichoretic unity of the divine persons will not allow the unity and authority of the church to be concentrated in a single person (e.g., a pope).[36] In contrast, "the

---

[28]Ibid., p. 646.
[29]Jürgen Moltmann, *The Trinity and the Kingdom* (Minneapolis: Fortress, 1993), p. 150.
[30]Ibid., p. 130.
[31]Ibid., p. 131.
[32]Ibid., p. 150.
[33]Ibid., pp. 175-76.
[34]Ibid., pp. 198-200.
[35]Ibid, p. 197.
[36]Ibid., p. 201.

doctrine of the Trinity constitutes the church as a 'community free of dominion.'"[37] The forms of church government that best reflect the social Trinity include "the presbyterial and synodal church order based on brotherly advice."[38]

Trinity and ecology. In an essay titled "Trinitarian Ecology" David Williams asserts that the doctrine of the Trinity provides a model for the proper functioning of the environment.[39] According to Williams, "God's very being as immanent Trinity also has ecological implications."[40] Although it may be too much "to expect to see every facet of Trinitarian belief as reflected in ecology," the "essential nature of the Trinity is to be found, and is indeed valuable in understanding how the world should interrelate."[41] The central insight of this doctrine is that both unity and distinctiveness must coexist in the divine life.[42] Just as distinctiveness and oneness are equally essential to the divine life such that "neither may be affirmed at the expense of the other," so "the heart of a correct ecology" is found in a proper balance between interrelatedness and diversity. Just as interrelatedness exists among the divine persons, so interrelatedness must obtain among living things. Furthermore, just as intratrinitarian relationships are stable and eternal, so also the world should have a stable ecosystem.[43] According to Williams, important parallels exist between the two great trinitarian heresies (Arianism and Sabellianism) and improper attitudes toward the environment. For example, just as Arianism improperly subordinated the Son to the Father, "Ecological Arianism" improperly subordinates certain elements of the created order to human beings by failing to recognize that human beings and the rest of creation "share an equality of essence" inasmuch as

---

[37]Ibid., p. 202.
[38]Ibid.
[39]David T. Williams, "Trinitarian Ecology," *Scottish Bulletin of Evangelical Theology* 18 (2000): 142-59.
[40]Ibid., p. 148.
[41]Ibid., p. 149.
[42]Ibid.
[43]Ibid., p. 153.

all things share "life."[44] A correct understanding of the Trinity can lead to greater care for the environment.

Trinity and marriage. In *Sexuality and the Christian Body: Their Way into the Triune God*, Eugene Rogers argues that Christian marriage—heterosexual or homosexual—should mirror the love of the Father for the Son, to which the Spirit bears witness.[45] Within creation, God "enables distant but appropriate correlates to the trinitarian love-in-freedom also for human love, structured by space and time."[46] Marriage, therefore, "bears an analogy to the trinitarian life" within the confines of time and space.[47] Because the ultimate analog for marriage is the life of the triune God, Rogers claims that heterosexual *and* homosexual marriages should be recognized as legitimate.[48] Similarly, in an essay titled "The Trinitarian Vocation of the Gay Community," Daniel Helminiak argues the intratrinitarian life of God constitutes the model for gay and lesbian Christians.[49] Helminiak identifies four parallels exist between the intratrinitarian relations and gay/lesbian relations: (1) relations in which gender is not an issue, (2) relations that constitute persons as persons, (3) relations in which persons are equal and (4) relations in which personal identity is not lost.[50] Gay and lesbian persons are called "to contribute to the fulfillment of a central aspect of Christ's work, to reproduce on earth the inner-trinitarian life of God in heaven."[51]

---

[44]Ibid., p. 154.

[45]Eugene F. Rogers Jr., *Sexuality and the Christian Body: Their Way into the Triune God* (Oxford: Blackwell, 1999).

[46]Ibid., pp. 202-3.

[47]Ibid., p. 201.

[48]"The 'family resemblance' by which same-sex marriages deserve to be called marriages is not primarily their resemblance to opposite-sex unions, although the family resemblance is close enough, with children or without. The family resemblance by which same-sex unions deserve to be called marriages is the same resemblance by which Christians justify calling opposite-sex unions marriages: their resemblance to the marriage of Christ and the Church" (Rogers, *Sexuality and the Christian Body*, p. 211).

[49]Daniel A. Helminiak, "The Trinitarian Vocation of the Gay Community," *Pastoral Psychology* 36 (1987): 100.

[50]Ibid., pp. 105-7.

[51]Ibid., p. 109.

Trinity and mission. Wanting to relate Trinity and mission, David Bjork asserts that the perichoretic unity of the divine persons provides a blueprint for how Protestant missionaries (such as himself) should relate to Catholics in post-Christian France: "My thesis is that a proper understanding of how the one, living and true God has manifested himself as a trinity of persons within a fundamental and absolute unity (as described by the Greek word *perichoresis*) furnishes us with a paradigm which might inform missionary endeavors in post-Christendom lands."[52] To this end Bjork identifies five missional implications that follow from a proper understanding of the unity of the divine persons. First, unity between evangelicals and Catholics in France must be "interpersonal, not organizational."[53] Second, unity between evangelicals and Catholics should be marked by "constantly interacting cooperation."[54] Just as Father, Son and Spirit work together in the economy of salvation, so also Catholics and evangelicals should work together. Third, the form of unity that exists must "preserve intact the identity and properties of each other."[55] As a result, two distinct forms of witness in France (Catholic and evangelical) are both legitimate. Fourth, unity between evangelicals and Catholics must "build interdependence whereby the members are defined based on their relationships with the others."[56] One group (e.g., evangelicals) should not try to define itself apart from another (e.g., Catholics). Finally, unity reflecting divine perichoresis should involve "pouring ourselves into the other."[57]

Immanent Trinity as blueprint: Methodological problems. For Leonardo Boff the immanent Trinity offers a blueprint for the ideal society. For Jürgen Moltmann, the immanent Trinity offers a blueprint for proper political and ecclesial structures; for David Williams, the proper

---

[52]David Bjork, "Toward a Trinitarian Understanding of Mission in Post-Christendom Lands," *Missiology* 27 (1999): 232.
[53]Ibid., p. 237.
[54]Ibid., p. 238.
[55]Ibid., p. 239.
[56]Ibid.
[57]Ibid., p. 240.

functioning of the environment; for Daniel Helminiak, for gay marriage; for David Bjork, for relations between Protestant missionaries and Catholic leaders. Each proposal employs a similar methodology: they appeal directly to some aspect of God's immanent life (e.g., perichoresis) in order to ground specific claims (e.g., necessity of egalitarian political structures).[58] There are at least six problems with direct movement from a doctrine of the immanent Trinity to created realities as in these proposals.[59]

First, apart from explicit scriptural warrant, how do we know what implications follow from specific metaphysical features of God's immanent life? Consider the triunity of God. Theologians like Moltmann frequently argue that hierarchical political and ecclesial structures are incompatible with the perichoretic unity and equality of the three divine persons. But why not argue that the threeness of God constitutes the blueprint for governmental structures with three "equal" yet "distinct" branches of authority: an executive branch (corresponding to the Father), a legislative branch (corresponding to the Word) and a judicial branch (corresponding to the Spirit, who is described in John's Gospel as "Counselor")? On this basis we could claim that the American government is an image of the Trinity! Apart from specific scriptural guidance, how do we determine what implications follow from God's inner architecture? Mark Heim makes just such an unwarranted move when he argues that *plurality* in the divine life grounds the validity of a *plu-*

---

[58]In the analysis that follows my concern lies not with the content of these proposals but rather with their trinitarian methodology. It is important to distinguish the use of trinitarian doctrine in these proposals from the constructive claims they make. Christians, for example, should be concerned about the environment and good theological reasons exist for affirming creation care. Nevertheless, David Williams's use of the Trinity—as I will demonstrate below—is deeply problematic.

[59]For a discussion of problems with modeling human relations after the immanent Trinity, see Tanner, *Christ the Key*, pp. 207-46. As Tanner explains, "the applicability of relations among persons of the trinity to human relationships is not so simple or direct" as is often assumed (ibid., p. 208). Although Tanner's discussion focuses on the application of trinitarian relations to politics, several problems she identifies parallel those I identify below. For example, she points out that many attempts to employ trinitarian relations as a model for human relations do not take into account the implications of the Creator-creature distinction nor do they take into consideration the reality that human relations (unlike divine relations) are marked by sin.

rality of religious perspectives. According to Heim, "Trinitarian conviction rules out the view that among all the possible claimed manifestations of God, one narrow strand is authentic."[60] As a result, "Christians
can find validity in other religions because of the conviction that the
Trinity represents a universal truth about the way the world and God
actually are."[61]

Second, many proposals which treat the immanent Trinity as a blueprint fail to take into account the implications of the Creator-creature
distinction.[62] The Creator-creature distinction disallows direct movement from divine relations to human relations. As Miroslav Volf rightly
notes, there can be no straight line from Trinity to society. Certain
"mediations" are required because human beings "can correspond to
God only in a *creaturely* fashion."[63] An egregious example of violating
the Creator-creature distinction can be seen in the case of David Williams's attempt to ground environmental ethics in trinitarian doctrine.
Williams not only argues that the immanent life of the triune God offers a model for the proper functioning of the environment, but he also
posits direct parallels between trinitarian heresies like Arianism and
Sabellianism and improper ecological attitudes.[64] Williams moves directly from divine life to creaturely life in ways that violate the Creator-
creature distinction.

This brings us to a third problem with treating the immanent Trinity as blueprint—namely, the problem of projection. Karen Kilby sug-

---

[60]S. Mark Heim, *The Depth of the Riches: A Trinitarian Theology of Religious Ends*, Sacra Doctrina (Grand Rapids: Eerdmans, 2001), p. 127.

[61]Ibid.

[62]"No matter how close the similarities between human and divine persons, and between a human society and the unity of the trinity, differences always remain—God is not us—and this sets up the major problem for theologies that want to base conclusions about human relationships on the trinity" (Tanner, *Christ the Key*, p. 221).

[63]Miroslav Volf, *After Our Likeness: The Church as the Image of the Trinity* (Grand Rapids: Eerdmans, 1998), p. 199. Although Volf acknowledges these limitations *in principle*, he appears to abandon them at crucial points *in practice*. His critique of the ecclesiologies of Joseph Ratzinger (Benedict XVI) (Catholic) and John Zizioulas (Orthodox) appears to draw a straight line from particular (mis)conceptions of the immanent Trinity to particular (mis)understandings of the church.

[64]See Williams, "Trinitarian Ecology," p. 154.

gests that this problem can be seen most clearly in the work of some contemporary social trinitarians who treat the perichoretic unity of the divine persons as a "resource for combating individualism, patriarchy, and oppressive forms of political and ecclesiastical organization."[65] Appeals to perichoresis among social trinitarians frequently involve three steps.[66] First, perichoresis is identified as that which constitutes the unity of Father, Son and Holy Spirit. Next, perichoresis is defined by projecting some aspect of human relatedness into God's immanent life. Finally, perichoresis is commended as an exciting resource Christians have to offer the world. "Projection, then, is particularly problematic in at least some social theories of the Trinity because what is projected onto God is immediately reflected back onto the world, and this reverse projection is said to be what is in fact *important* about the doctrine."[67] Catherine LaCugna offers a similar analysis:

> In the desire to remedy some of the great problems of the day, the temptation is to use the doctrine of the Trinity as "an autonomous datum and even premise for theology" that is applied to a particular problem, for example, unequal distribution of resources. It is as if the goal is to figure out God "*in se*"—the number of persons, relations and processions and how they are configured—and then project this "intradivine" structure onto human community, or vice versa. But as we have seen, this strategy, whether it supports a hierarchical *or* egalitarian vision, inevitably appears to be a transcendental projection of human preferences onto God.[68]

The problem of projection can be clearly seen in the theology of religions. Whereas some social trinitarians project aspects of human relatedness into the immanent life of the triune God, Panikkar projects

---

[65]Karen Kilby, "Perichoresis and Projection: Problems with Social Doctrines of the Trinity," *New Blackfriars* 81 (2000): 438.

[66]Ibid., p. 442.

[67]Ibid.

[68]Catherine Mowry LaCugna, *God for Us: The Trinity and Christian Life* (San Francisco: HarperSanFrancisco, 1992), pp. 379-80. Readers will need to decide for themselves whether LaCugna adequately takes this problem into account in her own constructive proposal.

human religious experience into the immanent life of the triune God and then reinterprets the doctrine of the Trinity on this basis. This represents at least one instance in which Ludwig Feuerbach's critique was right on target: when this kind of projection takes place, theology is ineluctably reduced to anthropology.[69] We are no longer speaking about God but only about ourselves.[70]

Fourth, by treating the *immanent* Trinity as a ready-made blueprint for various societal structures, some theologians sever moorings between the Trinity and God's self-revelation in Scripture. In the examples outlined earlier, a straight line is drawn from the immanent Trinity to created realities in ways that bypass (and, in some cases, undermine) the economy of salvation revealed in Scripture. The immanent Trinity is established as a paradigm and then "oughts" are directly deduced from metaphysical aspects of God's life apart from scriptural reflection. As Alister McGrath rightly notes, problems inevitably arise any time trinitarian speculation "los[es] its moorings in the language of Scripture."[71] For example, moorings to Scripture are severed when theologians build an entire social project on a speculative account of the unity of the divine persons (e.g., *perichoresis*). Another example of severed moorings can be seen in the attempt to use trinitarian doctrine to ground the legitimacy of same-sex unions. Since both same-sex and opposite-sex unions are said to mirror the perichoretic love of the Father, Son and Holy Spirit (who themselves are beyond gender), both types of unions (gay and straight) are said to be legitimate. Severed moorings between Trinity and Scripture are prevalent in theology of

---

[69]See Ludwig Feuerbach, *The Essence of Christianity*, trans. George Eliot (New York: Harper, 1957).

[70]Karl Barth rightly recognized the significance of Feuerbach's critique. See Barth's introductory essay to the 1957 edition of Feuerbach's book (ibid., pp. x-xxxii). Discussions of Feuerbach's critique can also be found at various points in the *Church Dogmatics* (see Karl Barth, *Church Dogmatics* 2/1, *The Doctrine of God*, trans. T. H. L. Parker et al. [Edinburgh: T & T Clark, 1957], pp. 292-93, 448-50, 467).

[71]Alister McGrath, "The Doctrine of the Trinity: An Evangelical Reflection," in *God the Holy Trinity: Reflections on Christian Faith and Practice*, ed. Timothy George (Grand Rapids: Baker Academic, 2006), p. 30.

religions. For example, Michael Ipgrave's trinitarian approach to interfaith dialogue depends on a fundamental distinction between "Trinity" and "trinity."[72] The former represents the Father, Son and Holy Spirit of Christian revelation, while the latter "serves as a generic name for any triadic account of divinity sharing to some recognizable extent in the patterns of Christian understanding of the Trinity."[73] The heavy lifting in Ipgrave's proposal is done not by the Christian doctrine of the Trinity but by the trinity. More specifically, Ipgrave employs six structural elements of trinity (plurality, personality, threeness, equality, necessity and immanence) that have been severed from the Trinity of Christian confession and worship.

Moorings to Scripture are also severed when "trinitarian" doctrine is used to undermine key christological or pneumatological claims. An example of this can be seen in a development that took place within the ecumenical movement in the late 1960s. There was a conscious shift away from a Christocentric understanding of mission toward a trinitarian understanding of mission. In response to Konrad Raiser's endorsement of this shift, Lesslie Newbigin expressed the following concern:

> What gives ground for anxiety here is the positing of a trinitarian model *against* the model of Christocentric universalism. . . . To set a trinitarian paradigm over against a Christological one, and to commend it as corresponding to an egalitarian climate of opinion, would surely be a disastrous mistake.[74]

It was only through its recognition that Jesus is Lord that the church eventually came to confess that God is Trinity.[75] Similar problems can be seen in the work of Dupuis and Yong. Dupuis uses trinitarian claims to undermine Christian teaching regarding the person and work of Christ, while Yong uses trinitarian claims to undermine Christian

---

[72]Michael Ipgrave, *Trinity and Inter Faith Dialogue: Plenitude and Plurality*, Religions and Discourse 14 (New York: Peter Lang, 2003).

[73]Ibid., p. 12.

[74]Lesslie Newbigin, "The Trinity as Public Truth," in *The Trinity in a Pluralistic Age*, ed. Kevin J. Vanhoozer (Grand Rapids: Eerdmans, 1997), p. 7.

[75]Ibid., p. 8.

teaching about the unity of the two hands of the Father.[76] Only when theological reflection is "bound by the actual details of God's self-revelation in economy" will the kind of problems identified above be avoided.[77]

Fifth, at best, appeals to the immanent Trinity support only the most general claims. We can say, "God is one; therefore, the church should be one" and this is true (cf. Jn 17).[78] But what specific ecclesial structures can we say legitimately reflect (or do not reflect) divine unity?[79] We can say, "Father, Son and Holy Spirit love each other; therefore, Christians should love each other," and this is true. But how do we know what this love should look like? The answer is not difficult. Scripture directs us to imitate the Father, Son and Holy Spirit *as they relate to us in the economy of salvation* (i.e., the economic Trinity). Notice how Paul directs us to imitate the *incarnate* Son: "Therefore be imitators of God, as beloved children. And walk in love, *as Christ loved us and gave himself up for us, a fragrant offering and sacrifice to God*" (Eph 5:1-2, italics added). The model for Christian love is the self-giving of the Son on the cross (i.e., in the economy of salvation). The model and motivation for Christian forgiveness is also found in the cross: "As the

---

[76]Perhaps the most blatant attempt to use trinitarian doctrine to undermine key christological claims can be seen in John Hick's call for a "Copernican revolution" in which he urges Christians to move from being Christocentric to theocentric (see John Hick, *God and the Universe of Faiths: Essays in the Philosophy of Religion* [London: Macmillan, 1973], pp. 120-32).

[77]LaCugna, *God for Us*, p. 365.

[78]From a different angle, it is also helpful to ask, What constitutes the unity Christ prays for in John 17? This unity of the church is not constituted by the church becoming a platonic reflection of the intratrinitarian unity of the Father, Son and Holy Spirit. Rather, this unity is constituted by communion with and participation in the salvific work of the triune God through the mission of the Son and Spirit. Communion—not imitation—is the central focus. Ironically, by treating the immanent Trinity as a model for the church, one (unintentionally) severs Trinity and church (see John Behr, "The Trinitarian Being of the Church," *St. Vladimir's Theological Quarterly* 48 [2004]: 67-88, esp. p. 70).

[79]It is one thing to affirm, in a general sense, that the unity of the church analogically reflects the unity the divine persons (as Jn 17 implies). It is quite another to specify the precise ontological content of this divine unity and then draw a straight line from a speculative conception of this unity to specific directives (e.g., David Bjork's claim that Catholics and Protestants should maintain distinctive ecclesial identities in France on the basis of hypostatic distinction of the divine persons).

Lord has forgiven you, so you also must forgive" (Col 3:13). The blueprint for Christian humility is not some kind of intratrinitarian kenosis (à la Hans Urs von Balthasar) but the *economic* self-emptying of the Son, who "humbled himself by becoming obedient to the point of death, even death on a cross" (Phil 2:8). The model for Christian compassion is the mercy humans experience from their heavenly Father: "Be merciful, even as your Father is merciful" (Lk 6:36).[80] In other words, when Holy Scripture invites us to imitate the Trinity, it directs us toward our relationship with the triune God in redemption. It is a covenantal relation with and experience of the triune God that provides model, motivation and ground for human imitation.[81]

These references to the cross highlight an additional reason why our relationship with the Trinity in the economy of salvation must constitute the focal point for Christian imitation. In this life we imitate God under the condition of sin. No sin marks the immanent life of God. How, therefore, do we know what it looks like to imitate God under sin? The answer is found by observing how the triune God relates to rebellious human beings. Thus, it should not be surprising that Ephesians 5:1-2 exhorts believers to imitate the love of God expressed in the cross because it is precisely in the cross that we observe God's love displayed under the condition of sin. When we forgive those who sin against us we are not directly imitating the relations among the Father, Son and Holy Spirit *in se* (as no forgiveness marks these relationships); instead we are imitating the forgiveness we ourselves have experienced from the triune God in the economy of salvation (i.e., the economic Trinity).

---

[80]In the immediate context, it is clear that Jesus has in mind the mercy God expresses toward rebellious human beings (i.e., economic Trinity). Christians are to love their enemies specifically because God "is kind to the ungrateful and the evil" (Lk 6:35).

[81]Kathryn Tanner rightly argues that we should not think about the relationship between Trinity and humanity in terms of the Trinity providing an external model but rather in terms of human beings sharing in the life of the Trinity: "The trinity in the economy does not close the gap by making trinitarian relations something like human ones, but by actually incorporating the human into its very own life through the incarnation. We are therefore not called to imitate the Trinity by way of the incarnation but brought to participate in it" (Tanner, *Christ the Key,* p. 234).

These themes come together nicely in 1 John 3:16: "By this we know love, that he laid down his life for us, and we ought to lay down our lives for the brothers." From an epistemological perspective John reminds us that the cross (i.e., the economic self-revelation of the triune God) enables us to comprehend the nature of true love. From an ontological perspective it is clear, in the broader context, that the love we experience in the cross (analogically) reflects the immanent life of God. John tells us that "God is love" (1 Jn 4:8). Nevertheless, we only know about this love, and see it displayed under conditions of sin, through the cross. Moreover, John's ethical injunction ("we ought to lay down our lives for the brothers" [1 Jn 3:16]) is grounded in our experience of Christ laying down his life for us. We might say that an *imitatio trinitatis* proves to be an *imitatio Christi*.[82]

Finally, in many cases, other Christian doctrines seem far more germane to many of the issues these theologians are attempting to address. Against the direction of a growing consensus, I have argued that no road exists from the Christian doctrine of the Trinity to an affirmation of the validity of non-Christian religions, and that issues surrounding religious diversity are better inflected through the doctrines of creation, Fall and redemption. A similar point could be made about ecology. Are not the doctrines of creation, Fall and redemption more relevant to a Christian understanding of the environment than direct appeal to the immanent life of the triune God? The same could be said regarding marriage. Are not the doctrines of creation (which provides the pattern for marriage) and the Fall (which highlights distortions of this pattern) more relevant to questions regarding the legitimacy of same-sex unions than direct appeal to the immanent Trinity? Why must ethical claims

---

[82]As Kathryn Tanner explains, "Jesus' relations with other people constitute the sort of human relations that the economy of the trinity itself specifies. Jesus' way of life toward other people as we share in it *is* the trinitarian form of human social life" (Tanner, *Christ the Key*, pp. 236-37). Notice how Augustine emphasizes modeling our lives after Christ: "Thus, to conclude, it is not surprising that scripture should be speaking about the Son when it speaks about wisdom, on account of the model which the image who is equal to the Father provides us with that we may be refashioned to the image of God; for we follow the Son by living wisely" (*De trinitate*, 7.5, p. 223).

be anchored directly in a speculative aspect of trinitarian ontology in order to be legitimate? In many of these proposals the assumption seems to be that if Christians can only understand some aspect of formal trinitarian doctrine (e.g., that the Trinity is a loving community) they will live differently (e.g., be more loving toward others). This assumption rests on a deficient anthropology. According to the New Testament, love arises not from *understanding* some aspect of divine ontology (e.g., *perichoresis*) but from a covenantal *relation* with the triune God. Human beings imitate the Trinity not by following an external model provided by the immanent Trinity but by being drawn into the life of the Trinity through the work of the Son and the Holy Spirit. Finally, as Richard Fermer rightly notes, in many cases the words and actions of Christ seem far more suitable for promoting virtues these theologians want to commend rather than direct appeal to the immanent Trinity.[83]

RETHINKING THE RELEVANCE OF THE TRINITY: AUGUSTINIAN REFLECTIONS

Although the contemporary quest to relate trinitarian doctrine to a wide variety of issues is praiseworthy, some of the methods for executing it are not. It is precisely at this point that Augustine may be able to offer us further assistance. In this final section, I want to consider how Augustine (whose trinitarian theology has—somewhat ironically—been dismissed as irrelevant by his critics) might challenge us to think more clearly about the relevance of trinitarian doctrine.

Six purposes of trinitarian doctrine. The trinitarian teaching of Augustine has value not only in helping evaluate use of the Trinity in the theology of religions but also thinking clearly about how trinitarian doctrine should function. To this end, I will highlight six purposes for trinitarian doctrine.[84]

---

[83]See Richard M. Fermer, "The Limits of Trinitarian Theology as a Methodological Paradigm," *Neue Zeitschrift für Systematische Theologie und Religionsphilosophie* 41 (1999): 186. See also Tanner, *Christ the Key*, pp. 234-46.

[84]Augustine himself does not identify these six purposes. They simply reflect my inductive summary of some of the ways that trinitarian doctrine functions in his theology.

Theological purpose. First and foremost, the doctrine of the Trinity is a teaching about God. We might describe this as the *theo*-logical purpose of the doctrine. It summarizes biblical teaching about God as Father, Son and Holy Spirit in the form of ontological claims and provides a regulative grammar that guides Christian speech addressed *to* God (e.g., worship and prayer) as well as Christian speech *about* God (e.g., theology, preaching, evangelism).[85] The theological purpose of this doctrine can be subtly obscured when its significance is reduced to its ability to provide a blueprint for ecclesial, societal or interreligious structures.

Doxological purpose. A second purpose of trinitarian doctrine might be described as "doxological." Why is it important that we think rightly about the Trinity? Simply so we may rightly honor the triune God in our worship. As Claude Welch explains, the doctrine of the Trinity "has importance in determining the pattern of worship so that it shall be truly directed to him who is known to us in Christ."[86] To state it negatively: if Christ is not God, then Christian worship of Christ is nothing short of blasphemous idolatry. Trinitarian teaching shapes the liturgical practices of the church including gospel proclamation, baptism, prayer, worship, preaching and communion.[87]

---

[85]By invoking the image of doctrine as "grammar," I am not suggesting that the doctrine of the Trinity should be seen merely as a second-order doctrine that structures Christian belief. The doctrine of the Trinity should also be seen as a first-order doctrine that makes ontological claims about the nature of the triune God. The theological purpose of this doctrine is undermined when it is reduced to a second-order grammar. On this point, see Matthew Levering, *Scripture and Metaphysics: Aquinas and the Renewal of Trinitarian Theology*, Challenges in Contemporary Theology (Malden, Mass.: Blackwell, 2004), esp. pp. 236-41; and Levering, "Friendship and Trinitarian Theology: Response to Karen Kilby," *International Journal of Systematic Theology* 9 (2007): 39-54. It is clear in *De trinitate* that Augustine is not merely interested in articulating a coherent trinitarian grammar; he views his trinitarian teaching as making first-order claims about God (without in any way undermining the ultimate incomprehensibility of God). Even in this life, humans are able to know the triune God—albeit in a limited way.

[86]Claude Welch, *In This Name: The Doctrine of the Trinity in Contemporary Theology* (New York: Charles Scribner's, 1952), p. 292.

[87]For discussion of trinitarian nature of the liturgical practices of the church, see Geoffrey Wainwright, *Worship with One Accord: Where Liturgy and Ecumenism Embrace* (New York: Oxford University Press, 1997), pp. 237-50; and Wainwright, *Doxology: The Praise of God in Worship, Doctrine and Life* (New York: Oxford University Press, 1980).

That trinitarian doctrine ultimately serves a doxological purpose can be seen quite clearly in *De trinitate*. Notice how Augustine underscores the necessity of praising God while, at the same time, acknowledging the difficulty of speaking about God:

> Now since we ought to think about the Lord our God always, and can never think about him as he deserves; since at all times we should be praising him and blessing him, and yet no words of ours are capable of expressing him, I begin by asking him to help me understand and explain what I have in mind and to pardon any blunders I may make. (*De trinitate* 5.1, 189)

A concrete example of the doxological role of trinitarian theology can be seen in a dispute that arose between pro-Nicene and anti-Nicene factions in Greek-speaking churches of the fourth century. Alongside the doxology "Glory to the Father *through* [*dia*] the Son *in* [*en*] the Holy Spirit," Basil of Caesarea (and other pro-Nicene Christians) also used the following doxology: "Glory to the Father *with* [*meta*] the Son *together with* [*syn*] the Holy Spirit."[88] Anti-Nicenes asserted that the latter doxology was inappropriate and should not be used in public worship. In response, Basil argues that both doxologies are necessary in order to express suitable honor to the Father, Son and Holy Spirit. The first doxology (using the Greek prepositions *dia* and *en*) is helpful in expressing the economic activity of the divine persons, while the second doxology (using the prepositions *meta* and *sun*) is helpful in expressing their intratrinitarian relations.[89]

---

[88]See St. Basil the Great, *On the Holy Spirit* 1.3, trans. David Anderson (Crestwood, N.Y.: St. Vladimir's Seminary Press, 1980), pp. 17-18.

[89]"The Spirit is said to dwell *in* created things in many and various ways, but as far as His relationship to the Father and Son is concerned, it is more appropriate to say that He dwells *with* them, rather than *in* them. Those who are worthy receive His grace, and He works within them. However, we cannot contemplate His pre-eternal existence and permanent presence with the Son and the Father unless we search for words which suitably express such an everlasting union. Truly precise *co-existence* can only be predicated of things which are mutually inseparable. . . . Therefore, when we consider the Spirit's *rank*, we think of him as present *with* the Father and the Son, but when we consider the working of His grace on it recipients, we say that the Spirit is *in* us" (Basil, *On the Holy Spirit* 26.63, pp. 95-96).

In a study of the trinitarian content of twenty-eight worship albums produced by Vineyard Music from 1999 to 2004, Robin Parry discovered that only 1.4 percent of the songs explicitly named Father, Son and Holy Spirit together, 8.8 percent addressed two of the divine persons, 38.7 percent addressed only one person, and 51 percent could be described as "you Lord" songs.[90] To the extent Parry's findings are indicative of broader trends in the church, it appears there is room for substantial improvement. The problem is not so much that contemporary songs violate trinitarian faith. Rather, contemporary worship sometimes fails properly to highlight the identity of the God to whom praise is directed.[91] This reality stands in stark contrast to someone like Charles Wesley, who wrote hundreds of hymns that are explicitly shaped by (and expressing) a trinitarian grammar.[92] Not every song needs explicitly to name the three persons to be trinitarian, but a proper "trinitarian syntax" should shape the composition of worship songs.[93]

Hermeneutical purpose. Third, the doctrine of the Trinity serves a *hermeneutical* purpose in as much as it helps us rightly read Scripture. In books 1-4 Augustine helps his community rightly read Scripture—especially in response to Latin Homoian misreadings. To this end he outlines a series of canonical rules that should shape Christian reading. Broadly speaking, three rules shape Augustine's reading of Scripture in its witness to the triune God: (1) a rule regarding a distinction between the Son in the "form of God" and the Son in the "form of a servant," (2) a rule applying to texts like John 5:19, John 5:26 and "sending" passages that reveal not that one divine person is less than another but simply that one person proceeds from another, and (3) a rule regarding the inseparable action of the divine persons. These rules serve impor-

---

[90]Robin Parry, *Worshipping Trinity: Coming Back to the Heart of Worship* (Waynesboro, Ga.: Paternoster Press, 2005), p. 143.

[91]Ibid., p. 133.

[92]The texts of these hymns can be found in George Osborn, ed., *The Poetical Works of John and Charles Wesley* (London: Wesleyan-Methodist Conference Office, 1870), 7:201-348.

[93]For a helpful discussion of how "trinitarian syntax" might properly shape the composition of worship songs, see Parry, *Worshipping Trinity*, pp. 122-46.

tant hermeneutical functions: they help the faithful rightly read Scripture and protect the church from falling into heresy.

The contemporary move toward reading Scripture in light of the "rule of faith" (as commended by proponents of "theological interpretation") can rightly be seen as an attempt to recover the hermeneutical function of trinitarian doctrine.[94] Augustine's writings provide a concrete model for a *ruled* reading of Scripture and highlight the benefits (and challenges) of such a reading for those who are committed to wedding biblical exegesis with theological orthodoxy.[95]

Anthropological purpose. A fourth purpose of trinitarian doctrine might be described as *anthropological.* A reciprocal relationship exists for Augustine between the knowledge of self and the knowledge of the Trinity. The *imago Dei* (which Augustine understands to be trinitarian) constitutes the basis for this reciprocal relationship. By reflecting on the Trinity, humans come to know themselves better as those who are made in God's image. Conversely, through the divine image in the soul (which has been fashioned in the image of the triune God) humans come to know the triune God and share in God's life (the central focus of books 8-15).[96] In chapter five I argued that Augustine's search for traces of the Trinity in the divine image in the soul must be seen fundamentally as an expression of his quest to seek God's face (cf. Ps 105:3-4) in the context of Christ's redemptive work. In *De trinitate,* anthropology is never divorced from soteriology—a point to which I will return shortly. It should be noted that the anthropological purpose is

---

[94]A helpful survey of these developments can be found in Daniel J. Treier, *Introducing Theological Interpretation of Scripture: Recovering a Christian Practice* (Grand Rapids: Baker, 2008).

[95]For a discussion of Augustine's reading of John 5 as an example of a ruled reading, see Keith E. Johnson, "Augustine's 'Trinitarian' Reading of John 5: A Model for the Theological Interpretation of Scripture?" *Journal of the Evangelical Theological Society* 52 (2009): 799-810.

[96]"This trinity of the mind is not really the image of God because the mind remembers and understands and loves itself, but because it is also able to remember and understand and love him by whom it was made. And when it does this, it becomes wise. If it does not do it, then even though it remembers and understands and loves itself, it remains foolish. Let it then remember its God to whose image it was made, and understand and love him. To put it in a word, let it worship the uncreated God by whom it was created for a capacity for him and able to share in him" (Augustine, *De trinitate,* 14.15, p. 383).

abused in contemporary theology when theologians make simplistic appeals to "image" doctrine to ground a wide variety of claims (as some of the previous examples attest).

Formative purpose. A fifth purpose of trinitarian doctrine relates to spiritual formation.[97] One of the central themes in *De trinitate* is "contemplation." The centrality of contemplation can be seen in at least two ways. First, contemplation of the triune God represents the ultimate goal of salvation:

> Contemplation in fact is the reward of faith, a reward for which hearts are cleansed through faith, as it is written, *cleansing their hearts through faith* (Acts 15:9). Proof that it is that contemplation for which hearts are cleansed comes from the key text, *Blessed are the clean of heart, for they shall see God* (Mt 5:8). (*De trinitate* 1.17, 77)

Augustine interprets the promise of Matthew 5:8 eschatologically: the "pure in heart" will be brought into a direct contemplation of the Father, Son and Holy Spirit when Christ hands the kingdom over to the Father (1 Cor 15:24). Mary sitting at Jesus' feet offers a proleptic picture of this future joy (*De trinitate* 1.20, 79-80). Second, "contemplation" plays a central role in Christian growth. In order to share in God's life, we must grow in "contemplation" of God; however, because of our love for temporal things we are "incapable of grasping eternal things, and weighed down by the accumulated dirt of our sins" (*De trinitate*, 4.24, 169). To overcome this problem, our minds must be purified (*De trinitate*, 1.2, 66-67). As Michel Barnes explains, "Theological language has no other ultimate purpose than to strip from the mind the material form and content of its thinking about God and to

---

[97]Others have noted the formative purpose of trinitarian doctrine in Augustine. See Lewis Ayres, "The Christological Context of Augustine's *De trinitate* XIII: Toward Relocating Books VIII-XV," *Augustinian Studies* 29 (1998): 111-39; Ayres, "Augustine on God as Love and Love as God," *Pro Ecclesia* 5 (1996): 470-87; Mary T. Clark, "Augustinian Spirituality," *Augustinian Studies* 15 (1984): 83-92; and A. N. Williams, "Contemplation: Knowledge of God in Augustine's *De trinitate*," in *Knowing the Triune God: The Work of the Spirit in the Practices of the Church*, ed. James J. Buckley and David S. Yeago (Grand Rapids: Eerdmans, 2001), pp. 121-46.

shape the heart in love for God; together these actions constitute the purification of the heart."[98] Augustine's investigation of the divine image in the soul in books 8 to 15 must, therefore, be seen in the context of the necessity of contemplation for Christian growth.[99] It is by means of the divine image that humans remember, understand and love God. In order for this to happen, the divine image must be refashioned. An important relationship exists for Augustine between "seeing" and "becoming." Commenting on 1 Corinthians 13:12, 2 Corinthians 3:18 and 1 John 3:2, Augustine explains, "From this it is clear that the image of God will achieve its full likeness of him when it attains to the full vision of him—though this text from the apostle John might also appear to be referring to the immortality of the body" (*De trinitate*, 14.24, 390). Among contemporary theologians, Ellen Charry has drawn significant attention to this formative function of trinitarian doctrine.[100] Commenting on *De trinitate*, Charry explains, "A central goal of Augustine's treatise is to persuade the reader that revelation and doctrine work together to reshape our minds and affections and thereby our identity."[101]

Soteriological purpose. Finally, trinitarian doctrine serves a *soteriological* purpose in that it provides the key to explicating the gospel message. "The gospel can neither be truly stated, nor the Word truly proclaimed," writes Claude Welch, "without affirming what is made explicit in the doctrine of the Trinity."[102] One of the most important reasons we must

---

[98]Michel R. Barnes, "The Logic of Augustine's Trinitarian Theology," unpublished paper presented at the Aquinas the Augustinian Conference, in Naples, Florida, on February 4, 2005, p. 12.

[99]Thus, a strong case could be made that the anthropological purpose I have described should be seen as a subset of the formative purpose.

[100]See Ellen T. Charry, *By the Renewing of Your Minds: The Pastoral Function of Christian Doctrine* (New York: Oxford University Press, 1997), pp. 121-52; Charry, "The Soteriological Importance of the Divine Perfections," in *God the Holy Trinity: Reflections on Christian Faith and Practice*, ed. Timothy George (Grand Rapids: Baker Academic, 2006), pp. 129-47.

[101]Charry continues, "In this sense, the mechanisms by which God chooses to convey himself to us are agents of spiritual cleansing that allow us to arrive at our true destiny: enjoyment of God and ourselves" (Charry, *By the Renewing of Your Minds*, p. 133).

[102]Welch, *In This Name*, p. 290.

think rightly about the Trinity, according to Thomas Aquinas, is so "we may think rightly concerning the salvation of the human race, accomplished by the Incarnate Son, and by the gift of the Holy Ghost."[103] In *The Drama of Doctrine*, Kevin Vanhoozer nicely captures this purpose of trinitarian doctrine:

> In sum, the gospel is ultimately unintelligible apart from Trinitarian theology. Only the doctrine of the Trinity adequately accounts for how those who are not God come to share in the fellowship of the Father and Son through the Spirit. The Trinity is both the Christian specification of God and a summary statement of the gospel, in that the possibility of life with God depends upon the person and work of the Son and the Spirit. The doctrine of the Trinity thus serves both as an identification of the *dramatis personae* and as a précis of the drama itself.[104]

Behind the church's condemnation of heresy is a recognition that the truth of the Christian message depends on a proper identification of the *dramatis personae*.[105] Only if the Son is God can he reveal the Father and atone for sin. Similarly, only if the Spirit is God can he unite humans to the Father and Son.[106] In sum, the gospel requires a triune God. Moreover, distorted understandings of the divine persons undermine the gospel. Arian theology, for example, "made it impossible to affirm that Jesus is 'God with us' or 'God for us,'" and this represented a direct challenge to the gospel message."[107] The soteriological function of trinitarian doctrine accounts for the polemical concern that drives much of Augustine's discussion in *De trinitate*. In books 2-4, he devotes extensive attention to the sendings of the Son

---

[103]Thomas Aquinas, *Summa Theologiae* I, Q. 32, a. 1, ad. 3.

[104]Kevin J. Vanhoozer, *The Drama of Doctrine: A Canonical-Linguistic to Christian Theology* (Louisville: Westminster John Knox, 2005), pp. 43-44.

[105]Ibid., p. 82.

[106]Ibid., p. 43.

[107]Ibid., p. 83. "Failure to identify the divine persons correctly leads to a misconstrual of the divine action, which in turn impedes our ability to participate in it. Heresies are dangerous because they are unable to proclaim the gospel—'God in Christ; Christ in us'—coherently and do not draw us into the saving action of the triune God. Heresies keep us from the way, the truth and the life. The early church was therefore right to deem heresy harmful to one's spiritual health."

and the Spirit within the drama of salvation. It is clear that a reciprocal relation exists for Augustine between a proper understanding of
the identity of the Son and Spirit and a proper understanding of their
salvific work.

One theologian who excelled in mining the soteriological purpose of
trinitarian doctrine is Hermann Bavinck.[108] Bavinck's (Augustinian)
trinitarianism shapes every facet of his explanation of the work of Christ
and soteriology in his *Reformed Dogmatics*.[109] For example, in his introduction to the *ordo salutis*, Bavinck explains, "There is room for an order
of salvation in a scriptural, Christian, and Reformed sense only on the
foundation of trinitarian confession."[110] First, it follows from Christian
confession of the Trinity that that the "acquisition" of salvation and the
"application" of salvation must be distinguished.[111] The distinction between salvation accomplished and applied is grounded in the hypostatic
distinction between the Son and the Holy Spirit.[112] Second, implied in
Christian confession of the Trinity is that the Spirit's work of applying
salvation—though distinct from the Son's accomplishment of redemption—cannot be separated from it.[113] Just as the Holy Spirit is one in
essence with the Father and Son, so his working is united with the work
of the Father and the Son in salvation. The incarnate Son was equipped
by the Spirit for his work on earth. Then, on the day of Pentecost,

---

[108]Another theologian who reflected deeply on the relationship of Trinity and soteriology was
Hans Urs von Balthasar (see Hans Urs von Balthasar, *The Theo-Drama: Theological Dramatic
Theory*, 5 vols., trans. Graham Harrison [San Francisco: Ignatius Press, 1990-1998], esp. vols.
2-4.

[109]Herman Bavinck, *Reformed Dogmatics*, vol. 1-4, ed. John Bolt, trans. John Vriend (Grand
Rapids: Baker Academic, 2003-2008). For a discussion of Bavinck's doctrine of the Trinity
see Bavinck, *Reformed Dogmatics*, vol. 2, *God and Creation*, pp. 256-334.

[110]Herman Bavinck, *Reformed Dogmatics*, vol. 3, *Sin and Salvation in Christ*, ed. John Bolt, trans.
John Vriend (Grand Rapids: Baker Academic, 2006), p. 569.

[111]Ibid., p. 570.

[112]Although the Spirit is one with the Father and Son, the Spirit "has his own way of existing,
his own manner of working. Although it is true that all the external works of God [*opera Dei
ad extra*] are undivided and inseparable, in creation and re-creation one can nevertheless observe an economy that gives us the right to speak of the Father and our creation, the Son and
our redemption, the Spirit and our sanctification" (ibid.).

[113]Ibid., p. 571.

Christ sent the Holy Spirit in order to apply all the benefits he acquired to the church. As the Son glorifies the Father, so the Holy Spirit glorifies the Son by distributing to the elect the benefits of Christ and bringing people to the Son and, through the Son, to the Father.[114] In so doing, he acts in a way that reflects his hypostatic identity as the one who proceeds from the Father and the Son. Elsewhere summarizing the trinitarian nature of salvation, Bavinck explains, "The essence of the Christian religion consists in this, that the creation of the Father, ruined by sin, is restored in the death of the Son of God, and re-created by the grace of the Holy Spirit into a kingdom of God."[115]

The soteriological purpose of trinitarian doctrine explains why the preceding critique of the trinitarian theologies of Mark Heim, Jacques Dupuis, Amos Yong and Raimundo Panikkar are so important. One might be tempted to dismiss this critique simply by asking, "Why does it really matter if these theologians present speculative accounts of the Trinity that are not in accord with classical theology?" However, such a conclusion would be disastrous. Augustine rightly recognized that distorted accounts of the divine persons lead to distorted understandings of the gospel. This is because Trinity and gospel are inseparably linked.[116] By reinterpreting the Trinity, Heim, Dupuis, Yong and Panikkar, in various ways and to varying degrees, undermine the gospel of Jesus Christ.

---

[114]Ibid., p. 572.

[115]Bavinck, *Reformed Dogmatics*, vol. 1, *Prolegomena*, p. 112.

[116]For a helpful discussion of the relationship between the Trinity and the gospel, see Fred Sanders, *The Deep Things of God: How the Trinity Changes Everything* (Wheaton, Ill.: Crossway, 2010). As Sanders explains, "The central argument of this book is that the doctrine of the Trinity inherently belongs to the gospel itself. It is not merely the case that this is a doctrine that wise minds have recognized as necessary for defense of the gospel, or that a process of logical deduction leads from believing the gospel to affirming the doctrine of the Trinity, or that people who believe the gospel should also believe whatever the God of the gospel reveals about himself. No, while all these statements are true, they do not say enough, because there is a Trinity-gospel connection much more intimate than those loose links suggest. Trinity and gospel are not just bundled together so that you can't have one without the other. They are internally configured toward each other. Even at the risk of being misunderstood before the full argument emerges in later chapters, let me say as concisely as possible: the gospel is Trinitarian, and the Trinity is gospel" (ibid., pp. 9-10).

CONCLUSION

"The Christian remains unsatisfied until all of existence is referred back to the triune God and until the confession of God's Trinity functions at the center of our thought and life."[117] Herman Bavinck commends an impulse that would resonate with Augustine. Part of the challenge in living out Bavinck's vision is determining "how all of existence is referred back to the triune God." It is ironic that some attempts to refer human existence to the Trinity (e.g. theology of religions) may actually have the opposite effect—namely, displacing the triune God as "the center of our life and thought." From an Augustinian perspective, the relevancy of this doctrine may be seen in the way it enables us rightly to speak about God, the way it helps us rightly worship God, the way it helps us read Scripture, the way it helps us understand ourselves, the way it draws us into the life of the triune God, and finally in the way it helps explicate the gospel. The doctrine of the Trinity, therefore, is a "mystery of salvation" not in the sense that it provides a ready-made blueprint for ecclesial, societal, political or even interreligious structures, but in the sense that it helps us rightly to reflect and enjoy the glory of the one who called us "out of darkness into his marvelous light" (1 Pet 2:9).

---

[117]Bavinck, *Reformed Dogmatics*, vol. 2, *God and Creation*, p. 330.

APPENDIX

RECLAIMING AUGUSTINE ON THE TRINITY

◆

Augustine has rightly been recognized in the Western church as a reliable authority whose teaching on the Trinity reflects the teaching of Scripture and the creeds. Our engagement with Augustine's theology in the preceding chapters reinforces the wisdom of this judgment. Although his teaching on the Trinity has exerted a dominant influence in the West, not everyone views Augustine's influence as positive. According to critics, Augustine begins with a unity of divine substance (which he allegedly prioritizes over the persons), his trinitarian doctrine is negatively influenced by Neo-Platonic philosophy, his psychological analogy is modalistic, and he severs the life of Trinity from the economy of salvation by focusing on the immanent Trinity. Viewed in this light, appropriating Augustine's trinitarian doctrine may seem about as prudent as boarding a sinking ocean liner after most of the passengers have wisely abandoned ship. Indeed, any appeal to Augustine may, in the minds of some readers, serve to solidify the impression that this project should be viewed with suspicion. Implicit answers to many of these criticisms can be found in the exposition of Augustine's trinitarian doctrine that I have offered in chapters two to six.[1] Nevertheless, the frequency and severity of these criticisms require that they

---

[1]Compelling responses to these and other criticisms can also be found in Lewis Ayres, *Augustine and the Trinity* (Cambridge: Cambridge University Press, 2010).

be addressed directly. Detailed response to these criticisms could fill an entire book (or several volumes). My aim in this appendix is much more modest. I have chosen simply to engage one articulate representative of these criticisms in order to draw attention to some of the ways Augustine is characteristically misread in contemporary theology. Alongside addressing specific criticisms, I will also explore factors that fuel misreadings of his trinitarian doctrine.

COLIN GUNTON'S CRITICISMS OF AUGUSTINE'S TRINITARIAN THEOLOGY

Few contemporary theologians have been more critical of Augustine's trinitarian theology than Colin Gunton. In *The Promise of Trinitarian Theology*, Gunton offers a wide-ranging critique of Augustine's teaching on the Trinity.[2] According to Gunton, Augustine develops an account of the Trinity which differs radically from that of the Cappadocians. Whereas the Cappadocians understand the Father, Son and Holy Spirit as a divine *community*, Augustine focuses on a single *substance* underlying the persons. Moreover, the single greatest influence on Augustine's doctrine of the Trinity was not the teaching of Scripture and the church but Neo-Platonism.[3] According to Gunton, the negative influence of Neo-Platonic thought can be seen in the way Augustine prioritizes the divine substance over the persons, in his fear of the material world, in his search for trinitarian analogies and in his doctrine of the Spirit.

Although similar criticisms can be found in the writings of Cornelius Plantinga, Catherine LaCugna, Karl Rahner and others, Gunton is an ideal interlocutor because the majority of contemporary criticisms of Augustine found sprinkled through the writings of others are nicely

---

[2]Colin E. Gunton, *The Promise of Trinitarian Theology* (Edinburgh: T & T Clark, 1991).

[3]See ibid., pp. 38-39. Similar criticisms can be found in Cornelius Plantinga Jr., "Social Trinity and Tritheism," in *Trinity, Incarnation, and Atonement: Philosophical and Theological Essays*, ed. Ronald J. Feenstra and Cornelius Plantinga Jr. (Notre Dame, Ind.: University of Notre Dame Press, 1989), p. 33; and Plantinga, "The Threeness/Oneness Problem of the Trinity," *Calvin Theological Journal* 23 (1988): 37-53.

summarized by Gunton. Gunton's criticisms of Augustine in *The Prom-ise of Trinitarian Theology* therefore will represent the focal point of my discussion.[4] Readers need not be familiar with Gunton's work to ap-preciate these criticisms as they reflect assumptions that can be found in popular summaries of the historical development of trinitarian doc-trine. Many of these criticisms do not originate with Gunton. He is simply an ardent spokesperson for them. Hence, my interest is not with Gunton's theology *per se* but simply with him as representative of con-temporary misreadings of Augustine. My criticisms of his interpreta-tion of Augustine's theology should not be read as an indictment on Gunton or his theology. Colin Gunton was a fine theologian and made many important contributions to contemporary trinitarian revival. This represents one reason his criticisms of Augustine need to be addressed. Following Gunton's lead, I have grouped his criticisms in five catego-ries. Although he discusses a wide range of issues (Neo-Platonism, on-tology, Christology, pneumatology, etc.), readers should bear in mind that Gunton discusses these topics in order to demonstrate the inade-quacy of Augustine's trinitarian theology. One important assumption underlying many of Gunton's criticisms is that Augustine and the Cap-padocians (Basil of Caesarea, Gregory of Nyssa, Gregory of Nazianzus) articulate radically different doctrines of the Trinity. As I will argue here, this represents one of the fundamental flaws with his reading of Augustine.

Substance and person in the Trinity. According to Gunton, Augus-tine failed to understand the conceptual revolution ushered in by the Cappadocians.[5] More specifically, he failed to comprehend the onto-logical implications of the distinction the Cappadocians drew between

---

[4]Similar criticisms can also be found in Gunton's book *The One, the Three, and the Many: God, Creation, and the Culture of Modernity* (New York: Cambridge University Press, 1993). Ayres and Barnes do not engage Gunton's reading of Augustine, as Gunton was a theologian and not a historian.

[5]Gunton's reading of the Cappadocians draws heavily upon the work of John Zizioulas. See John D. Zizioulas, *Being as Communion: Studies in Personhood and the Church* (Crestwood, N.Y.: St. Vladimir's Seminary Press, 1985), pp. 27-65.

hypostasis and *ousia*. By distinguishing *hypostasis* and *ousia*, the Cappadocians not only provided a grammar for distinguishing the oneness and threeness of God but they also developed a radically new ontology in which the being of God (*ousia*) was understood to be constituted by a communion of persons. The Cappadocians recognized there is no substance that the persons share apart from the "dynamic of persons in relation."[6] Gunton believes that the Cappadocians were fully aware of the conceptual revolution they ushered in—a revolution which "stood in opposition to all Greek ontology."[7]

"Because he failed to appropriate the ontological achievement of his Eastern colleagues," Augustine "allowed the insidious return of Hellenism in which being is not communion, but something underlying it."[8] As proof of the latter, Gunton cites a text in which Augustine acknowledges that he does not comprehend the distinction that the "Greeks" draw between *hypostasis* and *ousia*.[9] Although Augustine realizes that different concepts are required to express the reality that God is both one and three, his "adoption of the correct Latin equivalents does not enable him to get the point," says Gunton, because later in the same section of book 5 Augustine acknowledges that he uses the term *person* (*persona*) to describe the Father, Son and Holy Spirit only so that he is not reduced to silence.[10] Further evidence that Augustine did not understand the "Cappadocian revolution" can be seen in the way he describes the divine relations. Augustine's discussion is driven by a different question than the Cappadocians. According to Gunton, Augustine does not ask, What kind of being is this, that God is to be found in the relations of Father, Son and Spirit? but, What kind of sense can be made of the apparent logical oddity of the threeness of the one God in

---

[6]Gunton, *Promise of Trinitarian Theology*, p. 10.

[7]Ibid., p. 9.

[8]Ibid., p. 10.

[9]"The Greeks also have another word, *hypostasis*, but they make a distinction that is rather obscure to me between *ousia* and *hypostasis*, so that most of our people who treat of these matters in Greek are accustomed to say *mia ousia, treis hypostaseis*, which is literally one being, three substances" (Augustine, *De trinitate* 5.10, 196).

[10]Gunton, *Promise of Trinitarian Theology*, p. 40.

terms of Aristotelian subject-predicate logic?"[11] Beginning, as he does, with the one God as "substance," Augustine has a difficult time fitting in the three persons. "Relation" (which must be distinguished from "substance" and "accident") merely provides Augustine with a theoretical basis for plurality in God.[12] He is simply "unable to break out of the stranglehold of the dualistic ontology which underlies the logic."[13] As a result, the relations do not qualify the persons ontologically. This represents "a clear step back" from the teaching of the Cappadocians:

> For them, the three persons are what they are in their relations, and therefore the relations qualify them ontologically, in terms of what they are. Because Augustine continues to use relation as a logical rather than an ontological predicate, he is precluded from being able to make claims about the being of the *particular* persons, who, because they lack distinguishable identity, tend to disappear into the all-embracing oneness of God.[14]

For this reason Augustine's trinitarian theology (as well as the Western theology that follows him) tends to be "modalist."[15] Unlike the Cappadocians who view the being of God as the "unfolding" of the three persons, Augustine views the true being of God as somehow "underlying" the three persons.[16]

Materiality and the incarnation. A second example of the negative influence of Neo-Platonism on his trinitarian theology can be seen in Augustine's attitude toward the material world: "It is well known that Augustine was suspicious of the material world."[17] Along with other Platonists, he found it difficult to believe that the material realm could be a vehicle of genuine knowledge. Although the incarnation plays an important role in his theology, it is clear that "the doctrine of the di-

---

[11]Ibid.
[12]Ibid.
[13]Ibid., p. 41.
[14]Ibid., pp. 41-42.
[15]Ibid., p. 74.
[16]Ibid., p. 42.
[17]Ibid., p. 33.

vinity of Christ is more important to Augustine than that of the humanity."[18] As a result, his Christology possesses a docetic character.[19] Although "anti-Arian zeal" may be partially responsible for this lacuna, this problem is so pervasive that other factors must also be involved—particularly "neoplatonic assumptions of the material order's incapacity to be really and truly the bearer of divinity."[20] Gunton claims that "anti-incarnational platonism" can be seen in Augustine's discussion of the Old Testament theophanies.[21] Augustine appears to be "embarrassed by too close an involvement of God in matter."[22] In Augustine's theology, angels replace the Son as mediators of God's relation with the world. Not only does this reflect his tendency to spiritualize, but "by losing the mediatorship of the Word" Augustine also "distances God from the creation and flattens out the distinctions between the persons of the Trinity."[23] By making these moves Augustine breaks with a tradition that can be traced to Irenaeus in which the Father relates directly to the world through the Son and Spirit. Augustine replaces this tradition with an "unknown God working through angels."[24]

A second example of "anti-incarnational platonism" can be found in Augustine's discussion of the baptism of Jesus in which he does not give due weight to Jesus' humanity.[25] As evidence of the latter, Gunton cites a passage in book 15 in which Augustine explains that the Spirit was already upon Jesus prior to his baptism.[26] Had Augustine given due weight to the humanity of Jesus, he would have recognized that Jesus

---

[18]Ibid., p. 34.
[19]Ibid.
[20]Ibid., p. 35.
[21]Ibid.
[22]Ibid.
[23]Ibid., p. 36.
[24]Ibid., p. 37.
[25]Ibid.
[26]"It would be the height of absurdity to believe that he only received the Holy Spirit when he was already thirty years old—that was the age at which he was baptized by John; no, we must believe that just as he came to that baptism without any sin, so he came to it not without the Holy Spirit" (Augustine, *De trinitate* 15.46, 431).

"entered a new form of relationship with the Spirit" at his baptism.[27] Augustine, however, "appears to treat the Spirit, in anticipation of a long tradition of Western thought, substantially rather than personally and relationally: as if the Spirit was a substantial presence, given in the womb and, so to speak, preprogramming Jesus' life, rather than the means by which his humanity was realized in relationship to the Father."[28] Although these may seem like relatively minor points, Gunton assures his readers they are part of a larger negative pattern in Augustine's theology.

One final example of Augustine's fear of the material world can be seen in his unwillingness to search for analogies of the Trinity in the material realm. The doctrine of the incarnation should lead us to view the material world as possessing "theological meaning."[29] If God is present in the human form in Jesus Christ, then the world must also possess special theological meaning; however, Augustine does not really believe that God is fully present in the humanity of Christ. If he did believe this, he would not view the material world as the "least adequate source" for analogies of the Trinity.[30]

Trinitarian analogies. Gunton rejects the view that Augustine's trinitarian "analogies are merely illustrative of the church's dogma, a penetration into its inner logic."[31] On the contrary, Augustine's analogies "impose upon the doctrine of the Trinity a conception of the divine threeness which owes more to neoplatonic philosophy than to the triune economy, and that the outcome is, again, a view of an unknown substance *supporting* the three persons rather than being *constituted* by their relatedness."[32] The foundation for Augustine's trinitarian doctrine is not the economy of salvation but a particular "conception of a three-

---

[27]Gunton, *Promise of Trinitarian Theology*, p. 37.
[28]Ibid.
[29]Ibid., p. 38.
[30]Ibid.
[31]Ibid., p. 42.
[32]Ibid., pp. 42-43.

fold mind."[33] One of the odd features about *De trinitate* is the fact that Augustine spends very little time explaining what the doctrine of the Trinity actually is. Instead he only offers a few brief summaries. This reinforces the perception that Augustine does not want to explain the teaching of the church but rather to illustrate it by means of something external.

Two features characterize Augustine's search for trinitarian analogies: individualism and intellectualism. Evidence of the former can be seen in the fact that, unlike Richard of St. Victor, Augustine does not search for analogies of the Trinity in human community but rather in the individual person. Evidence of the latter can be seen in Augustine's decision to treat the human mind as the best analogy for the Trinity. His individualism serves to reinforce the oneness of God, while his intellectualism treats God as a kind of "supermind."[34]

Gunton also contests Augustine's assertion that his most important triad is not memory, understanding and will *in itself* but the mind as it remembers, understands and loves God: "I believe, against all this, that the triad of memory, understanding and will is determinative for Augustine's conception of the Trinity."[35] A definitive piece of evidence includes the following: when Augustine attempts to distinguish the Son from the Spirit in book 15, he ultimately appeals to memory, understanding and will (in itself). Thus, *"The crucial analogy for Augustine is between the inner structure of the human mind and the inner being of God, because it is in the former that the latter is made known, this side of eternity at any rate, more really than in the 'outer' economy of grace."*[36] That this is the case simply reflects Augustine's dependence on "a platonizing doctrine of knowledge as recollection."[37] The Father (likened to memory) becomes the storehouse of knowledge while the Word (likened to understanding) becomes part of the content of the divine mind. The

---

[33]Ibid., p. 43.
[34]Ibid., p. 44.
[35]Ibid., p. 45.
[36]Ibid.
[37]Ibid.

Spirit, in this context, is likened to will. No justification exists for the latter in the economy of salvation. Thus, Augustine's choice to associate the Spirit with the will can only be explained in terms of the negative influence of Neo-Platonic philosophy. Augustine's stress on the mind as image of the Trinity led to "fateful consequences" in Western theology by directing attention away from the economy of salvation toward the mind as the source of divine knowledge.

Trinitarian pneumatology. Gunton claims that Augustine's conception of the Holy Spirit represents "the Achilles' heel" of his trinitarian theology. Although Augustine attempts to marshal biblical support, his doctrine of the Spirit is shaped "by his need to have a third person corresponding to the will in the threefold mind."[38] While he acknowledges that biblical warrant exists for speaking of Spirit as "gift," Gunton insists, nonetheless, that "gift" does not provide an adequate basis for distinguishing the Spirit from the Son (particularly in light of the fact that Scripture also uses "gift" language to describe the sacrifice of the Son). Similar problems also arise in Augustine's attempt to posit "love" as a distinguishing characteristic of the Spirit. No scriptural warrant exists for attributing love exclusively to the Spirit. These problems simply reflect Augustine's single-minded desire to fit the Spirit into a predetermined conceptual framework that bypasses the economy of salvation.

By operating within a dualistic framework that limits the work of the Spirit to connecting individuals to God, Augustine misses the biblical emphasis on the "eschatological dimension" of the Spirit's work as well as the role of the Spirit in creating community.[39] This leads him to conceptualize the church as an "institution mediating grace to the individual rather than the community formed on the analogy of the Trinity's *interpersonal* relationships."[40] Because his doctrine of the Spirit largely brackets the economy of salvation, Au-

---

[38]Ibid., p. 48.
[39]Ibid., p. 50.
[40]Ibid., p. 51.

gustine is unable "to give personal distinctiveness to the being of the Spirit in the inner Trinity."[41]

In his discussion of Augustine's teaching on the procession of the Holy Spirit from the Father and Son, Gunton dismisses the claim that significant continuities exist between Augustine's account of procession of the Spirit from the Father and the Son, and the Eastern view that the Spirit proceeds from the Father *through* the Son. In light of the fact that "major differences" exist between Augustine and the Cappadocians on other points, significant differences must exist here as well.[42] Although the procession of the Spirit from the Father and Son may provide a conceptual apparatus for distinguishing the Son and Spirit, readers must consider whether Augustine "is able to handle the ontological revolution that is required by a theology of the Trinity."[43] Gunton insists that the answer to this question is no. By failing to comprehend the Cappadocian revolution (i.e., that God's being consists in communion), Augustine locates the ultimate principle of being somewhere else. What is ultimately real about the Trinity for Augustine, therefore, is not a community constituted by Father, Son and Holy Spirit but simply the "divine substance."[44]

The abysmal legacy of Augustine's trinitarian theology. In addition to problems plaguing the content of Augustine's trinitarian theology, Gunton identifies several negative effects of Augustine's legacy: "Augustine's work is so brilliant that it blinded generations of theologians to its damaging weaknesses."[45] By severing the life of the triune God from the economy of salvation, Augustine paved the way for the mar-

---

[41]Ibid.

[42]Ibid., p. 52.

[43]Ibid., p. 53.

[44]Gunton approvingly cites Wolfson's claim that while Tertullian, Nicaea and Basil identify the Father as the substratum of God, Augustine teaches that the Son and Spirit "derive only their existence, not their divinity," from the Father. See H. A. Wolfson, *The Philosophy of the Church Fathers* (Cambridge, Mass.: Harvard University Press, 1956), p. 397. This leads to the conclusion that the "divine substance" displaces the Father as the "basis of the being of God" (Gunton, *Promise of Trinitarian Theology*, p. 54).

[45]Gunton, *Promise of Trinitarian Theology*, p. 39.

ginalization of the doctrine of the Trinity. [46] Under the influence of Augustine's legacy the Trinity became "dogma to be believed rather than as the living focus of life and thought,"[47] as well as a problem to be solved rather than a summary of the gospel.[48]

Moreover, by "flattening out" the distinctiveness of the divine persons, failing to understand the Cappadocian account of *hypostasis*, and seeking analogies of the Trinity in an individual human mind, Augustine paved the way for modern individualism. In fact, a direct link can be seen between Augustine and Descartes: "Again and again in the *De Trinitate* the godlikeness of the human person is located in the mind, and there is in this respect a direct link between Augustine and modern tradition stemming from Descartes."[49] By way of contrast, a relational understanding of the human person can be traced to the Cappadocians (especially Basil of Caesarea): "By giving priority to the concept of person in their doctrine of God, they transform at once the meaning of both concepts. The being of God is not now understood in the way characteristic of Greek metaphysics, but in terms of communion."[50] Gunton explicitly cites Basil as describing the triune God as a kind of "indivisible community."[51]

Finally, Augustine's trinitarian theology forms the basis for a deficient ecclesiology. Although we should not draw a straight line from the immanent Trinity to ecclesial practice, Gunton believes that there is an important sense in which the being of the church indirectly "echoes" the relations of the divine persons.[52] In such a context the trinitarian theologies of Augustine and the Cappadocians (which might respectively be characterized as "modalist" and "relational") lead to "correspondingly different ecclesiologies."[53] Read in terms of ecclesiol-

---

[46]Ibid., p. 3. Catherine LaCugna offers a similar criticism (see LaCugna, *God for Us*, p. 81).
[47]Gunton, *Promise of Trinitarian Theology*, p. 3.
[48]Ibid., p. 31.
[49]Ibid., p. 95.
[50]Ibid., p. 96.
[51]Ibid.
[52]Ibid., p. 74.
[53]Ibid., p. 74.

ogy, Augustine's trinitarian theology "conceives of the being of the church as in some sense anterior to the concrete historical relationships of the visible community."[54] This ecclesiology involves a Platonized view of the church in which the "invisible church" (and, hence, the "real church") exists "ontologically prior" to, and apart from, the historical community.[55] In contrast, Cappadocian trinitarian theology leads to a very different (and clearly preferable) understanding of the church as a "visible" community that echoes the "perichoretic interrelation" of the three divine persons.[56]

REREADING AUGUSTINE

In the discussion that follows I will argue that Gunton's criticisms rest upon fundamental misunderstandings of Augustine's trinitarian theology. Before I respond to Gunton's criticisms, it is important to consider *why* Augustine is frequently misread. At least four factors drive contemporary misreadings of Augustine's theology.[57] First, contemporary readings of Augustine's trinitarian theology are often held captive to the "de Régnon paradigm." As Michel Barnes notes, "Nothing is more common in contemporary systematics than the inability to read Augustine outside of de Régnon's paradigm."[58] Théodore de Régnon (1831-1893) was a French Jesuit who wrote a multivolume history of trinitarian doctrine titled *Études de théologie positive sur la Sainte Trinité*.[59] Ironically, de Régnon is both "the most influential and yet least known of Catholic historians of doctrine."[60] De Régnon believed that doctrinal history could be divided into specifics eras marked by particular

---

[54]Ibid., pp. 74-75.

[55]Ibid., p. 75.

[56]Ibid., p. 83.

[57]I know of no single essay in which Michel Barnes explicitly groups these four points the way I have. This list represents my own synthetic summary of the problems Barnes identifies in several different essays.

[58]Michel R. Barnes, "Augustine in Contemporary Trinitarian Theology," *Theological Studies* 56 (1995): 239.

[59]Théodore de Régnon, *Études de théologie positive sur la Sainte Trinité* (Paris: Victor Retaux, 1892, 1898).

[60]Michel R. Barnes, "De Régnon Reconsidered," *Augustinian Studies* 26 (1995): 51.

"doctrinal paradigms" (Barnes's term).[61] De Régnon drew a distinction between *patristic* and *scholastic* paradigms. In the patristic paradigm (exemplified by the Cappadocians), "the divine is always encountered in or as person" while in the scholastic paradigm (exemplified by Augustine), "divinity is always understood in or as a nature."[62] It is de Régnon's paradigm, therefore, that stands behind the claim that Augustine prioritized the divine nature over the persons (while the Cappadocians allegedly prioritized the persons over the divine nature).[63] Interestingly, belief in "Greek" versus "Latin" paradigms represents a modern phenomenon: "only theologians of the last one hundred years have ever thought it was true," according to Barnes.[64] Although numerous works arrange their history of trinitarian theology around this paradigm, "none of them shows any awareness that the paradigm needs to be demonstrated, or that it has a history."[65] Although the de Régnon paradigm is deeply flawed, we certainly cannot deny its effectiveness in the classroom. After all, patristic trinitarian theology is a complicated affair. The de Régnon paradigm comes to the rescue by offering a simple hook for students struggling to understand the theological landscape of the fourth century. It's not difficult to understand why this paradigm has been slow to die off despite lack of evidence to support it.

Another factor that drives contemporary misreadings is a tendency to read Augustine's trinitarian theology in isolated pieces, combined with a failure to contextualize his thought.[66] The former practice began in the medieval period when portions of *De trinitate* (e.g., bks. 5-7)

---

[61]Ibid., p. 53.

[62]Ibid., p. 54.

[63]Ibid., p. 51.

[64]Barnes, "Augustine in Contemporary Trinitarian Theology," p. 238.

[65]Ibid. Whereas much English-language scholarship uncritically assimilated de Régnon's paradigm, French scholarship had a running argument over its validity (Barnes, "De Régnon Reconsidered," p. 55).

[66]Michel R. Barnes, "Rereading Augustine's Theology of the Trinity," in *The Trinity: An Interdisciplinary Symposium on the Trinity*, ed. Stephen T. Davis, Daniel Kendall and Gerald O'Collins (New York: Oxford University Press, 1999), p. 147.

circulated independent of the whole. In more subtle ways this practice continues in contemporary theology. Augustine's trinitarian theology is frequently mediated through a handful of dismembered citations. Moreover, even when all his trinitarian writings are read as a whole, they are frequently read out of context. Barnes suggests that four contexts are crucial: (1) Augustine's entire corpus on the Trinity, (2) other contemporary Latin trinitarian writings in the late fourth and early fifth centuries, (3) contemporary Latin polemical writings during the same period, and (4) prior authoritative trinitarian teaching from the second and third centuries.[67] Although we might imagine that numerous studies have been done attempting to locate Augustine's trinitarian theology in these contexts, in reality, "studies of this sort can hardly be found at all."[68] One is hard pressed, for example, to find detailed studies chronicling Augustine's debt to Latin Christian predecessors such as Tertullian.[69] On the contrary, most efforts at contextualizing Augustine's trinitarian theology focus almost exclusively upon his debt to Neo-Platonism (in the context of the de Régnon paradigm). This "contextualization" leads to the mistaken conclusion that Augustine's *emphasis* on divine unity is the result of Neo-Platonic influence. As Barnes notes, the latter claim is dependent on the work of Oliver du Roy:

> For many theologians writing about Augustine's trinitarian theology, the larger "external" narrative is simply de Régnon's grand scheme of "western trinitarian theology *begins with* (in the sense of 'presumes' and 'is ultimately concerned with') divine unity (i.e., the essence) while eastern trinitarian theology *begins with* divine diversity (i.e., the persons)." The narrative provided by de Régnon's paradigm is filled in, as it were, with du Roy's work to provide the following "historical context": "the

---

[67]Ibid.

[68]Ibid., p. 151.

[69]"Such discussions as there are reduce Augustine to Tertullian, or position this debt in terms of de Régnon's paradigm: e.g., how does Augustine's theory of relations differ from that of Gregory of Nazianzus? We are brought to the odd position that, according to many systematic theologians, the influence of philosophy in religious doctrine is fundamental, while the influence of prior expositions of religious doctrines is not" (Barnes, "Augustine in Contemporary Trinitarian Theology," p. 244).

emphasis in Augustine's trinitarian theology on divine unity is indebted to the influence of neoplatonism."[70]

Although exploration of the "Neo-Platonic" character of Augustine's theology may once have served to contextualize his theology in terms of its doctrinal development, it no longer functions that way. Rather than opening possibilities for understanding Augustine, thinking of him as a Neo-Platonist "has shut down possibilities for reading him."[71]

A third factor that influences misreadings of Augustine's trinitarian theology is a failure to distinguish between the teaching of Augustine and later developments. Later developments sometimes constitute the basis for (unjustified) criticisms. Augustine, for example, is frequently criticized for his "psychological analogy" of the Trinity. This criticism wrongly assumes that Augustine's psychological analogy plays a dominant role in his trinitarian theology. In an essay exploring the core elements of Augustine's trinitarian doctrine, Michel Barnes argues that the triad of memory, understanding and will should *not* be numbered among the core elements of his thought.[72] Although this mental triad plays an important role in *De trinitate*, there are "many significant discussions by Augustine of the Trinity in which the triad makes no appearance whatsoever."[73] Augustine's use of this triad is merely "opportunistic, not fundamental and necessary."[74] This reality stands in contrast with later medieval trinitarian thought in which the mental triad clearly plays a dominant role (e.g., Thomas Aquinas). To read Augustine's psychological analogy as a core element of his trinitarian thought is to transform Augustine into a medieval figure. This is pre-

---

[70]Barnes, "Rereading Augustine's Theology of the Trinity," p. 152.

[71]Michel R. Barnes, "The Logic of Augustine's Trinitarian Theology," unpublished paper presented at the Aquinas the Augustinian Conference, in Naples, Florida, on February 4, 2005, p. 2. Augustine's relationship to Neo-Platonism is complex. For a helpful discussion of the influence of Neo-Platonism on Augustine's trinitarian theology, see Ayres, *Augustine and the Trinity*, pp. 13-41.

[72]See Barnes, "The Logic of Augustine's Trinitarian Theology," pp. 7-11.

[73]Ibid., p. 11.

[74]Ibid., p. 9.

cisely what de Régnon's typology does when it locates Augustine as an exemplar of a "scholastic" era over and against the Cappadocians who represent the "patristic" era. Another instance of reading later developments into Augustine's thought can be seen in Karl Rahner's famous essay on the Trinity. Rahner claims that the marginalization of the Trinity in contemporary theology is attributable, at least in part, to the practice of treating the doctrine of God under two headings in theology manuals: (1) *De Deo Uno*, and (2) *De Deo Trino*. Although Rahner acknowledges that this practice did not explicitly arise until the medieval period, he appears to trace its origin back to Augustine.[75] In so doing, he reads de Régnon's paradigm back into Augustine.[76] Augustine, however, makes no distinction between God and Trinity.[77] On the contrary, when summarizing Christian teaching on the triune God in book 1, Augustine speaks about the "Trinity which God is" (*De trinitate* 1.7, 69).[78]

A final factor that fuels misreadings of Augustine is a failure to engage contemporary Augustinian scholarship. Ironically, at the same time some contemporary theologians have been vilifying him, scholars have been criticizing and revising the standard depictions of Augustine's thought. "Unfortunately," as Lewis Ayres explains, "the critiques of Augustine's trinitarianism found in much modern theological writing do not occur actively *against* this trend in Augustinian scholarship—engaging directly and in detail with original texts and attempting to refute these new scholarly arguments—but largely in *ignorance* of it."[79] Thus, the description of Augustine's trinitarian theology in many

---

[75]Karl Rahner, *The Trinity*, trans. Joseph Donceel (New York: Crossroad, 1999), p. 17.

[76]Edmund Hill, "Karl Rahner's 'Remarks on the Dogmatic Treatise *De trinitate* and St. Augustine," *Augustinian Studies* 2 (1971): 68-69.

[77]Michel R. Barnes and Lewis Ayres, "God," in *Augustine Through the Ages: An Encyclopedia*, ed. Allan D. Fitzgerald (Grand Rapids: Eerdmans, 1999).

[78]This phrase is not used by any of Augustine's predecessors and represents an important alternative to merely affirming the Father as *Deus* (see Ayres, *Augustine and the Trinity*, p. 100).

[79]Lewis Ayres, "The Fundamental Grammar of Augustine's Trinitarian Theology," in *Augustine and his Critics: Essays in Honour of Gerald Bonner*, ed. Robert Dodaro and George Lawless (New York: Routledge, 2000), p. 51.

popular theological works simply rehashes old accounts that are no longer tenable. Progress will be made only when contemporary writers engage in a close reading of Augustine's writings in their proper historical context bracketing the larger narrative.[80]

Gunton's reading of Augustine exhibits all four of the problems outlined above. Although he nowhere cites Théodore de Régnon, his reading of Augustine (as well as the Cappadocians) reflects the de Régnon paradigm. In addition, Gunton makes no effort to contextualize Augustine with reference to Latin trinitarian writings either prior to or contemporary with Augustine. On the contrary, he asserts that everything that is significant about Augustine's trinitarian theology can be understood with reference to Neo-Platonism. Furthermore, he fails to distinguish Augustine's trinitarian teaching from later Augustinian developments. This can be seen in the way he draws a straight line from Augustine to modern individualism via Descartes. Finally, Gunton's reading of Augustine fails to engage contemporary Augustinian scholarship (which would challenge many—if not most—of his assertions about the character of Augustine's thought). With this background in mind, I will respond to Gunton's criticisms following the five categories introduced earlier.

Substance and person: Misreading the Cappadocians. At the root of Gunton's criticism of Augustine is an assumption that significant differences exist between Augustine's trinitarian ontology (in which the divine nature somehow *underlies* the persons) and the ontology of the Cappadocians (in which the being of God is *constituted by* a community of divine persons). Since most of Gunton's criticisms of Augustine regarding the relationship of substance and person are dependent on a problematic reading of the Cappadocians, we will first consider Gunton's reading of the Cappadocians.

Nowhere does Gunton offer any substantive exposition of trinitarian texts of Basil, Gregory of Nyssa or Gregory of Nazianzus in *The*

---

[80]Ibid., p. 52.

Promise of Trinitarian Theology. He simply employs a reading of the Cappadocians that can be found in John Zizioulas's *Being as Communion*.[81] A detailed analysis of the trinitarian theology of the Cappadocians is outside the scope of our present investigation; however, a brief examination of recent scholarship on Gregory of Nyssa will suffice to illustrate some of the problems that plague the Gunton-Zizioulas reading. Among the Cappadocians, Gregory of Nyssa is regularly heralded as the prototypical social trinitarian, which renders him an ideal candidate.

In 2002 an entire issue of *Modern Theology* was devoted to a discussion of the trinitarian theology of Gregory of Nyssa. Contributors included Sarah Coakley, David Hart, Lewis Ayres, Michel Barnes and others.[82] Several important themes emerge in these essays. First, these scholars are in unanimous agreement that the de Régnon paradigm must be rejected and that popular misreadings of Gregory's theology owe much to the negative influence of this paradigm.[83] In other words, the de Régnon typology fuels not only misreadings of Augustine but also the Cappadocians.

Second, these scholars collectively argue that Gregory's approach to the Trinity should *not* be characterized as "social" either in the sense that Gregory begins with the three persons or in the sense that he pri-

---

[81]John D. Zizioulas, *Being as Communion: Studies in Personhood and the Church* (Crestwood, N.Y.: St. Vladimir's Seminary Press, 1985).

[82]Sarah Coakley, "Re-thinking Gregory of Nyssa: Introduction—Gender, Trinitarian Analogies, and the Pedagogy of The Song," *Modern Theology* 18 (2002): 431-43; David B. Hart, "The Mirror of the Infinite: Gregory of Nyssa on the *Vestigia Trinitatis*," *Modern Theology* 18 (2002): 541-61; Lewis Ayres, "On Not Three People: The Fundamental Themes of Gregory of Nyssa's Trinitarian Theology as Seen in 'To Ablabius: On Not Three Gods,'" *Modern Theology* 18 (2002): 445-74; Michel R. Barnes, "Divine Unity and the Divided Self: Gregory of Nyssa's Trinitarian Theology in its Psychological Context," *Modern Theology* 18 (2002): 475-96; and Lucian Turcescu, "'Person' Versus 'Individual,' and Other Modern Misreadings of Gregory of Nyssa," *Modern Theology* 18 (2002): 527-39. Brian Daley and Martin Laird also contributed essays to this volume.

[83]See Coakley, "Re-thinking Gregory of Nyssa," pp. 431-34; Hart, "Mirror of the Infinite," pp. 541-42; Ayres, "Fundamental Themes of Gregory of Nyssa's Trinitarian Theology," pp. 445-46; Turcescu, "'Person' Versus 'Individual,'" p. 527.

oritizes the persons over the divine essence.[84] Although social readings
frequently appeal to a "three men" analogy, which appears in *Ad Ablabium* as proof of Gregory's social orientation, Lewis Ayres points out
that these readings fail to take into account the polemical context of *Ad
Ablabium:* "Gregory's opponents are alleging that the relationship between substance and person deployed by the Cappadocians is suscep-
tible to the logic that applies to the case of three people."[85] In this context, Gregory wants to lead the reader away from a social analogy and
toward an answer to this criticism through a complex analysis of "divine power."[86]

Third, although it is true that the Cappadocians draw an important
distinction between *hypostasis* and *ousia*, this distinction does not represent one of the fundamental themes in Gregory's theology. Ayres argues that the core of Gregory's trinitarian theology can be found in his
notion of "divine power."[87] It is through the latter that Gregory approaches the problem of relating unity and diversity in God's life:
"Gregory's theology of the infinite and simple divine power is the context within which he can articulate the possibility of eternally distinct
hypostases within one divine power."[88] Gregory's analysis of divine
power, therefore, provides the key to his response to critics who assert

---

[84]See Coakley, "Re-thinking Gregory of Nyssa," p. 434; Hart, "Mirror of the Infinite," p. 542;
Ayres, "Fundamental Themes of Gregory of Nyssa's Trinitarian Theology," pp. 446-47;
Turcescu, "'Person' Versus 'Individual,'" pp. 527-37; Barnes, "Divine Unity and the Divided
Self," pp. 475-76.

[85]Ayres, "Fundamental Themes of Gregory of Nyssa's Trinitarian Theology," p. 447.

[86]Ibid., p. 446.

[87]"I will argue that we should not attempt to understand Gregory by reference primarily to the
development of particular terminological formulations (such as one *ousia*, three *hypostases*).
Nor should we attempt to understand Gregory by reading his thought against the background
of a division of pro-Nicene theologians into general 'eastern' and 'western' groups according to
their supposed preference for 'beginning from' unity or diversity in the Godhead. I will suggest that Gregory's Trinitarian theology is best approached by focusing on the ways in which
he makes a particular contribution to the emergence of a pro-Nicene 'grammar' of divinity
though developing his complex account of divine power" (Ayres, "Fundamental Themes of
Gregory of Nyssa's Trinitarian Theology," pp. 445-46). For a detailed analysis of *power* in
Gregory's theology, see Michel R. Barnes, *The Power of God:* Dunamis *in Gregory of Nyssa's
Trinitarian Theology* (Washington D.C.: Catholic University of America Press, 2001).

[88]Ayres, "Fundamental Themes of Gregory of Nyssa's Trinitarian Theology," p. 467.

that the way pro-Nicene theologians distinguish the divine persons re-flects to the logic of differentiation involved in the case of three people. In *Ad Ablabium*, Gregory argues that affirming three hypostases does not imply three gods, because the nature of divinity is such that it cannot be divided. That divinity cannot be divided is established through a complex analysis of divine action.

Gregory's argument builds on the assumption that natures and their inherent powers are known through the operation of these powers. Since divine operations are always seen to be one, the divine power (and nature) that gives rise to these operations must also be one.[89] Gregory anticipates a problem that arises from his line of argumentation. What about the case of three *separate* orators (i.e., three natures) who speak at the same time (i.e., one action)? To address this problem, Gregory must establish a stronger link between divine causality and external operation.[90] To this end, he distinguishes the "inseparable union of the divine persons in their activity" from the "accidental or coincidental activity of human persons undertaking some common project or business."[91] The divine persons do not merely work together like three humans performing the same task; rather, "they function inseparably to constitute any and every divine activity toward the creation."[92] Every action issues *from* the Father passes *through* the Son and is brought to perfection *by* the Spirit. Ayres notes that many have misunderstood Gregory on this point, interpreting his description of divine action as an example of the alleged personal character of Gregory's theology as if the divine persons merely cooperated, under the Father's direction, in bringing about various actions. Although Gregory in no way denies the hypostatic distinction that exists between the persons, he does not present the three "as possessing distinct actions toward a common goal, but as together constituting *just one distinct action* (because they are one

---

[89]Ibid., p. 452.
[90]Ibid., p. 461.
[91]Ibid.
[92]Ibid.

power)."[93] When we examine God's work in the world, we see a single power acting "by a unitary causal sequenced activity of the three persons."[94] We cannot, therefore, speak of three gods, because we do not see three distinct operations. The divine power is one, yet the persons are distinct.

Finally, these theologians argue that Gregory's trinitarian theology does not possess the kind of "personal" or "social" character ascribed to it by Gunton, Zizioulas and others. In an essay exploring the relationship between Gregory's psychology and his trinitarian thought, Michel Barnes points out that many contemporary scholars read Gregory's trinitarian writings through the lens of certain psychological concerns and conclude that Gregory understands the Trinity in terms of "personal relationship" or that he locates "consciousness(es)" within the Trinity—without ever consulting Gregory's psychology to see how psychological concerns may or may not have influenced his trinitarian theology.[95] An examination of Gregory's psychology clearly reveals "that *personal relationship* or *consciousness* are not the important, substantial psychological concepts for Gregory."[96] Moreover, Barnes insists that Gregory's use of *hypostasis* does not mean "person" in the modern sense of a conscious individual subject.[97] His understanding of *hypostasis* must be derived from the broader context of his trinitarian theology. Whereas Athanasius uses a doctrine of divine generation to ground the *common* nature of the Father and Son (on the assumption that like begets like), Gregory uses a doctrine of generation to ground the *distinction* between the Father and Son.[98] Barnes explains that the difference in existence between the Father and the Son is expressed by Gregory in language of "causality" (i.e., the Father is *Cause* [αιτιος] and the Son is *of the Cause*

---

[93]Ibid.

[94]Ibid., p. 462.

[95]Barnes, "Divine Unity and the Divided Self," p. 476.

[96]Ibid.

[97]"Gregory uses *hypostasis* to mean an existent with real and separate existence, and he does not use the term to refer to or to name a subject of cognition or volition" (Barnes, "Divine Unity and the Divided Self," p. 482).

[98]Ibid., pp. 483-84.

[εκ του αιτου]) and the reality of this difference is expressed using the term *hypostasis*.[99]

One of the most important links between Gregory's psychology and his trinitarian theology can be seen in his account of the will. The divided nature of the human will represents one of his key psychological concerns. For Gregory, "the will is ineffective in its attachment to the good; this lack of effectiveness is due to what is experienced as a conflict in the will; and this conflict suggests divisions in the will, i.e., the will is not meaningfully—as a moral agent—one with itself."[100] Not surprisingly, the efficacy of divine will plays an important role in his trinitarian thought: "The integrity and effectiveness of the wills of the Son and Spirit stands in direct contrast to the state of our human wills. Our will is not one, or rather, we do not have only one will: we have many, and the conflict among them sabotages our own decisions."[101] Perfect unity of will (both among wills and within a will) is possible only for will with a divine nature.[102] Although Gregory believes that Father, Son and Spirit each possess a will (and the faculty that enacts it), "we must be careful not to impose the implications of a later concept of 'person' (e.g., Boethian or Cartesian) upon Gregory" and draw false conclusions.[103] For Gregory, the wills of the Father, Son and Spirit are not three *separate* wills. It would be better to understand them as "Three Individuals, but One Will throughout the Three, or, as Gregory puts it, 'the motion of the di-

---

[99]Ibid., p. 484. What distinguishes Gregory's causal language from that of his opponent Eunomius is that Gregory applies the language of cause exclusively to the relations of the *persons* and never to the divine *nature:* "When we speak of a cause and that which depends on it, we do not, by these words, refer to nature. For no one would hold that cause and nature are identical. Rather we indicate a different manner of existence" (Gregory of Nyssa, "An Answer to Ablabius: That We Should Not Think of Saying There Are Three Gods," in *Christology of the Later Fathers*, Library of Christian Classics, ed. Edward R. Hardy [Louisville: Westminster John Knox Press, 1954], p. 266).

[100]Barnes, "Divine Unity and the Divided Self," p. 480.

[101]Ibid., p. 488.

[102]"Perfect unity among wills, like unity within a will ('freedom'), is true only of wills with a divine nature—if this were otherwise then Gregory's argument that *unity of operations reveals unity of nature* would have no standing" (ibid., p. 489).

[103]Ibid.

vine will from the Father, through the Son, to the Spirit.' "[104]

In light of the preceding analysis, it appears that Gunton has misread the Cappadocians (at least as represented by Gregory of Nyssa) and unjustifiably criticizes Augustine for failing to comprehend something that they do not actually affirm.

Substance and person: Misreading Augustine. We already examined the relationship between substance and person in Augustine's trinitarian theology in chapter four. For the purposes of the present discussion, the following should be noted.[105] First, Augustine does not begin with the divine substance (as opposed to beginning with the persons). His starting point—if we must even speak in such unhelpful terms—is neither the divine substance nor the persons; it is the scriptural teaching on the triune God.[106] This can be seen in book 1 when Augustine begins his discussion of the Trinity with a brief summary of "Catholic" teaching on the Trinity (*De trinitate* 1.7, 69-70). Moreover, in discussing the "fundamental grammar" of Augustine's trinitarian theology (Ayres's term), I argued in chapter four that inseparable operation should be seen as one of the core elements of his theology.[107]

Second, Gunton misunderstands Augustine's discussion of the Greek terms *hypostasis* and *ousia*. Gunton reads Augustine's acknowledged difficulty in understanding the distinction Greek theologians make between *hypostasis* and *ousia* as evidence that he failed to understand the conceptual revolution ushered in by the Cappadocians. It is important to recognize, however, that Augustine's difficulty was not conceptual

---

[104]Ibid.

[105]For a helpful discussion of Augustine's mature trinitarian ontology, see Ayres, *Augustine and the Trinity*, chaps. 7-10.

[106]See Neil Ormerod, *The Trinity: Retrieving the Western Tradition* (Milwaukee: Marquette University Press, 2005), pp. 35-36.

[107]Inseparable operation, as I noted in chap. 4, also represents a fundamental element of Cappadocian trinitarian theology. If one wants to argue that Augustine's account of inseparable operation constitutes a reason to reject his trinitarian theology, then one must be consistent and affirm that it also constitutes a reason to reject the trinitarian theology of the Cappadocians.

but linguistic. The formal Latin equivalents to the Greek terms *hypostasis* and *ousia* are *substantia* ("substance") and *essentia* ("being"). Because *substantia* and *essentia* possess virtually synonymous meaning in Latin, they are not suitable for expressing, among native Latin speakers, the distinctions that exist among the Father, the Son and the Holy Spirit.[108] Latin speaking pro-Nicene Christians preferred to express this conceptual distinction in terms of a distinction between one being (*essentia*) or substance (*substantia*) and three persons (*persona*). Augustine's linguistic confusion, therefore, is completely understandable. No warrant, therefore, exists for inferring conceptual confusion from Augustine's justifiable linguistic confusion.

Furthermore, Gunton misinterprets Augustine's ambivalence regarding the term *person* (*persona*). From his reserve, we should not infer that Augustine somehow failed to affirm real distinctions among the Father, Son and Holy Spirit.[109] At least two factors play an important role in Augustine's ambivalence regarding the Latin term *persona:* his distinction between "faith" and "understanding" and the Creator-creature distinction. Notice how these two factors are intertwined in Augustine's discussion of *person* in book 7:

> That there are three is declared by the true faith, when it says that the
> Father is not the Son, and the Holy Spirit which is the gift of God is
> neither the Father nor the Son. So when the question is asked "Three
> what?" we apply ourselves to finding some name of species or genus

---

[108]"But because we have grown accustomed in our usage to meaning the same thing by 'being' (*essentiam*) as by 'substance' (*substantiam*), we do not dare say one being, three substances (*unam essentiam, tres substantias*). Rather, one being or substance (*unam essentiam, vel substantiam*), three persons (*tres autem personas*) is what many Latin authors, whose authority carries weight, have said when treating of these matters, being able to find no more suitable way of expressing in words what they understood without words" (Augustine, *De trinitate* 5.10, 196). The language Augustine employs to speak about unity and distinction in the triune God (i.e., *una substantia, tres persona*) can be traced back to Tertullian.

[109]This criticism cannot be squared with the strong anti-Monarchian and anti-Sabellian themes that emerge in Augustine's *De fide et symbolo* (see Ayres, *Augustine and the Trinity*, pp. 72-92). Ayres points out that Augustine's strong anti-Monarchian language signifies permanent relationships among the divine persons. "Latin anti-Monarchian terminologies are intended to defend the principle that the divine names must be understood as implying the real existence of the agents and relationships they name" (ibid., p. 76).

which will comprise these three, and no such name occurs to our minds, because the total transcendence of the godhead quite surpasses the capacity of ordinary speech.[110]

"Faith" (i.e., the Scriptures read by the church) requires one to affirm that the Father is not the Son and the Son is not the Father.[111] A problem, however, arises in how to express to our understanding what "faith" requires us to affirm (i.e., that the Father is not the Son and the Son is not the Father). The latter problem is further compounded by Creator-creature distinction. As Augustine explains, "the total transcendence of the godhead quite surpasses the capacity of ordinary speech." As a result, any human term we choose to express the reality that the Father is not the Son and that the Son is not the Father will ultimately fall short.[112] Thus, we should not interpret Augustine's ambivalence regarding *persona* as undermining genuine hypostatic distinctions that exist among the Father, Son and Holy Spirit. In chapter four I argued that Augustine grounds real distinctions among the divine persons in relations of origin: the Son is distinct from the Father by virtue of his generation while the Spirit is distinct from the Father (and the Son) by virtue of his procession from the Father and the Son (as from one principle).[113]

Gunton also fails to recognize the polemical context of Augustine's discussion of *persona* in books 5-7. Unlike the Cappadocians, who allegedly developed a "relational" ontology by carefully reflecting on the being of God, Gunton insists that Augustine's discussion of *person* is driven by the "apparent logical oddity of the threeness of the one God,"

---

[110]Augustine, *De trinitate* 5.7, 224.

[111]It is important to note that Augustine's summary of Latin teaching on the Trinity does not use the term *persona* but simply affirms that the Father is not the Son because the Father begot the Son and the Son is not the Father because the Son is begotten by the Father (see Augustine, *De trinitate* 1.7, 69-70).

[112]*Person* can never be used univocally of humans and God. One of the questions to be raised regarding Gunton's notion of divine "person" is whether it adequately addresses the Creator-creature distinction.

[113]Although differences exist between Augustine and the Cappadocians, it is important to recognize that the Cappadocians also root distinctions between the persons in relations of origin that obtain in the immanent life of God.

which Augustine expresses "in terms of Aristotelian subject-predicate logic."[114] Augustine, however, is not in a speculative moment wrestling with an apparent logical oddity of imputing threeness to the one God. On the contrary, Augustine is answering the criticisms of Latin Homoian theologians.[115] Homoians argued that since there can be no accidents (*accidentia*) in God, all divine predicates must be substantial. Since, as predicates, unbegotten (*ingenitum*) and begotten (*genitum*) ostensibly name different substances, these Homoians asserted that the substance of the Father must be different from the substance of the Son (*De trinitate* 5.4, 191). Augustine answered this criticism by pointing out that while God can have no accidents, it does not follow that every statement about God must be a substance statement. Some predications (e.g., "begotten" and "unbegotten") indicate a relation (*relatiuum*).[116] "So although begotten [*genitus*] differs from unbegotten [*ingenitus*], it does not indicate a different substance, because just as son refers to father, and not son to not father, so begotten must refer to begetter, and not begotten to not begetter" (*De trinitate* 5.8, 194). In short, Augustine is offering a *philosophical* solution to a *philosophical* problem. The Cappadocians faced a comparable challenge (most notably from Eunomius) and offered a similar conceptual solution (namely, that "Father" and "Son" name relations that do not modify the essence of God).[117]

---

[114]Gunton, *Promise of Trinitarian Theology*, p. 40.

[115]See Michel R. Barnes, "The Arians of Book V, and the Genre of '*de Trinitate*,'" *Journal of Theological Studies* 44 (1993): 185-95.

[116]"With God, though, nothing is said modification-wise, because there is nothing changeable with him. And yet not everything that is said of him is said substance-wise. Some things are said with reference to something else, like Father with reference to Son and Son with reference to Father; and this is not said modification-wise, because the one is always Father and the other always Son—not 'always' in the sense that he is Son from the moment he is born or that the Father does not cease to be Father from the moment the Son does not cease to be Son, but in the sense that the Son is always born and never began to be Son" (Augustine, *De trinitate* 5.5, 192).

[117]Eunomius insisted that "ungenerateness" (*agennesia*) constituted the essence of God. In response to Eunomius, the Cappadocians argued that "ingenerateness" (*agennesia*) signifies the Father in relation to the Son. The Son is distinct from the Father by virtue of his generation by the Father. The Spirit is distinct from the Father by virtue of his procession from the Father (see Gregory of Nazianzus, "The Fifth Theological Oration—On the Spirit," in *Christology of the Later Fathers*, Library of Christian Classics, ed. Edward R. Hardy [Louisville:

Finally, Gunton fundamentally misunderstands the role of the Father in Augustine's trinitarian theology. He claims that for Augustine the "true being of God" somehow underlies the persons. On this reading, the divine substance—rather than the Father—constitutes the substratum of God. This, in turn, constitutes the basis for Gunton's claim that Augustine's trinitarian theology is modalist. In response it should be noted that although he speaks unequivocally about Father, Son and Holy Spirit as a unity of substance, Augustine also affirms clearly that the Father is the *principium* (source). Lewis Ayres argues that Augustine's mature account of the Trinity involves "an ordered communion of equals established by the Father."[118] Thus, the immanent life of the triune God "is founded in the Father's activity as the one from whom the Son is eternally born and the Spirit proceeds."[119]

Materiality and the incarnation. Gunton claims that Augustine is afraid of the material world and that this fear (reflecting the negative influence of Neo-Platonism) leads him toward an "anti-incarnational" and "docetic" Christology, which fails to give full weight to the humanity of Christ. Although this criticism may not appear to be related to Augustine's teaching on the Trinity,[120] it is directly related in the sense it constitutes alleged evidence for the negative influence of Neo-Platonism on Augustine's trinitarian theology.

Contra Gunton, this criticism cannot be established simply through guilt by association (i.e., since all Neo-Platonists were afraid of the material world and Augustine was a Neo-Platonist, he must have been

---

Westminster John Knox Press, 1954], p. 199).

[118]Ibid., p. 197. For further discussion of the nature of this divine communion, see Ayres, *Augustine and the Trinity*, chaps. 7-10.

[119]Ayres, *Augustine and the Trinity*, p. 3.

[120]We also need to remember that Augustine (along with all early Christian theologians) makes no methodological distinction between "trinitarian theology" and "Christology." For a helpful discussion of this reality along with its implications for how we should read patristic theology, see John Behr, *The Formation of Christian Theology*, vol. 2, *The Nicene Faith* (Crestwood, N.Y.: St. Vladimir's Seminary Press, 2004), pp. 1-17, 475-81. Interestingly, recent scholarship on Augustine has been paying greater attention to how christological themes shape his trinitarian theology. A vivid example of this can be seen in the case of what Ayres describes as Augustine's "Christological epistemology" (see Ayres, *Augustine and the Trinity*, pp. 142-70).

fearful of the material world). Gunton's claim can only be established through a close reading of Augustine's writings in their historical context. Read in context, the examples Gunton cites simply do not support his assertions.

In order to understand why Gunton's assessment is wrong, we must first understand the role that "divine immateriality" plays in Augustine's trinitarian theology. Not only does the doctrine of God's immaterial nature represent one of the foundational features of Augustine's trinitarian theology, but the role that this doctrine plays in his thought is also "without antecedents in Latin or Greek Christianity" deriving from Augustine's unique intellectual development.[121] Augustine's doctrine of divine immateriality serves as a way of articulating a central concern of pro-Nicene theologians—namely, protecting the Creator-creature distinction. Pro-Nicene theologians wanted to establish a clear distinction between divine nature and all other natures (i.e., created natures). As a result, they ruled out the possibility of any kind of middle nature(s).[122] What is distinctive about Augustine, therefore, is the way that he employs divine immateriality "to emphasize the distinction between uncreated and created natures."[123] Augustine's emphasis on divine immateriality, therefore, should not be seen as reflecting a fear of the material world but rather as grounding the distinction between God and creation. With this in mind, we will consider Gunton's evidence.

First, Gunton's assertion that Augustine's discussion of the Old Testament theophanies represents an instance of "anti-incarnational platonism" is unsustainable. Gunton reasons that if Augustine really believed in the incarnation, we would be able to see antecedents of this in his explanation of Old Testament theophanies. Instead, Augustine allegedly limits divine appearances to the work of angels in order to avoid associating God with matter. Although it is true that Augustine believes that the divine appearances in the Old Testament were mediated

---

[121]Barnes, "Logic of Augustine's Trinitarian Theology," p. 6.
[122]Ibid.
[123]Ibid.

by angels, it is wrong to conclude that this reality reflects negatively on his understanding of the incarnation. Precisely the opposite is the case. In books 2-4, Augustine wants to establish that the Son was not sent until the New Testament (and he is on solid biblical ground in wanting to affirm this). For this reason, he clearly distinguishes the appearance of the incarnate Son from earlier divine manifestations. In making this move Augustine breaks with an earlier theological tradition which interpreted all Old Testament theophanies as Christophanies. This move is motivated both by exegetical and theological considerations. From an exegetical perspective Augustine does not believe adequate warrant exists for interpreting all Old Testament theophanies as Christophanies. From a theological perspective Augustine believes that identifying the Son as the uniquely visible person of the Trinity (in contrast to the Father, who is invisible) leads to a subordinationist understanding of the Son that is incompatible with New Testament teaching regarding the equality of the Son with the Father.[124]

Second, Gunton's claim that Augustine's account of the baptism of Jesus represents a second instance of "anti-incarnational platonism" is also untenable. According to Gunton, Augustine cannot accept the obvious implication of this narrative that Jesus entered into a new relationship with the Spirit following his baptism. Gunton, however, appears to have misunderstood Augustine's point. Augustine's explanation of this story (specifically his claim that "It would be the height of absurdity to believe that he only received the Holy Spirit when he was already thirty years old" [De trinitate 15.46, 431]) does not reflect anti-incarnational Platonism. Rather, the "supposition that Augustine rejects as the height of absurdity was in fact made by the Adoptionist heresy, which declared that Jesus (a mere human being) was *adopted* as Son of God at his baptism, when the Holy Spirit came upon him."[125]

---

[124]On a related note Augustine does not, contra Gunton, lose the mediatorship of the Word in his account of the theophanies. On the contrary, mediation plays a central role in Augustine's discussion of the mission of the Son in book 4.

[125]Augustine, *The Trinity*, trans. Edmund Hill (Brooklyn: New City Press, 1991). p. 442 n. 125.

Third, Gunton is mistaken in his claim that Augustine undermines the value of the material realm as a bearer of theological meaning by locating the divine image in the mind. He fails to understand the purpose of the second half of *De trinitate*. Augustine believes that traces of the Trinity (*vestigia trinitatis*) can be found throughout creation. In this sense, Augustine affirms precisely what Gunton wishes he would affirm—namely, that the created world possesses theological meaning; however, in the second half of *De trinitate* Augustine is not searching for analogies of the Trinity. His interest lies with the divine image, which he believes has been created in the image of the Trinity. More specifically, Augustine wants to contemplate the triune God through the divine image in the human soul (*mens*). He believes he has scriptural warrant (especially in Paul) for locating the divine image in soul. To insist that by locating the divine image in the soul, Augustine undermines the value of the material realm is, therefore, without warrant. Moreover, Gunton's claim that the material world does not bear theological meaning cannot be reconciled with Augustine's rich account of *sacramentum*. For Augustine *sacramenta* are material objects that constitute sacred signs pointing to deeper realities. Augustine does not limit *sacramenta* to baptism and Eucharist, but also includes numerous Old Testament events, places and objects (e.g., sabbath, circumcision, altars, etc.) as well as key elements of New Testament faith (e.g., Easter, Pentecost, sign of the cross, feasts, garments, etc.). It is important to note that these elements are not mere "signs" for Augustine but *sacramenta* that correspond to deeper spiritual realities. Although these material realities have no intrinsic power, they mediate the power of the Word of God.[126]

Finally, it is one thing to acknowledge that Augustine, through his

---

[126]"From these responses of Augustine a sacramental principle comes to clarification: sacraments are the visible word of God to be received in faith. The sacrament is composed of both the material element and the word of God. The power of the sacrament comes from the word of God articulated in and through the church" Emmanuel J. Cutrone, "Sacraments," in *Augustine Through the Ages: An Encyclopedia*, ed. Allan D. Fitzgerald (Grand Rapids: Eerdmans, 1999).

polemical engagement with Latin Homoian theologians, may in this context place greater emphasis on Christ's deity than on his humanity. It is quite another to insist, as Gunton does, that Augustine somehow denies, or does not fully affirm, the humanity of Jesus Christ. Although he does not articulate the relation between the two natures of Christ in the precise technical language of later creedal developments (e.g., Chalcedon), Augustine clearly teaches that Christ possesses two natures (divine and human) and that these two natures are united in one subject.[127] On the one hand, Augustine draws a careful distinction between the Son in the "form of a servant" and the Son in the "form of God," insisting that neither of these natures was "turned or changed."[128] On the other hand, he insists that these two "forms" exist in one person.

Trinitarian analogies. Gunton claims that in his search for trinitarian "analogies," Augustine imposes a Neo-Platonic conception of divine unity on the Trinity, with the result that an unknown substance underlies the persons. In so doing, Augustine purportedly abandons the economy of salvation and turns God into a kind of "supermind." Moreover, by searching for trinitarian analogies in the mind, Augustine purportedly paves the way for individualism and intellectualism. These criticisms are rooted in Gunton's assumption that Augustine possesses an ontology that differs radically from that of the Cappadocians. I have already demonstrated that this claim (which is parasitic upon de Régnon's paradigm) is unsustainable.[129] In addition, we must recognize

---

[127]"Augustine insists throughout his career that the humanity of Jesus, even though united to and possessed by the Word of God, remains complete in both its corporeal and its psychological dimensions" (Brian E. Daley, "Christology," in *Augustine Through the Ages: An Encyclopedia*, ed. Allan D. Fitzgerald [Grand Rapids: Eerdmans, 1999]). Daley suggests that four emphases can be discerned in Augustine's writings about Christ: (1) emphasis on the integrity of the humanity of Christ, (2) emphasis on the divine person of the Word as the source of unity between the natures, (3) emphasis on Christ as Mediator, and (4) Christ's mediation as an expression of God's unmerited grace.

[128]"In conclusion then, because the form of God took on the form of a servant, each is God and each is man, but each is God because of God taking on, and each is man because of man taken on. Neither of them was turned or changed into the other by that 'take-over'; neither godhead changed into creature and ceasing to be godhead, nor creature changed into godhead and ceasing to be creature" (Augustine, *De trinitate* 1.14, 75).

[129]Obviously differences exist between the trinitarian theologies of Augustine and the Cappa-

that *analogy* is the wrong term to describe what Augustine is doing in the second half of *De trinitate*. Lewis Ayres points out that some scholars have somewhat imprecisely used the term *analogy* to describe the likenesses for which Augustine searches in books 8-15.[130] Although he sometimes searches for analogies (*analogia*) of the inseparable working of the persons, "Augustine *never* directly uses *analogia* or *proportio* to describe the relationship between God and any aspect of the creation (and interestingly neither term even appears in *trin*)."[131] Instead Augustine employs the term *similitudo* (likeness) to describe the relationship that obtains between God and creation. With this context in mind, we will critically examine the evidence Gunton adduces in support of his interpretation of Augustine's trinitarian "analogies."

First, in his search for the divine image in the human soul, Augustine does not impose a foreign concept of divine threeness upon the Trinity. Not only does his reading of Scripture prompt him to see the image of God in the human soul as a reflection of the Trinity, but it is also scriptural teaching about the Trinity (as outlined in the first half of *De trinitate*) that provides the blueprint for the trinitarian image in soul and as well as the basis for evaluating the viability of trinities he identifies. Furthermore, Augustine is not unique in locating the divine image in the soul. David Hart points out that important similarities exist between Gregory of Nyssa and Augustine in seeing the individual human soul as the locus of the divine image: "One should also note, at the outset, that for Gregory, no less than for Augustine, the divine image is first and foremost the possession of each individual soul, in the mystery of her simultaneous unity of essence and diversity of acts."[132]

Second, Augustine does not abandon the economy of salvation in his

---

docians. The problem with Gunton's reading is not an assumption that differences exist but that Gunton attempts to locate these differences in areas which Augustine and the Cappadocians share in common.

[130]Lewis Ayres, "'Remember That You Are Catholic' (Serm 52.2): Augustine on the Unity of the Triune God," *Journal of Early Christian Studies* 8 (2000): 59.

[131]Ibid., p. 61.

[132]Hart, "Mirror of the Infinite," p. 543.

search for reflections of the Trinity in the divine image in the soul. To the contrary, Augustine is engaged in a vital search to know and understand the triune God. The redemptive work of Christ plays a crucial role in this search. Augustine focuses on the image in the soul not out of a desire to liken God to a "supermind" but because the divine image represents the locus of God's redemptive work. The centrality of the economy of salvation can be seen in books 12-14 in which Augustine chronicles the effacement of the divine image by sin, its restoration through the work of Christ, and its future perfection.

Third, Gunton's critique fails to recognize the continuity that exists between Augustine and the Cappadocians in their search for psychological "likenesses" to the Trinity.[133] Gregory of Nyssa sometimes applies "psychological categories to the Trinity," and when he does so "we often find him happily doing so with reference to the Godhead as analogous to *one* person, the Father's constitution of the Triune Godhead being treated as analogous to one who speaks an intelligible word on his breath or spirit (*Catechetical Oration* 1-2 is paradigmatic here)."[134] In the text to which Lewis Ayres refers, Gregory is attempting to explicate the distinction of divine persons in their unity. Notice, in this text, how Gregory explicates the unity and distinction of the Father and Son by likening the generation of the Son to the production of a mental word:

> In our own case we say that a spoken word comes from the mind, and is neither entirely identical with it nor altogether different. For by being derived from something else, it is different and not identical with it. Yet, since it reflects the mind, it can no longer be thought to be different from it, but is one with it in nature, though distinct as a subject. So the Word of God, by having its own subsistence, is distinct from him from whom it derives its subsistence. On the other hand, by manifesting in itself the attributes to be seen in God, it is identical in nature with Him who is recognized by the same characteristics.[135]

---

[133]Ibid., p. 44.

[134]Ayres, "On Not Three People," p. 447.

[135]Gregory of Nyssa, "Address on Religious Instruction," in *Christology of the Later Fathers*, Library of Christian Classics, ed. Edward R. Hardy (Louisville: Westminster John Knox Press,

Remarkable similarities therefore exist between Augustine and
Gregory in their application of psychological categories to the Trinity.
Hence, if the presence of trinitarian likenesses to the mind constitutes
a reason to reject Augustine's trinitarian theology, then it would also
appear to represent a reason to reject the theology of the Cappadocians
(at least as represented by Gregory of Nyssa) as well.

Trinitarian pneumatology. Gunton asserts that Augustine's pneumatology represents one of the core weaknesses of his doctrine of the
Trinity. At least four problems shape Gunton's analysis. First, Gunton
is wrong when he claims that "Augustine has given us little reason to
believe that God is to be known as he is from his manifestation in the
economy."[136] In chapter three I demonstrated that significant continuity exists for Augustine between what, in contemporary theological
terms, we call the "economic" Trinity and the "immanent" Trinity. The
economy of salvation, contra Gunton, plays a crucial role in the development of Augustine's doctrine of the Spirit.[137] One of Augustine's contributions to the Western tradition is his notion that the Spirit proceeds
from the Father and the Son. It is from the bestowal of the Spirit by
the Son *in the economy of salvation* that Augustine was led to infer that
the Spirit proceeds from the Father and the Son in the immanent life
of the triune God. The logic of this is quite clear: if sending reveals
procession, and if the Son sent the Spirit, then the Spirit must proceed
from the Son (as well as from the Father). Moreover, Augustine sees
biblical warrant for the procession of the Spirit from the Son in the way
that Scripture speaks about the Holy Spirit as the "Spirit of the Father
and the Son." Thus, Gunton's claim that Augustine's doctrine of the

---

1954), p. 272. In the following section Gregory also explains his method: "Our knowledge of
the Word comes from applying, in a raised degree, our own attributes to the transcendent
nature" (ibid.).

[136]Gunton, *Promise of Trinitarian Theology*, p. 53.

[137]As Barnes notes, "Augustine reads virtually all statements about the relationship of the Son
and the Spirit as also signifying aspects of their eternal relationship" (Barnes, "Augustine's
Last Pneumatology," p. 225). John 20:22 represents a case in point. From the Son's "breath-
ing" on the disciples, Augustine's infers a role for the Son in the eternal procession of the
Spirit.

Spirit is "strongly affected by his need to have a third person corresponding to the will in the threefold mind" is unwarranted.

Second, Gunton is also mistaken when he claims that Augustine is unable to provide an adequate account of the personal nature of the Holy Spirit: "The overall result is that because the doctrine of the Spirit has inadequate economic hypostatic weight in Augustine, the father of Western theology also lacks the means to give personal distinctiveness to the being of the Spirit in the inner Trinity."[138] As evidence of the latter, he cites Augustine's description of the Spirit as "gift" and "love." These two concepts allegedly lack biblical support. Moreover, from a trinitarian perspective, they do not provide an adequate basis for distinguishing the Spirit from the Son. In response, it must be noted that the hypostatic distinction between the Son and Spirit in Augustine's trinitarian theology does not ultimately depend on his analysis of "gift" and "love." Augustine grounds real distinctions between the divine persons in relations of origin that obtain in the immanent Trinity. The Son is distinct from the Father by virtue of his *generation* while the Spirit is distinct from the Father and the Son by virtue of *procession* from the Father and the Son as from one principle. *Gift* and *love* represent an attempt, on Augustine's part, to describe the relationships that obtain at an intra-trinitarian level by drawing inferences from the activity of the Spirit in the economy. Thus, even if we were to acknowledge with Gunton that these concepts, as employed by Augustine, lack adequate biblical support,[139] it does not follow that Augustine fails to give adequate hypostatic weight to the Spirit.[140]

Third, we must recognize that Gunton's critique of Augustine's pneu-

---

[138]Gunton, *Promise of Trinitarian Theology*, p. 51.

[139]From an economic perspective, there does seem to be a unique sense in which the New Testament speaks of the Holy Spirit as "gift"—especially in the preaching of the gospel in Acts (Acts 2:38; 8:20; 10:45; 11:17). Moreover, although Paul applies the language of gift to salvation in Christ (Rom 5:15; 2 Cor 9:15), he expresses the concept of the gift of the Spirit in terms of the language of promise (see Gal 3:14; Eph 1:13). Interestingly, Luke also uses promise in relation to the Spirit in Acts as well (Acts 1:4; 2:33; 2:39).

[140]For a helpful discussion of the Holy Spirit in Augustine's trinitarian theology, see Ayres, *Augustine and the Trinity*, chap. 10.

matology is dependent on his misreading of the Cappadocians. This misreading leads Gunton to dismiss the claim made by the editors of the Library of Christian Classics edition of *De trinitate* that continuity exists between Augustine's understanding of procession of the Spirit from the Father and Son, and the Eastern doctrine that the Spirit proceeds from the Father through the Son.[141] According to Gunton, "We have already seen, however, that there are major differences all along the line between Augustine and the Cappadocian Fathers. There are bound to be differences here also."[142] Aside from reminding his readers of the "ontological revolution" ushered in by the Cappadocians, Gunton offers no exposition of the Cappadocian doctrine of the Spirit; nor does he explain how this doctrine differs from Augustine. It should be noted, however, that significant continuity exists between Augustine and the Cappadocians in the sense that both use generation and procession as the basis for distinguishing the Son and the Spirit from the Father.[143] Furthermore, both acknowledge the Father as the ultimate "source" of the Son and the Spirit. The Cappadocians express this reality through the language of *monarchia* (Greek), while Augustine expresses it through the language of *principium* (Latin). Although he believes that the Spirit proceeds from the Father *and the Son,* Augustine is equally insistent that the Holy Spirit proceeds principally from the Father because the Father is the source of deity (*De trinitate* 4.29, 174).[144] Having acknowledged these points of continuity, we must recognize an important point

---

[141]Gunton, *Promise of Trinitarian Theology*, p. 52.

[142]Ibid.

[143]Unlike later Western trinitarian theology (e.g., Thomas Aquinas), Augustine never speaks in terms of "two processions." Procession (*processio*) is used exclusively in *De trinitate* in reference to the Spirit.

[144]Although Gunton is aware of this feature in Augustine's doctrine of the Spirit, he responds not by criticizing Augustine's specific formulation but by appealing to later developments as the basis for his criticism: "We cannot escape the history of the matter, and that is that although Augustine was aware of the need to qualify the *Filioque* with a *principaliter*, the tradition which built upon his work eventually developed a doctrine of God which was materially different from that of its Eastern colleagues" (Gunton, *Promise of Trinitarian Theology*, p. 53). It is difficult to see how later trinitarian developments (which Gunton does not spell out) constitute a reason for rejecting Augustine's doctrine of the Spirit.

of *discontinuity* between Augustine and the Cappadocians. Although the Cappadocians recognized that the procession of the Spirit clearly differed from the generation of the Son (such that it would be inappropriate to speak of the Spirit as a second Son), they were largely at a loss to offer a rationale for this distinction. For example, although Gregory of Nazianzus clearly wants to distinguish procession and generation, he is unable to offer any explanation of how they differ or why the Holy Spirit is not a second son:

> What, then, is procession? Do you tell me what is the unbegottenness of the Father, and I will explain to you the physiology of the generation of the Son and the procession of the Spirit, and we shall both of us be frenzy-stricken for prying into the mystery of God. And who are we to do these things, we who cannot even see what lies at our feet, or number the sand of the sea, or the drops of rain, or the days of eternity, much less enter into the depths of God, and supply an account of that nature which is so unspeakable and transcending all words?[145]

Augustine provided an answer by suggesting that the Holy Spirit proceeds jointly from the Father and the Son as from one principle (see discussion in chap. 4). Of course, with Gregory, Augustine would want to affirm that generation and procession are ultimately incomprehensible to the human mind.

What remains of Gunton's claim that Augustine's trinitarian theology is responsible for many of the contemporary problems that plague both Western culture (e.g., individualism) and the church (e.g., deficient ecclesiology)? Gunton's analysis of the legacy of Augustine's thought is marked by least two weaknesses. First, it rests on a deficient understanding of Augustine's trinitarian theology. Second, his analysis employs a reductionist (genealogical) view of history. All phenomena of interest (e.g., ecclesiology and anthropology) are said to depend genetically on two differing concepts of the Trinity. This is simply untenable.

---

[145]Gregory of Nazianzus, "The Fifth Theological Oration" 8, pp. 198-99.

CONCLUSION

Although his teaching on the Trinity has exerted a dominant influence in the West, not everyone views Augustine's influence as positive. According to critics, Augustine prioritizes a unity of substance over the divine persons, his psychological "analogy" is modalistic, his trinitarian teaching reflects the negative influence of Neo-Platonism, and he separates the life of the triune God from the economy of salvation. I have not attempted to survey all the theologians who share these criticisms but rather focused on one articulate representative of these criticisms, Colin Gunton, in order to draw attention to some of the ways Augustine is characteristically misread in contemporary theology. Four factors fuel contemporary misreadings of Augustine: (1) the inability to read Augustine and the Cappadocians outside the de Régnon paradigm, (2) a tendency to read Augustine's theology in isolated pieces, combined with a failure to contextualize his thought, (3) a failure to distinguish between the teaching of Augustine and later developments, and (4) failure to engage contemporary Augustinian scholarship. As long as these factors continue to persist (especially the influence of the de Régnon paradigm), it is unlikely criticisms of Augustine's trinitarian theology, such as those we have examined here, will abate. This is unfortunate as Augustine's trinitarian theology represents one of the theological treasures of the church in guiding her to know and enjoy the triune God.

BIBLIOGRAPHY

◆

Aleaz, K. P. "Pluralism Calls for Pluralistic Inclusivism," pp. 162-75. In *The Myth of Religious Superiority: Multifaith Explorations of Religious Pluralism.* Edited by Paul F. Knitter. Maryknoll, N.Y.: Orbis, 2005.

Arnold, Johannes. "Begriff und heilsökonomische Bedeutung der göttlichen Sendungen in Augustinus' *De Trinitate*." *Recherches Augustiniennes* 25 (1991): 3-69.

Augustine of Hippo. *Corpus Christianorum Series Latina.* Vol. 50. Turnholt: Brepols, 1968.

———. *Tractates on the Gospel of John, 11-27.* Fathers of the Church 79. Translated by John W. Rettig. Washington D.C.: Catholic University of America, 1988.

———. *Tractates on the Gospel of John, 55-111.* Fathers of the Church 90. Translated by John W. Rettig. Washington D.C.: Catholic University of America Press, 1994.

———. *The Trinity.* Translated by Edmund Hill. Brooklyn: New City Press, 1991.

———. *The Works of Saint Augustine: A Translation for the 21st Century.* Vol. 3.3, *Sermons III (51-94) on the New Testament.* Translated by Edmund Hill. Edited by John E. Rotelle. Brooklyn: New City Press, 1991.

Ayres, Lewis. *Augustine and the Trinity.* Cambridge: Cambridge University Press, 2010.

———. "Augustine on God as Love and Love as God." *Pro Ecclesia* 5 (1996): 470-87.

———. "Augustine on the Rule of Faith: Rhetoric, Christology and the Foundation of Christian Thinking." *Augustinian Studies* 36 (2005): 33-49.

———. "Between Athens and Jerusalem: Prolegomena to Anthropology in *De Trinitate*." *Modern Theology* 8 (1992): 53-73.

———. "The Christological Context of Augustine's *De Trinitate* XIII: Toward Re-locating Books VIII-XV." *Augustinian Studies* 29 (1998): 111-39.

———. "The Fundamental Grammar of Augustine's Trinitarian Theology," pp. 51-76. In *Augustine and his Critics: Essays in Honour of Gerald Bonner*. Edited by Robert Dodaro and George Lawless. London: New York: Routledge, 2000.

———. *Nicaea and Its Legacy: An Approach to Fourth-Century Trinitarian Theology*. New York: Oxford University Press, 2004.

———. "On Not Three People: The Fundamental Themes of Gregory of Nyssa's Trinitarian Theology as Seen in 'To Ablabius: On Not Three Gods.'" *Modern Theology* 18 (2002): 445-74.

———. "'Remember That You Are Catholic' (Serm. 52.2): Augustine on the Unity of the Triune God." *Journal of Early Christian Studies* 8 (2000): 39-82.

Badock, Gary. "Karl Rahner, the Trinity, and Religious Pluralism," pp. 143-54. In *The Trinity in a Pluralistic Age*. Edited by Kevin J. Vanhoozer. Grand Rapids: Eerdmans, 1997.

Baer, Helmut D. "The Fruit of Charity: Using the Neighbor in *De Doctrina christiana*." *Journal of Religious Ethics* 24 (1996): 47-64.

Bailleux, E. "Dieu trinité et son œuvre." *Recherches augustiniennes* 7 (1971): 189-218.

Balthasar, Hans Urs von. *The Theo-Drama: Theological Dramatic Theory*. Vol. 2, *Dramatis Personae: Man in God*. Translated by Graham Harrison. San Francisco: Ignatius Press, 1990.

———. *The Theo-Drama: Theological Dramatic Theory*. Vol. 3, *Dramatis Personae: Persons in Christ*. Translated by Graham Harrison. San Francisco: Ignatius Press, 1992.

———. *The Theo-Drama: Theological Dramatic Theory*. Vol. 4, *The Action*. Translated by Graham Harrison. San Francisco: Ignatius Press, 1994.

———. *The Theo-Drama: Theological Dramatic Theory*. Vol. 5, *The Last Act*. Translated by Graham Harrison. San Francisco: Ignatius Press, 1998.

Barnes, Michel R. "The Arians of Book V, and the Genre of '*de Trinitate*.'" *Journal of Theological Studies* 44 (1993): 185-95.

———. "Augustine and the Limits of Nicene Orthodoxy." *Augustinian Studies* 38 (2007): 189-202.

———. "Augustine in Contemporary Trinitarian Theology." *Theological Studies* 56 (1995): 237-50.

———. "Augustine's Last Pneumatology." *Augustinian Studies* 39 (2008): 223-34.

———. "De Régnon Reconsidered." *Augustinian Studies* 26 (1995): 51-79.

———. "De Trinitate VI and VII: Augustine and the Limits of Nicene Orthodoxy." *Augustinian Studies* 39 (2007): 189-202.

———. "Divine Unity and the Divided Self: Gregory of Nyssa's Trinitarian Theology in its Psychological Context." *Modern Theology* 18 (2002): 475-96.

———. "Exegesis and Polemic in Augustine's *De Trinitate* I." *Augustinian Studies* 30 (1999): 43-52.

———. "The Fourth Century as Trinitarian Canon," pp. 47-67. In *Christian Origins: Theology, Rhetoric and Community*. Edited by Lewis Ayres and Gareth Jones. New York: Routledge, 1998.

———. "The Logic of Augustine's Trinitarian Theology." Unpublished paper presented at the Aquinas the Augustinian Conference, Naples, Florida, February 4, 2005.

———. "One Nature, One Power: Consensus Doctrine in Pro-Nicene Polemic," pp. 205-23. In *Studia Patristica*. Vol. 29, *Historica, Theologica et Philosophica, Critica et Philologica*. Edited by Elizabeth A. Livingstone. Louvain: Peeters, 1997.

———. *The Power of God: Dunamis in Gregory of Nyssa's Trinitarian Theology*. Washington D.C.: Catholic University of America Press, 2001.

———. "Rereading Augustine's Theology of the Trinity," pp. 145-76. In *The Trinity: An Interdisciplinary Symposium on the Trinity*. Edited by Stephen T. Davis, Daniel Kendall, and Gerald O'Collins. New York: Oxford University Press, 1999.

———. "The Visible Christ and the Invisible Trinity: Mt. 5:8 in Augustine's Trinitarian Theology of 400." *Modern Theology* 19 (2003): 329-55.

Barth, Karl. *Church Dogmatics*. Vol. I/1, *The Doctrine of the Word of God*. 2nd ed. Translated by G. W. Bromiley. Edinburgh: T & T Clark, 1975.

———. *Church Dogmatics*. Vol. II/1, *The Doctrine of God*. Translated by T. H. L. Parker et al. Edinburgh: T & T Clark, 1957.

Basil of Caesarea. *On the Holy Spirit*. Translated by David Anderson. Crestwood, N.Y.: St. Vladimir's Seminary Press, 1980.

Bauckham, Richard. *Jesus and the God of Israel: God Crucified and Other Studies on the New Testament's Christology of Divine Identity*. Grand Rapids: Eerdmans, 2008.

———. "Jürgen Moltmann's *The Trinity and the Kingdom of God* and the Question of Pluralism," pp. 155-64. In *The Trinity in a Pluralistic Age*. Edited by Kevin J. Vanhoozer, 155-64. Grand Rapids: Eerdmans, 1997.

Bavinck, Herman. *Reformed Dogmatics*. Vol. 2, *God and Creation*. Translated by John Vriend. Grand Rapids: Baker Academic, 2004.

Behr, John. *The Formation of Christian Theology*. Vol. 1, *The Way to Nicaea*. Crestwood, N.Y.: St. Vladimir's Seminary Press, 2001.

———. *The Formation of Christian Theology*. Vol. 2, *The Nicene Faith*. Crestwood, N.Y.: St. Vladimir's Seminary Press, 2004.

———. "The Trinitarian Being of the Church." *St. Vladimir's Theological Quarterly* 48 (2004): 67-88.

Benner, Drayton C. "Augustine and Karl Rahner on the Relationship between the

Immanent and the Economic Trinity." *International Journal of Systematic Theology* 9 (2007): 24-38.

Bernhardt, Reinhold. "The Real and the Trinitarian God," pp. 194-210. In *The Myth of Religious Superiority: Multifaith Explorations of Religious Pluralism*. Edited by Paul F. Knitter. Maryknoll, N.Y.: Orbis, 2005.

————. "Trinitätstheologie als Matrix einer Theologie der Religionen." *Ökumenische Rundschau* 49 (2000): 287-301.

Bjork, David. "Toward a Trinitarian Understanding of Mission in Post-Christendom Lands." *Missiology* 27 (1999): 231-44.

Boff, Leonardo. *Holy Trinity, Perfect Community*. Maryknoll, N.Y.: Orbis, 2000.

————. *Trinity and Society*. Maryknoll, N.Y.: Orbis, 1988.

Bourassa, François. "Sur le Traité de la Trinité." *Gregorianum* 47 (1966): 254-85.

————. "Théologie trinitaire chez Saint Augustin." *Gregorianum* 58 (1977): 675-716.

Boyer, Steven D. "Articulating Order: Trinitarian Discourse in an Egalitarian Age." *Pro Ecclesia* 18 (2009): 255-72.

Braaten, Carl E. "Christocentric Trinitarianism vs. Unitarian Theocentrism: A Response to Mark Heim." *Journal of Ecumenical Studies* 24 (1987): 17-21.

————. "The Triune God: the Source and Model of Christian Unity and Mission." *Missiology* 18 (1990): 415-427.

Brachtendorf, Johannes. "'. . . prius esse cogitare quam credere': A Natural Understanding of 'Trinity' in St. Augustine?" *Augustinian Studies* 29 (1998): 35-46.

Brague, Rémi. "On the Christian Model of Unity: The Trinity." *Communio* 10 (1983): 149-166.

Brom, Luco J. van den. "God, Gödel and Trinity: A Contribution to the Theology of Religions," pp. 56-75. In *Christian Faith and Philosophical Theology: Essays in Honour of Vincent Brümmer Presented on the Occasion of the Twenty-Fifth Anniversary of his Professorship in the Philosophy of Religion in the University of Utrecht*. Edited by Gijsbert van den Brink, Luco J. van den Brom, and Marcel Sarot. Kampen, Netherlands: Kok Pharos, 1992.

Brown, Stephen F. *Bonaventure: The Journey of the Mind to God*. Translated by Philotheus Boehner. Indianapolis: Hackett, 1993.

Brück, Michael von. "Advaita and Trinity: Reflections on the Vedantic and Christian Experience of God with Reference to Buddhist-Non-Dualism." *Indian Theological Studies* 20 (1983): 37-60.

Bryant, M. Darrol. "Interfaith Encounter and Dialogue in a Trinitarian Perspective," pp. 3-20. In *Christianity and the Wider Ecumenism*. Edited by Peter C. Phan. New York: Paragon House, 1990.

Burnaby, John. *Amor Dei: A Study of the Religion of St. Augustine.* London, Hodder & Stoughton, 1938.

Campbell, Cynthia M. "The Triune God: A Model for Inclusion." *Austin Seminary Bulletin: Faculty Edition* 97 (1981): 13-20.

Cavadini, John. C. "The Quest for Truth in Augustine's *De Trinitate.*" *Theological Studies* 58 (1997): 429-40.

————. "The Structure and Intention of Augustine's *De Trinitate.*" *Augustinian Studies* 23 (1992): 103-23.

Cenkner, William. "Interreligious Exploration of Triadic Reality: The Panikkar Project." *Dialogue & Alliance* 4 (1990): 71-85.

Charry, Ellen T. *By the Renewing of Your Minds: The Pastoral Function of Christian Doctrine.* New York: Oxford University Press, 1997.

————. "The Soteriological Importance of the Divine Perfections," pp. 129-47. In *God the Holy Trinity: Reflections on Christian Faith and Practice.* Edited by Timothy George. Grand Rapids: Baker Academic, 2006.

————. "Spiritual Formation by the Doctrine of the Trinity." *Theology Today* 54 (1997): 367-80.

Clark, Mary T. "Augustine's Theology of the Trinity: Its Relevance." *Dionysius* 13 (1989): 71-84.

————. "Augustinian Spirituality." *Augustinian Studies* 15 (1984): 83-92.

————. "Image Doctrine." In *Augustine through the Ages: An Encyclopedia.* Edited by Allan D. Fitzgerald. Grand Rapids: Eerdmans, 1999.

————. "De Trinitate," pp. 91-102. In *The Cambridge Companion to Augustine.* Edited by Eleonore Stump and Norman Kretzmann. New York: Cambridge University Press, 2001.

Clendenin, Daniel B. *Many Gods, Many Lords: Christianity Encounters World Religions.* Grand Rapids: Baker, 1995.

Coakley, Sarah. "'Persons' in the 'Social' Doctrine of the *Trinity*: A Critique of Current Analytic Discussion," pp. 123-44. In *The Trinity: An Interdisciplinary Symposium on the Trinity.* Edited by Stephen T. Davis, Daniel Kendall and Gerald O'Collins. New York: Oxford University Press, 1999.

————. "Re-thinking Gregory of Nyssa: Introduction—Gender, Trinitarian Analogies, and the Pedagogy of The Song." *Modern Theology* 18 (2002): 431-43.

————, ed. *Re-Thinking Gregory of Nyssa.* Directions in Modern Theology. Malden, Mass.: Blackwell, 2003.

Coffey, David. *Deus Trinitas: The Doctrine of the Triune God.* New York: Oxford University Press, 1999.

Congar, Yves M. J. *I Believe in the Holy Spirit*. Translated by David Smith. New York: Seabury Press, 1983.

———. *The Word and the Spirit*. Translated by David Smith. San Francisco: Harper & Row, 1986.

Congregation for the Doctrine of the Faith. "Declaration *Dominus Iesus* on the Unicity and Salvific Universality of Jesus Christ and the Church." August 6, 2000.

Cooper, John. "The Basic Philosophical and Theological Notions of Saint Augustine." *Augustinian Studies* 15 (1984): 93-113.

Cousins, Ewert H. *Bonaventure and the Coincidence of Opposites*. Chicago: Franciscan Herald, 1978.

———. *Christ of the 21st Century*. Rockport, Mass.: Element, 1992.

———. "The Convergence of Cultures and Religions in Light of the Evolution of Consciousness." *Zygon* 34 (1999): 209-19.

———. "Introduction: The Panikkar Symposium at Santa Barbara." *Cross Currents* 29 (1979): 131-40.

———. "Judaism-Christianity-Islam: Facing Modernity Together." *Journal of Ecumenical Studies* 30 (1993): 417-25.

———. "Panikkar's Advaitic Trinitarianism," pp. 119-30. In *The Intercultural Challenge of Raimon Panikkar*. Edited by Joseph Prabhu. Maryknoll, N.Y.: Orbis, 1996.

———. "Raimundo Panikkar and the Christian Systematic Theology of the Future." *Cross Currents* 29 (1979): 141-55.

———. "The Trinity and World Religions." *Journal of Ecumenical Studies* 7 (1970): 476-98.

Cox, Harvey G., Jr. "Make Way for the Spirit," pp. 93-100. In *God's Life in Trinity*. Edited by Miroslav Volf and Michael Welker. Minneapolis: Fortress, 2006.

Crouse, R. D. "St. Augustine's *De Trinitate*: Philosophical Method." *Studia Patristica* 16 (1985): 501-510.

Crowe, Frederick E. "Son and Spirit: Tension in the Divine Missions?" *Lonergan Workshop* 5 (1985): 1-21.

———. "Son of God, Holy Spirit and World Religions," pp. 324-43. In *Appropriating the Lonergan Idea*. Edited by Michael Vertin. Washington, D.C.: Catholic University of America Press, 1989.

Cunningham, David S. "Interpretation: Toward a Rehabilitation of the *Vestigia* Tradition," pp. 179-202. In *Knowing the Triune God: The Work of the Spirit in the Practices of the Church*. Edited by James J. Buckley and David S. Yeago. Grand Rapids: Eerdmans, 2001.

———. *These Three are One: The Practice of Trinitarian Theology*. Challenges in Contemporary Theology. Malden, Mass.: Blackwell, 1998.

Davis, Stephen T., Daniel Kendall and Gerald O'Collins, eds. *The Trinity: An Interdisciplinary Symposium on the Trinity.* New York: Oxford University Press, 1999.

D'Costa, Gavin. "Christ, the Trinity and Religious Plurality," pp. 16-29. In *Christian Uniqueness Reconsidered: The Myth of a Pluralistic Theology of Religions.* Edited by Gavin D'Costa. Maryknoll, N.Y.: Orbis, 1990.

―――. "The Impossibility of a Pluralist View of Religions." *Religious Studies* 32 (1996): 223-32.

―――. *The Meeting of Religions and the Trinity.* Maryknoll, N.Y.: Orbis, 2000.

―――. *Theology and Religious Pluralism: The Challenge of Other Religions.* Oxford: Blackwell, 1986.

―――. "Theology of Religions," pp. 626-44. In *The Modern Theologians: An Introduction to Christian Theology in the Twentieth Century.* Edited by David F. Ford. 2nd ed. Cambridge, Mass.: Blackwell, 1997.

―――. "Towards a Trinitarian Theology of Religions," pp. 139-54. In *A Universal Faith? Peoples, Cultures, Religions and the Christ: Essays in Honor of Prof. Dr. Frank De Graeve.* Edited by Catherine Cornille and Valeer Neckebrouck. Grand Rapids: Eerdmans, 1992.

―――. "Whose Objectivity? Which Neutrality? The Doomed Quest for a Neutral Vantage Point from Which to Judge Religions." *Religious Studies* 29 (1993): 79-95.

Devdas, Nalini. "The Theandrism of Raimundo Panikkar and Trinitarian Parallels in Modern Hindu thought." *Journal of Ecumenical Studies* 17 (1980): 606-20.

DiNoia, Joseph A. *The Diversity of Religions: A Christian Perspective.* Washington, D.C.: Catholic University of America Press, 1992.

Dünzl, Franz. *A Brief History of the Doctrine of the Trinity in the Early Church.* Translated by John Bowden. New York: T & T Clark, 2007.

Dupuis, Jacques. *Christianity and the Religions: From Confrontation to Dialogue.* Translated by Phillip Berryman. Maryknoll, N.Y.: Orbis, 2002.

―――. *Jesus Christ at the Encounter of World Religions.* Maryknoll, N.Y.: Orbis, 1991.

―――. *Toward a Christian Theology of Religious Pluralism.* Maryknoll, N.Y.: Orbis, 1997.

―――. "Trinitarian Christology as a Model for a Theology of Religious Pluralism," pp. 83-97. In *The Myriad Christ: Plurality and the Quest for Unity in Contemporary Christology.* Edited by Terrence Merrigan and Jacques Haers. Sterling, Va.: Uitgeverij Peeters, 2000.

―――. "'The Truth Will Make You Free': The Theology of Religious Pluralism Revisited." *Louvain Studies* 24 (1999): 211-63.

Farley, Margaret A. "New Patterns of Relationship: Beginnings of a Moral Revolution." *Theological Studies* 36 (1975): 627-46.

Fermer, Richard M. "The Limits of Trinitarian Theology as a Methodological Paradigm." *Neue Zeitschrift für Systematische Theologie und Religionsphilosophie* 41 (1999): 158-86.

Fernando, Ajith. "The Church: The Mirror of the Trinity," pp. 239-56. In *Global Missiology for the 21st Century: The Iguassu Dialogue*. Edited by William D. Taylor. Grand Rapids: Baker Academic, 2000.

Flett, John G. "In the Name of the Father, the Son and the Holy Spirit: A Critical Reflection on the Trinitarian Theologies of Religion of S. Mark Heim and Gavin D'Costa." *International Journal of Systematic Theology* 10 (2008): 73-90.

Fortman, Edmund J. *The Triune God: A Historical Study of the Doctrine of the Trinity*. Philadelphia: Westminster Press, 1972.

Gallagher, Robert L. "The Holy Spirit in the World: In Non-Christians, Creation and Other Religions." *Asia Journal of Pentecostal Studies* 9 (2006): 17-33.

George, Timothy, ed. *God the Holy Trinity: Reflections on Christian Faith and Practice*. Grand Rapids: Baker Academic, 2006.

Gilson, Étienne. *The Christian Philosophy of Saint Augustine*. Translated by L. E. M. Lynch. New York. Random House, 1960.

Gioia, Luigi. *The Theological Epistemology of Augustine's De Trinitate*. Oxford Theological Monographs. Oxford: Oxford University Press, 2008.

Green, Brad. "The Protomodern Augustine? Colin Gunton and the Failure of Augustine." *International Journal of Systematic Theology* 9 (2007): 328-41.

Gregory of Nazianzus. "The Theological Orations," pp. 128-214. In *Christology of the Later Fathers*, Library of Christian Classics. Edited by Edward R. Hardy. Louisville: Westminster John Knox Press, 1954.

Gregory of Nyssa. "Against Eunomius," pp. 233-48. In *Nicene and Post-Nicene Fathers of the Christian Church*, Second series, vol. 5. Edited by Philip Schaff and Henry Wace. Grand Rapids: Eerdmans, 1979.

———. "An Answer to Ablabius: That We Should Not Think of Saying There Are Three Gods," pp. 256-67. In *Christology of the Later Fathers*, Library of Christian Classics. Edited by Edward R. Hardy. Louisville: Westminster John Knox Press, 1954.

Grenz, Stanley J. *Rediscovering the Triune God: The Trinity in Contemporary Theology*. Minneapolis: Fortress Press, 2004.

———. *The Social God and the Relational Self: A Trinitarian Theology of the Imago Dei*. Louisville: Westminster John Knox Press, 2001.

———. "Toward an Evangelical Theology of the Religions." *Journal of Ecumenical Studies* 31 (1994): 49-65.

Griffiths, Bede. *Universal Wisdom: A Journey Through the Sacred Wisdom of the World.* San Francisco: HarperSanFrancisco, 1994.

Griffiths, Paul J. *Problems of Religious Diversity.* Malden, Mass.: Blackwell, 2001.

Gunton, Colin E. "Augustine, the Trinity and the Theological Crisis of the West." *Scottish Journal of Theology* 43 (1990): 33-58.

———. *The One, the Three, and the Many: God, Creation, and the Culture of Modernity.* New York: Cambridge University Press, 1993.

———. *The Promise of Trinitarian Theology.* Edinburgh: T & T Clark, 1991.

———. "Trinity, Ontology and Anthropology: Towards a Renewal of the Doctrine of the *Imago Dei*," pp. 47-61. In *Persons, Divine, and Human: King's College Essays in Theological Anthropology.* Edited by Christoph Schwöbel and Colin E. Gunton. Edinburgh: T & T Clark, 1991.

———. *The Triune Creator: A Historical and Systematic Study.* New Series in Constructive Theology. Grand Rapids: Eerdmans, 1998.

Haight, Roger. "Trinity and Religious Pluralism." *Journal of Ecumenical Studies* 44 (2009): 525-40.

Hart, David B. "The Mirror of the Infinite: Gregory of Nyssa on the *Vestigia Trinitatis.*" *Modern Theology* 18 (2002): 541-61.

Hart, Trevor. "Karl Barth, the Trinity and Pluralism," pp. 124-42. In *The Trinity in a Pluralistic Age.* Edited by Kevin J. Vanhoozer. Grand Rapids: Eerdmans, 1997.

Haudel, Matthias. "The Relations Between Trinity and Ecclesiology as an Ecumenical Challenge and Its Consequences for the Understanding of Mission." *International Review of Mission* 90 (2001): 401-8.

Heim, S. Mark. *The Depth of the Riches: A Trinitarian Theology of Religious Ends.* Sacra Doctrina. Grand Rapids: Eerdmans, 2001.

———. "The Depth of the Riches: Trinity and Religious Ends." *Modern Theology* 17 (2001): 21-55.

———. "God's Diversity: A Trinitarian View of Religious Pluralism." *Christian Century* 118 (2001): 14-18.

———. *Is Christ the Only Way? Christian Faith in a Pluralistic World.* Philadelphia: Judson, 1989.

———. "Salvations: A More Pluralistic Hypothesis." *Modern Theology* 10 (1994): 343-60.

———. *Salvations: Truth and Difference in Religion.* Maryknoll, N.Y.: Orbis, 1995.

———. "Witness to Communion: A Trinitarian Perspective on Mission and Religious Pluralism." *Missiology* 33 (2005): 192-99.

Helminiak, Daniel A. "The Trinitarian Vocation of the Gay Community." *Pastoral Psychology* 36 (1987): 100-111.

Hick, John. *A Christian Theology of Religions: The Rainbow of Faiths*. Louisville: Westminster John Knox Press, 1995.

———. *Disputed Questions in Theology and Philosophy of Religion*. New Haven, Conn.: Yale University Press, 1993.

———. *God and the Universe of Faiths: Essays in the Philosophy of Religion*. London: Macmillan, 1973.

———. *God Has Many Names*. Philadelphia: Westminster Press, 1982.

———. *An Interpretation of Religion: Human Responses to the Transcendent*. New Haven, Conn.: Yale University Press, 1989.

———. *The Metaphor of God Incarnate: Christology in a Pluralistic Age*. Louisville: Westminster John Knox, 1993.

———. "Rethinking Christian Doctrine in the Light of Religious Pluralism," pp. 89-102. In *Christianity and the Wider Ecumenism*. Edited by Peter C. Phan. New York: Paragon House, 1990.

Hick, John, and Paul F. Knitter, eds. *The Myth of Christian Uniqueness: Toward a Pluralistic Theology of Religions*. Maryknoll, N.Y.: Orbis, 1987.

Hildebrand, Stephen M. *The Trinitarian Theology of Basil of Caesarea: A Synthesis of Greek Thought and Biblical Truth*. Washington, D.C.: Catholic University of America Press, 2007.

Hill, Edmund. "Karl Rahner's 'Remarks on the Dogmatic Treatise De Trinitate and St. Augustine.'" *Augustinian Studies* 2 (1971): 67-80.

———. *The Mystery of the Trinity*. Introducing Catholic Theology. London: Geoffrey Chapman, 1985.

———. "Our Knowledge of the Trinity." *Scottish Journal of Theology* 27 (1974): 1-11.

———. "St. Augustine's *De Trinitate*: The Doctrinal Significance of Its Structure." *Revue des études augustiniennes* 19 (1978): 277-86.

Hodgson, Peter C. "The Spirit and Religious Pluralism," pp. 135-50. In *The Myth of Religious Superiority: Multifaith Explorations of Religious Pluralism*. Edited by Paul F. Knitter. Maryknoll, N.Y.: Orbis, 2005.

———. "The Spirit and Religious Pluralism." *Horizons* 31 (2004): 22-39.

Holmes, Stephen R. "Trinitarian Missiology: Towards a Theology of God as Missionary." *International Journal of Systematic Theology* 8 (2006): 72-90.

Hunt, Anne. "Psychological Analogy and Paschal Mystery in Trinitarian Theology." *Theological Studies* 59 (1998): 197-218.

———. *Trinity: Nexus of the Mysteries of Christian Faith*. Theology in Global Perspective. Maryknoll, N.Y.: Orbis, 2005.

———. *What Are They Saying About the Trinity?* Mahway, N.J.: Paulist Press, 1998.

Husbands, Mark. "The Trinity Is Not Our Social Program: Volf, Gregory of Nyssa and Barth," pp. 120-41. In *Trinitarian Theology for the Church: Scripture, Community, Worship*. Edited by Daniel J. Treier and David Lauber. Downers Grove, Ill.: InterVarsity Press, 2009.

Ipgrave, Michael. *Trinity and Inter Faith Dialogue: Plenitude and Plurality*. Religions and Discourse 14. New York: Peter Lang, 2003.

Irenaeus. "Against the Heresies," pp. 309-567 In *The Ante-Nicene Fathers*. Vol. 1. Edited by Alexander Roberts and James Donaldson. Grand Rapids: Eerdmans, 1979.

James, Robison B. "The Trinity and Non-Christian Religions: A Perspective That Makes Use of Paul Tillich as Resource." *Perspectives in Religious Studies* 33 (2006): 361-73.

Jenson, Robert W. "Karl Barth," pp. 21-36. In *The Modern Theologians: An Introduction to Christian Theology in the Twentieth Century*. Edited by David F. Ford. 2nd ed. Cambridge, Mass.: Blackwell, 1997.

———. "What is the Point of Trinitarian Theology?" pp. 31-43. In *Trinitarian Theology Today: Essays on Divine Being and Act*. Edited by Christoph Schwöbel. Edinburgh: T & T Clark, 1995.

Johnson, Keith E. "Augustine's 'Trinitarian' Reading of John 5: A Model for the Theological Interpretation of Scripture?" *Journal of the Evangelical Theological Society* 52 (2009): 799-810.

———. "Divine Transcendence, Religious Pluralism and Barth's Doctrine of God." *International Journal of Systematic Theology* 5 (2003): 200-224.

———. "Does the Doctrine of the Trinity Hold the Key to a Christian Theology of Religions?" pp. 142-60. In *Trinitarian Theology for the Church: Scripture, Community, Worship*. Edited by Daniel J. Treier and David Lauber. Downers Grove, Ill.: InterVarsity Press, 2009.

———. "Theology of Religions," pp. 1126-28. In *Dictionary of the Ecumenical Movement*. Edited by Nicholas Lossky et al. 2nd ed. Geneva: WCC Publications, 2002.

Jowers, Dennis W. "Divine Unity and the Economy of Salvation in the *De Trinitate* of Augustine." *Reformed Theological Review* 60 (2001): 68-84.

———. *The Trinitarian Axiom of Karl Rahner: The Economic Trinity is the Immanent Trinity and Vice Versa*. Lewiston, N.Y.: Edwin Mellen, 2006.

Kaiser, Christopher. "The Ontological Trinity in the Context of Historical Religions." *Scottish Journal of Theology* 29 (1976): 301-10.

Kärkkäinen, Veli-Matti. "'How to Speak of the Spirit Among Religions': Trinitarian Prolegomena for a Pneumatological Theology of Religions," pp. 47-70. In *The Work of the Spirit: Pneumatology and Pentecostalism*. Edited by Michael Welker. Grand Rapids: Eerdmans, 2006.

————. *An Introduction to the Theology of Religions: Biblical, Historical and Contemporary Perspectives.* Downers Grove, Ill.: InterVarsity Press, 2003.

————. "Toward a Pneumatological Theology of Religions: A Pentecostal-Charismatic Inquiry." *International Review of Mission* 91 (April 2002): 187-98.

————. "Trinity and Religions: On the Way to a Trinitarian Theology of Religions." *Missiology: An International Review* 33 (2005): 159-74.

————. *Trinity and Religious Pluralism: The Doctrine of the Trinity in Christian Theology of Religions.* Burlington, Vt.: Ashgate, 2004.

Kasper, Walter. *The God of Jesus Christ.* Translated by Matthew J. O'Connell. New York: Crossroad, 1984.

Kelly, Anthony. *The Trinity of Love: A Theology of the Christian God.* New Theology. Wilmington, Del.: Michael Glazier, 1989.

Kendall, Daniel, and Gerald O'Collins, eds. *In Many and Diverse Ways: In Honor of Jacques Dupuis.* Maryknoll, N.Y.: Orbis, 2003.

Khodr, Georges. "Christianity and the Pluralistic World—The Economy of the Holy Spirit." *Ecumenical Review* 23 (1971): 118-28.

Kilby, Karen. "Aquinas, the Trinity and the Limits of Understanding." *International Journal of Systematic Theology* 7 (2005): 414-27.

————. "Perichoresis and Projection: Problems with Social Doctrines of the Trinity." *New Blackfriars* 81 (2000): 432-45.

————. "The Trinity: A New Wave?" *Reviews in Religion and Theology* 7 (2000): 378-81.

Kim, Heung-Gyu. *Prolegomena to a Christian Theology of Religions.* Lanham, Md.: University Press of America, 2000.

Knitter, Paul F. *Introducing Theologies of Religions.* Maryknoll, N.Y.: Orbis, 2002.

————. "A New Pentecost? A Pneumatological Theology of Religions." *Current Dialogue* 19 (1991): 32-41.

————. *No Other Name? A Critical Survey of Christian Attitudes Toward the World Religions.* American Society of Missiology 7. Maryknoll, N.Y.: Orbis, 1985.

————. *One Earth, Many Religions: Multifaith Dialogue and Global Responsibility.* Maryknoll, N.Y.: Orbis, 1995.

————. "Toward a Liberation Theology of Religions," pp. 178-202. In *The Myth of Christian Uniqueness: Toward a Pluralistic Theology of Religions.* Edited by John Hick and Paul F. Knitter. Maryknoll, N.Y.: Orbis, 1987.

Kraemer, Hendrik. *The Christian Message in a Non-Christian World.* New York: Harper & Row, 1938.

LaCugna, Catherine M. *God for Us: The Trinity and Christian Life.* San Francisco: HarperCollins, 1991.

LaCugna, Catherine M., and Kilian McDonnell. "Returning from 'The Far Country': Theses for a Contemporary Trinitarian Theology." *Scottish Journal of Theology* 41 (1988): 191-215.

Lai, Pan-Chiu. *Towards a Trinitarian Theology of Religions: A Study in Paul Tillich's Thought.* Studies in Philosophical Theology 8. Kampen, Netherlands: Kok Pharos, 1994.

Lash, Nicholas. "Considering the Trinity." *Modern Theology* 2 (1986): 183-96.

Leslie, Ben. "Does God Have a Life? Barth and LaCugna on the Immanent Trinity." *Perspectives in Religious Studies* 24 (1997): 377-98.

Letham, Robert. *The Holy Trinity: In Scripture, History, Theology and Worship.* Phillipsburg, N.J.: Presbyterian & Reformed, 2004.

Levering, Matthew. "Beyond the Jamesian Impasse in Trinitarian Theology." *The Thomist* 66 (2002): 395-420.

―――. "Friendship and Trinitarian Theology: Response to Karen Kilby." *International Journal of Systematic Theology* 9 (2007): 39-54.

―――. *Scripture and Metaphysics: Aquinas and the Renewal of Trinitarian Theology,* Challenges in Contemporary Theology. Malden, Mass.: Blackwell, 2004.

Lossky, Vladimir. *The Mystical Theology of the Eastern Church.* Translated by members of the Fellowship of St. Alban and St. Sergius. London: James Clarke, 1957.

Matthews, Charles. "Pluralism, Otherness and Augustinian Tradition." *Modern Theology* 14 (1998): 83-112.

McDermott, Gerald R. *Can Evangelicals Learn from World Religions? Jesus, Revelation & Religious Traditions.* Downers Grove, Ill.: InterVarsity Press, 2000.

McDonnell, Kilian. *The Other Hand of God: The Holy Spirit as the Universal Touch and Goal.* Collegeville, Minn.: Liturgical Press, 2003.

―――. "A Trinitarian Theology of the Holy Spirit?" *Theological Studies* 46 (1985): 191-227.

McGrath, Alister. "The Doctrine of the Trinity: An Evangelical Reflection," pp. 17-35. In *God the Holy Trinity: Reflections on Christian Faith and Practice.* Edited by Timothy George. Grand Rapids: Baker Academic, 2006.

―――. "A Particularist View: A Post-Enlightenment Approach," pp. 151-209. In *More Than One Way? Four Views of Salvation in a Pluralistic Word.* Edited by Dennis L. Okholm and Timothy R. Phillips. Grand Rapids: Zondervan, 1995.

Merriell, D. Juvenal. *To the Image of the Trinity: A Study in the Development of Aquinas' Teaching.* Toronto: Pontifical Institute of Mediaeval Studies, 1990.

Migliore, Daniel L. "The Trinity and the Theology of Religions," pp. 101-17. In *God's Life in Trinity.* Edited by Miroslav Volf and Michael Welker. Minneapolis: Fortress, 2006.

Molnar, Paul. *Divine Freedom and the Doctrine of the Immanent Trinity: In Dialogue with Karl Barth and Contemporary Theology.* Edinburgh: T & T Clark, 2002.

———. "The Function of the Immanent Trinity in the Theology of Karl Barth: Implications for Today." *Scottish Journal of Theology* 42 (1989): 367-99.

———. "Toward a Contemporary Doctrine of the Immanent Trinity: Karl Barth and Present Discussion." *Scottish Journal of Theology* 49 (1996): 311-57.

Moltmann, Jürgen. *The Trinity and the Kingdom.* Translated by Margaret Kohl. Minneapolis: Fortress, 1993.

Muller, Earl C. *Trinity and Marriage in Paul: The Establishment of a Communitarian Analogy of the Trinity Grounded in the Theological Shape of Pauline Thought.* American University Studies, Series 7: Theology and Religion 60. New York: Peter Lang, 1990.

Netland, Harold A. *Encountering Religious Pluralism: The Challenge to Christian Faith and Mission.* Downers Grove, Ill.: InterVarsity Press, 2001.

Newbigin, Lesslie. "The Basis, Purpose and Manner of Inter-Faith Dialogue." *Scottish Journal of Theology* 30 (1977): 253-70.

———. *The Gospel in a Pluralist Society.* Grand Rapids: Eerdmans, 1989.

———. *The Open Secret: An Introduction to the Theology of Mission.* Rev. ed. Grand Rapids: Eerdmans, 1995.

———. "The Quest for Unity Through Religion." *Journal of Religion* 35 (1955): 17-33.

———. "Religion for the Market Place," pp. 135-48. In *Christian Uniqueness Reconsidered: The Myth Of A Pluralistic Theology Of Religions.* Edited by Gavin D'Costa. Maryknoll, N.Y.: Orbis, 1990.

———. "Religious Pluralism: A Missiological Approach." *Studia Missionalia* 42 (1993): 227-44.

———. "Religious Pluralism and the Uniqueness of Jesus Christ." *International Bulletin of Missionary Research* 13 (April 1989): 50-54.

———. *Trinitarian Themes for Today's Mission.* London: Paternoster, 1998.

———. "The Trinity as Public Truth," pp. 1-8. In *The Trinity in a Pluralistic Age.* Edited by Kevin J. Vanhoozer. Grand Rapids: Eerdmans, 1997.

———. *Truth to Tell: The Gospel as Public Truth.* Grand Rapids: Eerdmans, 1991.

Niebuhr, H. Richard. "The Doctrine of the Trinity and the Unity of the Church." *Theology Today* 3 (1946): 371-86.

Okholm, Dennis L., and Timothy R. Phillips, eds. *More Than One Way? Four Views of Salvation in a Pluralistic World.* Grand Rapids: Zondervan, 1995.

Ormerod, Neil. "Augustine and the Trinity: Whose Crisis?" *Pacifica* (2003): 17-32.

————. "Augustine's *De Trinitate* and Lonergan's Realms of Meaning." *Theological Studies* 64 (2003): 773-94.

————. "The Psychological Analogy for the Trinity: At Odds with Modernity." *Pacifica* 14 (2001): 281-94.

————. *The Trinity: Retrieving the Western Tradition*. Milwaukee: Marquette University Press, 2005.

Osborn, Eric. *Irenaeus of Lyons*. Cambridge: Cambridge University Press, 2001.

Panikkar, Raimundo. *Blessed Simplicity: The Monk as Universal Archetype*. New York: Seabury Press, 1982.

————. *The Cosmotheandric Experience*. Emerging Religious Consciousness. Maryknoll, N.Y.: Orbis, 1993.

————. "Inter-Religious Dialogue: Some Principles." *Journal of Ecumenical Studies* 12 (1975): 407-9.

————. *Invisible Harmony: Essays on Contemplation and Responsibility*. Edited by Harry J. Cargas. Minneapolis: Augsburg Fortress, 1995.

————. "The Jordan, the Tiber and the Ganges: Three Kairological Moments of Christic Self-Awareness," pp. 89-116. In *The Myth of Christian Uniqueness: Toward a Pluralistic Theology of Religions*. ed. John Hick and Paul F. Knitter. Maryknoll, N.Y.: Orbis, 1987.

————. *The Silence of God: The Answer of the Buddha*. Maryknoll, N.Y.: Orbis, 1989.

————. "Toward an Ecumenical Theandric Spirituality." *Journal of Ecumenical Studies* 5 (1968): 507-34.

————. *The Trinity and the Religious Experience of Man: Person-Icon-Mystery*. Maryknoll, N.Y.: Orbis, 1973.

————. *The Unknown Christ of Hinduism*. Rev. ed. London: Darton, Longman & Todd, 1984.

Pecknold, C. C. "How Augustine Used the Trinity: Functionalism and the Development of Doctrine." *Anglican Theological Review* 85 (2003): 127-41.

Pelikan, Jaroslav J. "*Canonica Regula*: The Trinitarian Hermeneutics of Augustine," pp. 329-43. In *Collectanea Augustiniana: Augustine—"Second Founder of the Faith."* Edited by Joseph C. Schnaubelt and Frederick Van Fleteren. New York: Peter Lang, 1990.

Pinnock, Clark H. *Flame of Love: A Theology of the Holy Spirit*. Downers Grove, Ill.: InterVarsity Press, 1996.

————. *A Wideness in God's Mercy: The Finality of Jesus Christ in a World of Religions*. Grand Rapids: Zondervan, 1992.

Plantinga, Cornelius, Jr. "Social Trinity and Tritheism," pp. 21-47. In *Trinity, Incarnation, and Atonement: Philosophical and Theological Essays*. Edited by Ronald J.

Feenstra and Cornelius Plantinga Jr. Notre Dame, Ind.: University of Notre Dame Press, 1989

———. "The Threeness/Oneness Problem of the Trinity." *Calvin Theological Journal* 23 (1988): 37-53.

Poupin, Roland. "Is there a Trinitarian Experience in Sufism?" pp. 72-87. In *The Trinity in a Pluralistic Age*. Edited by Kevin J. Vanhoozer. Grand Rapids: Eerdmans, 1997.

Race, Alan. *Christians and Religious Pluralism: Patterns in the Christian Theology of Religions*. Maryknoll, N.Y.: Orbis, 1982.

Rahner, Karl. *The Trinity*. Translated by Joseph Donceel. New York: Crossroad, 1997.

Reid, Duncan. "The Defeat of Trinitarian Theology: An Alternative View." *Pacifica* 9 (1996): 289-300.

Roeber, A. G. "Western, Eastern, or Global Orthodoxy? Some Reflections on St. Augustine of Hippo in Recent Literature." *Pro Ecclesia* 17 (2008): 210-23.

Rogers, Eugene F., Jr. *Sexuality and the Christian Body: Their Way into the Triune God*. Challenges in Contemporary Theology. Malden, Mass.: Blackwell, 1999.

Ruokanen, Miika. *The Catholic Doctrine of Non-Christian Religions According to the Second Vatican Council*. New York: Brill, 1992.

Samartha, Stanley J. "The Holy Spirit and People of Other Faiths." *Ecumenical Review* 42 (1990): 250-63.

Sanders, Fred. *The Deep Things of God: How the Trinity Changes Everything*. Wheaton, Ill.: Crossway, 2010.

———. "Entangled in the Trinity: Economic and Immanent Trinity in Recent Theology." *Dialog* 40 (2001): 175-82.

———. *The Image of the Immanent Trinity: Rahner's Rule and the Theological Interpretation of Scripture*. Issues in Systematic Theology 12. New York: Peter Lang, 2005.

———. "Trinity Talk, Again." *Dialog* 44 (2005): 264-72.

Sanders, John. *No Other Name: An Investigation into the Destiny of the Unevangelized*. Grand Rapids: Eerdmans, 1992.

———, ed. *What About Those Who Have Never Heard? Three Views on the Destiny of the Unevangelized*. Downers Grove, Ill.: InterVarsity Press, 1995.

Schmidt-Leukel, Perry. "Exclusivism, Inclusivism, Pluralism: The Tripolar Typology—Clarified and Reaffirmed," pp. 13-27. In *The Myth of Religious Superiority: Multifaith Explorations of Religious Pluralism*. Edited by Paul F. Knitter. Maryknoll, N.Y.: Orbis, 2005.

Schwöbel, Christoph. "Particularity, Universality, and the Religions: Toward a Christian Theology of Religions," pp. 30-48. In *Christian Uniqueness Reconsidered: The Myth of a Pluralistic Theology of Religions*. Edited by Gavin D'Costa. Maryknoll, N.Y.: Orbis Books, 1990.

————, ed. *Trinitarian Theology Today*. Edinburgh: T & T Clark, 1995.

Scirghi, Thomas J. "The Trinity: A Model for Belonging in Contemporary Society." *Ecumenical Review* 54 (2002): 333-42.

Sheridan, Daniel P. "Grounded in the Trinity: Suggestions for a Theology of Relationship to Other Religions." *Thomist* 50 (1986): 260-78.

Sigurdson, Ola. "Is the Trinity a Practical Doctrine?" pp. 115-25. In *The Concept of God in Global Dialogue*. Edited by Werner G. Jeanrond and Aasulv Lande. Maryknoll, N.Y.: Orbis, 2005.

Smart, Ninian, and Stephen Konstantine. *Christian Systematic Theology in World Context*. Minneapolis: Fortress, 1991.

Stackhouse, John G., ed. *No Other Gods Before Me? Evangelicals and the Challenge of World Religions*. Grand Rapids: Baker Academic, 2001.

Studer, Basil. *Augustins De Trinitate: eine Einführung*. Paderborn, Germany: Schöningh, 2005.

————. *The Grace of Christ and the Grace of God in Augustine of Hippo: Christocentrism or Theocentrism?* Collegeville, Minn.: Liturgical Press, 1997.

————. "History and Faith in Augustine's *De Trinitate*." *Augustinian Studies* 28 (1997): 7-50.

Sullivan, John E. *The Image of God: The Doctrine of St. Augustine and its Influence*. Dubuque, Ia.: Priory Press, 1963.

Thiemann, Ronald F. "Beyond Exclusivism and Absolutism: A Trinitarian Theology of the Cross," pp. 118-32. In *God's Life in Trinity*. Edited by Miroslav Volf and Michael Welker. Minneapolis: Fortress, 2006.

Thompson, John. *Modern Trinitarian Perspectives*. New York: Oxford University Press, 1994.

Thompson, Marianne Meye. *The God of the Gospel of John*. Grand Rapids: Eerdmans, 2001.

Thompson, Thomas R. "Trinitarianism Today: Doctrinal Renaissance, Ethical Relevance, Social Redolence." *Calvin Theological Journal* 32 (1997): 9-42.

Turcescu, Lucian. "'Person' versus 'Individual', and Other Modern Misreadings of Gregory of Nyssa." *Modern Theology* 18 (2002): 527-39.

Vanderspoel, John. "The Background to Augustine's Denial of Religious Plurality," pp. 179-93. In *Grace, Politics and Desire: Essays on Augustine*. Edited by Hugo Anthony Meynell. Calgary: University of Calgary Press, 1990.

Vanhoozer, Kevin J. "Does the Trinity Belong in a Theology of Religions? On Angling in the Rubicon and the 'Identity' of God," pp. 41-71. In *The Trinity in a Pluralistic Age*. Edited by Kevin J. Vanhoozer. Grand Rapids: Eerdmans, 1997.

———. *The Drama of Doctrine: A Canonical-Linguistic to Christian Theology*. Louisville: Westminster John Knox, 2005.

Viladesau, Richard. "The Trinity in Universal Revelation." *Philosophy and Theology* 4 (1990): 317-34.

Volf, Miroslav. *After Our Likeness: The Church as the Image of the Trinity*. Grand Rapids: Eerdmans, 1998.

———. "Being as God Is," pp. 3-12. In *God's Life in Trinity*. Edited by Miroslav Volf and Michael Welker. Minneapolis: Fortress, 2006.

———. "'The Trinity Is Our Social Program': The Doctrine of the Trinity and the Shape of Social Engagement." *Modern Theology* 13 (1998): 403-23.

Vroom, Hendrik. "Do All Religious Traditions Worship the Same God?" *Religious Studies* 26 (1990): 73-90.

Wainwright, Geoffrey. "The Doctrine of the Trinity: Where the Church Stands or Falls." *Interpretation* 45 (1991): 117-32.

———. *Doxology: The Praise of God in Worship, Doctrine and Life*. New York: Oxford University Press, 1980.

———. "The Ecumenical Rediscovery of the Trinity." *One in Christ* 34 (1998): 95-124.

———. Worship with One Accord: Where Liturgy and Ecumenism Embrace. New York: Oxford University Press, 1997.

Wassmer, Thomas. "The Trinitarian Theology of Augustine and His Debt to Plotinus." *Scottish Journal of Theology* 14 (1961): 248-55.

Webster, John. "Principles of Systematic Theology." *International Journal of Systematic Theology* 11 (2009): 56-71.

———. "Trinity and Creation." *International Journal of Systematic Theology* 12 (2010): 4-19.

Weinandy, Thomas. "The Immanent and Economic Trinity." *The Thomist* 57 (1993): 655-66.

Welch, Claude. *In This Name: The Doctrine of the Trinity in Contemporary Theology*. New York: Charles Scribner's, 1952.

Wilken, Robert L. "Is Pentecost a Peer of Easter? Scripture, Liturgy, and the *Proprium* of the Holy Spirit," pp. 158-77. In *Trinity, Time, and Church: A Response to the Theology of Robert W. Jenson*. Edited by Colin E. Gunton. Grand Rapids: Eerdmans, 2000.

Williams, A. N. "Contemplation: Knowledge of God in Augustine's *De Trinitate*," pp. 121-46. In *Knowing the Triune God: The Work of the Spirit in the Practices of the*

Church. Edited by James J. Buckley and David S. Yeago. Grand Rapids: Eerdmans, 2001.

Williams, David T. "Trinitarian Ecology." *Scottish Bulletin of Evangelical Theology* 18 (2000): 142-59.

Williams, Rowan. "*Sapientia* and the Trinity: Reflections on *De Trinitate*," pp. 317-32. In *Collectanea Augustiniana*. Edited by Bernard Bruning, J. van Houtem and Mathijs Lamberigts. Louvain: Leuven University Press, 1990.

————. "*De Trinitate*," pp. 845-51. In *Augustine Through the Ages: An Encyclopedia*. Edited by Allan D. Fitzgerald. Grand Rapids: Eerdmans, 1999.

————. "Trinity and Pluralism," pp. 3-15. In *Christian Uniqueness Reconsidered: The Myth of a Pluralistic Theology of Religions*. Edited by Gavin D'Costa. Maryknoll, N.Y.: Orbis, 1990.

Williams, Stephen. "The Trinity and 'Other Religions,'" pp. 26-40. In *The Trinity in a Pluralistic Age*. Edited by Kevin J. Vanhoozer. Grand Rapids: Eerdmans, 1997.

Wolfson, H. A. *The Philosophy of the Church Fathers*. Cambridge, Mass.: Harvard University Press, 1956.

Wright, David. "The Watershed of Vatican II: Catholic Approaches to Religious Pluralism," pp. 207-36. In *One God, One Lord: Christianity in a World of Religious Pluralism*. Edited by Andrew D. Clarke and Bruce W. Winter. 2nd ed. Grand Rapids: Baker, 1992.

Yeago, David. "The New Testament and the Nicene Dogma: A Contribution to the Recovery of Theological Exegesis." *Pro Ecclesia* 3 (1994): 152-64.

Yong, Amos. *Beyond the Impasse: Toward a Pneumatological Theology of Religions*. Grand Rapids: Baker Academic, 2003.

————. *Discerning the Spirit(s): A Pentecostal-Charismatic Contribution to a Christian Theology of Religions*. Journal of Pentecostal Theology, Supplement Series 20. Sheffield: Sheffield Academic Press, 2000.

————. "Oneness and the Trinity: The Theological and Ecumenical Implications of Creation *Ex Nihilo* for an Intra-Pentecostal Dispute." *Pneuma: The Journal of the Society for Pentecostal Studies* 19 (1997): 81-107.

————. *The Spirit Poured Out on All Flesh: Pentecostalism and the Possibility of Global Theology*. Grand Rapids: Baker Academic, 2005.

————. "The Turn to Pneumatology in Christian Theology of Religions: Conduit or Detour?" *Journal of Ecumenical Studies* 35 (1998): 39-65.

Zizioulas, John D. *Being as Communion: Studies in Personhood and the Church*. Crestwood, N.Y.: St. Vladimir's Seminary Press, 1985.

————. "The Church as Communion." *St. Vladimir's Theological Quarterly* 38 (1994): 3-16.

Author Index

Subject Index

Scripture Index